101 CLASSIC HIKES OF THE SOUTHWEST

HELP US KEEP THIS GUIDE UP TO DATE

Every effort has been made by the author and editors to make this guide as accurate and useful as possible. However, many things can change after a guide is published—regulations change, facilities come under new management, and so forth.

We would love to hear from you concerning your experiences with this guide and how you feel it could be improved and kept up to date. While we may not be able to respond to all comments and suggestions, we'll take them to heart, and we'll also make certain to share them with the author. Please send your comments and suggestions to falconeditorial@rowman.com.

Thanks for your input!

101 CLASSIC HIKES
OF THE SOUTHWEST

THE BEST HIKES IN SOUTHERN NEVADA, SOUTHEASTERN
CALIFORNIA, ARIZONA, WESTERN NEW MEXICO,
SOUTHWESTERN COLORADO, AND SOUTHERN UTAH

Bruce Grubbs

ESSEX, CONNECTICUT

FALCONGUIDES®

An imprint of Globe Pequot, the trade division of
The Rowman & Littlefield Publishing Group, Inc.
4501 Forbes Blvd., Ste. 200
Lanham, MD 20706
www.rowman.com

Falcon and FalconGuides are registered trademarks and Make Adventure Your Story is a
trademark of The Rowman & Littlefield Publishing Group, Inc.

Distributed by NATIONAL BOOK NETWORK

British Library Cataloguing in Publication Information available

Library of Congress Cataloging-in-Publication Data

Names: Grubbs, Bruce (Bruce O.), author.
Title: 101 classic hikes of the Southwest: the best hikes in southern Nevada, southeastern
    California, Arizona, western New Mexico, southwestern Colorado, and southern Utah / Bruce
    Grubbs.
Description: Essex, Connecticut: FalconGuides, [2024] | Includes index. |
Summary: "Focusing on the best hikes in the Four Corners states, this guide will take readers on
    an adventure across Arizona, Nevada, Utah, and New Mexico"— Provided by publisher.
Identifiers: LCCN 2023026115 (print) | LCCN 2023026116 (ebook) | ISBN 9781493071081
    (paperback) | ISBN 9781493071098 (epub)
Subjects: LCSH: Hiking—Southwest, New—Guidebooks. | Southwest, New--Guidebooks. | LCGFT:
    Guidebooks.
Classification: LCC GV199.42.S68 G78 2024 (print) | LCC GV199.42.S68 (ebook) | DDC
    796.510979—dc23/eng/20230616
LC record available at https://lccn.loc.gov/2023026115
LC ebook record available at https://lccn.loc.gov/2023026116

Printed in India

CONTENTS

THE HIKES

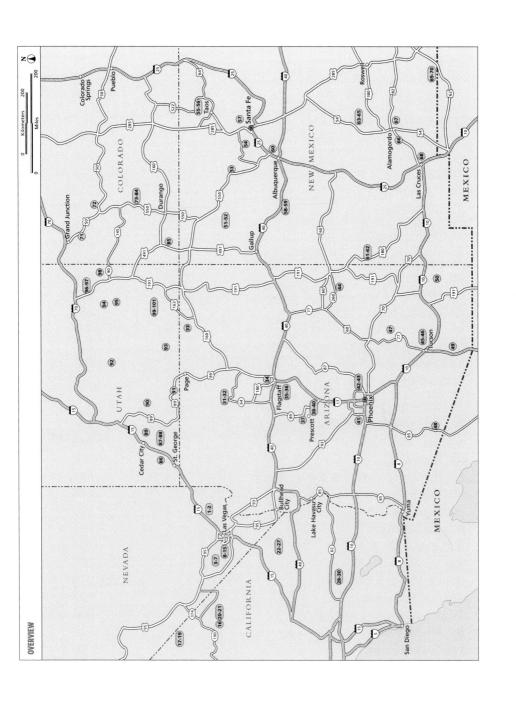

ACKNOWLEDGMENTS

I appreciate the efforts of the authors of other Falcon Guides covering the southwestern states in producing their excellent hiking guides, which I relied on for ideas on which hikes to include for areas in which I didn't have direct experience. Thanks also to my hiking friends who put up with my photography and trail mapping on hikes and backpack trips. Special thanks to Duart Martin for her unflagging support of this project, especially during the final stages of editing and map preparation. And finally, thanks to my editor, David Legere, and the rest of the staff at Falcon Guides for their patient efforts in making this new edition a reality.

INTRODUCTION

GEOLOGY AND GEOGRAPHY

The American Southwest as covered in this book includes southern Nevada, southeastern California, Arizona, western New Mexico, southwestern Colorado, and southern Utah. It is generally an arid region that includes portions of the four American deserts—the Sonoran, Chihuahuan, Great Basin, and Mojave. Each of these four deserts have distinct climates and landforms, where elevations range from below sea level to more than 10,000 feet. In addition, there are plateaus and mountains whose lofty elevations create a cooler and wetter climate above the deserts. From central Arizona south and west, the area known as the Basin and Range geological province consists of many parallel mountain ranges separated by desert plains. Many of these mountains are low desert ranges, while others are high enough to support forests. The Colorado Plateau, covering parts of Arizona, Utah, Colorado, and New Mexico, is one of the largest and highest plateaus on the planet and averages about 5,000 feet above sea level. The highest portions of the plateau reach over 12,000 feet. The plateau is named for the Colorado River, which along with its many tributaries, drains the western Rocky Mountains and has carved thousands of canyons into the sedimentary rock layers. Volcanic fields dot the plateau, creating isolated mountains. On the east, the Colorado Plateau is bounded by the southern Rocky Mountains, which feature the highest and most alpine hikes in this book, in the southwestern Colorado and western New Mexico sections of the book. Elevations here reach above 14,000 feet.

For the hiker, this beautiful region has it all—easy rambles across open desert plains with 100-mile views, rugged scrambles to the tops of desert peaks, hikes along lush riparian zones and through fantastic sandstone narrows, backpack trips into maze-like canyons, easy walks through pine forests, and trails that traverse high alpine terrain carved out by glaciers. For the author, the hard part was deciding which hikes to leave out, because there are tens of thousands of beautiful and rewarding trails in this region. So please look at this book as an introduction to this incredible piece of the American landscape—your invitation to exploration.

WILDFIRES

In recent years the Southwest has suffered a number of unusually large and destructive wildfires. While fire has always been part of the natural forest ecology in the West, a combination of drought, tree-killing insect epidemics, and dense forests caused by more than a century of poor management practices has led to fires not only burning hundreds of thousands of acres of forest but also burning large areas of desert as well. Recent large fires have affected a number of the hikes in this book, and more are sure to be affected in the future. Always call or e-mail the appropriate land-management agency before your hike, or at least check their website, for current conditions and possible area or trail closures.

WEATHER AND CLIMATE

While the lowest desert elevations in California's Mojave Desert may receive no moisture at all in the course of a year, the highest plateaus and mountains in Utah, Colorado, and New Mexico receive 200 inches or more of snow in a year. Temperatures vary from the record 130 degrees F set in Death Valley to minus 61 degrees in Colorado. But those are the extremes. In general, the low deserts in the Arizona, Nevada, and California portions of this book have their best hiking weather from late fall through spring, while the high plateaus and mountains are covered in deep snow. During the summer, while the low deserts are scorching hot, the high-country weather is cool and inviting. All this means that you can hike this region year-round.

Weather varies considerably from year to year, but the Southwest does have a distinct seasonal pattern. Early summer tends to be warm and dry, but around late June, seasonal moisture moves up from the south, a phenomenon known as the North American Monsoon. As the summer progresses, this moisture gradually moves northwest and sets off afternoon thunderstorms, especially over the high plateaus and mountains. Late in the summer, even the lower deserts usually see thunderstorm activity. Much of the area covered by this book receives half or more of its annual moisture from the monsoon. The good news is that the afternoon thunderstorms usually end by dark, leaving the nights and mornings clear and calm.

The monsoon ends around mid-September, leaving behind clear, cool, stable weather. Autumn is a delightful time to explore the entire region. While low desert days may be warm, and mountain nights nippy, the days are usually bright and clear.

Winter storms may strike Utah, Colorado, and northern Arizona as early as October, but serious snowfall usually holds off until late November. Once the winter pattern does set in, by the end of December most of the high country is under deep snow, making it the domain of the cross-country skier and the snowshoer. Meanwhile, much of the desert country starts to receive some rain, causing it to green up. In wet years the first desert flowers start to appear in January. By late winter, all but the lowest deserts will have received rain—the Sonoran Desert of southern Arizona and northern Mexico receives half its annual moisture from the winter rains. Winter weather moves north, away from the Southwest, in April, but the southern edge of storms sweeping across the Northwest bring spring winds in the Southwest, which can be strong enough to cause sand storms in the high deserts of southern Utah. Depending on the timing and amount of winter moisture, the deserts can produce unbelievable wildflower displays in the spring.

HOW TO USE THIS BOOK

Start: Directions to all the trailheads begin from a nearby town and the total distance from this point to the trailhead is listed here.

Distance: This is the total distance of the hike, whether out-and-back, around a loop, or one way with a car shuttle. Distances were measured with computer mapping software and websites. Although slightly shorter than distances measured on the ground with a trail wheel, the mileages are consistent throughout the book.

Hiking time: The time for an average hiker to do the hike. These times err on the conservative side but do not take into account rest stops, photography, and other non-hiking activities. Fast hikers will need less time, while slow or out-of-shape hikers may use more time.

Difficulty: All hikes are rated as easy, moderate, or strenuous, with reasons for the rating. Although this is necessarily a highly subjective rating, nearly anyone who can walk should be able to do an easy hike in just a few hours. Moderate hikes are longer—up to a full day—and may involve several hundred feet or more of elevation gain, and possibly cross-country hiking as well. Experienced hikers will have no problems; beginners should hike with someone more experienced and will have more fun if they are in reasonable shape. Strenuous hikes are very long, requiring a full day of hiking by fit hikers, or several days in the case of backpack trips. The hiking may involve cross-country or faint, rough trails that require good map and compass skills, and some rock scrambling may be required on rough terrain. Only fit, experienced hikers should tackle these hikes.

Trail surface: Most trails in the Southwest region are dirt and rocks. Other trail surface conditions are described here, including hikes on old roads, paved trails, and cross-country.

Best seasons: The best part of the year to do the hike, taking into account such conditions as winter snow and summer heat.

Water: For backpackers and for emergency use by day hikers, this section lists known water sources. Most springs and creeks should be considered seasonal, and you should never depend on a single source of water. All water should be purified before using it to drink or cook. Day hikers should carry all the water they'll need.

Other trail users: You may encounter horses and/or mountain bikes on some of the trails.

Canine compatibility: Many people like to hike with their furry friends, so this section mentions whether dogs are allowed, and restrictions, if any. All areas that are open to dogs require that they be under control, which for most dogs means on a leash. If your dog barks or runs up to other hikers, even in a friendly way, then it is not under control and must be kept on a leash. This is just common courtesy to other hikers, some of whom may have had bad experiences with dogs.

Fees and permits: If any fees, including entry fees, are required, they are mentioned here. Any permits required are also listed.

Schedule: If access is limited to certain times of the day or year for administrative reasons such as road closures, you'll find that information here.

Maps: The CalTopo.com MapBuilder Topo layer, the Gaia GPS map layer, and National Geographic Trails Illustrated paper maps that show the hike are listed here. With CalTopo's (caltopo.com) and Gaia GPS's (gaiagps.com) web-based maps, you can print custom maps for the area of your hike including any of the topo, street mapping, and satellite and aerial image layers. The Trails Illustrated paper maps are the most up-to-date trail maps, where they are available. Trails Illustrated maps are available as a layer in Gaia GPS.

Trail contacts: Look here for the name and contact information of the agency or organization responsible for managing the land crossed by the hike. It's a good idea to call or e-mail the land-management agency before your hike to check on road and trail conditions. Where possible, the contact information includes the mailing and street address, phone number, and website. E-mail addresses are not included because they change frequently; check the agency website for an e-mail address, generally found under a "Contact" link. Sometimes web addresses change as well, but you can usually find land-management units on the web with a search engine.

Finding the trailhead: This section gives driving directions from the nearest town, as well as the GPS coordinates in latitude and longitude.

The Hike: Here's the meat of the hike—a detailed description of the trail or route and the features and attractions along the way. I describe the route using landmarks as well as trail signs, when possible, because trail signs can be missing. Refer to the next section, "Miles and Directions," for a description with distances between key points.

Miles and Directions: This table lists the key points, such as trail intersections, or turning points on a cross-country hike, by miles and tenths. You should be able to find the route with this table alone. The mileages in this book do not necessarily agree with distances found on trail signs, agency mileages, and other descriptions, because trail miles are measured by a variety of methods and personnel. All mileages were carefully measured using digital topographic mapping software for accuracy and consistency within the book.

MAP LEGEND

Municipal

=〔15〕=	Interstate Highway
=〔181〕=	US Highway
=〔522〕=	State Road
=〔176〕=	County/Forest Road
= = = =	Gravel Road
= = = =	Unpaved Road
⊢—•—⊣	Railroad
▪▪▪▬▪▪▪	International Border
▪▪▪▪—▪▪▪▪	State Boundary

Trails

------	Featured Trail
------	Trail
··········	Cross-country Route

Water Features

⬭	Body of Water
∽	River/Creek
⌇	Intermittent Stream
⋚	Waterfall
∥	Rapids
⟳	Spring

Symbols

▲	Backcountry Campsite
⟐	Boat Launch
⏝	Bridge
▪	Building/Point of Interest
⛺	Campground
∴	Dunes
×	Elevation
∩	Natural Arch
🅿	Parking
⏝	Pass
▲	Peak
🏕	Picnic Area
⛑	Ranger Station/Park Office
🚻	Restroom
📷	Scenic View/Overlook
○	Town
①	Trailhead
❓	Visitor/Information Center

Land Management

▭	National Park/Forest/Recreation Area
▭	National Monument/Wilderness Area
▭	State Park/Forest, County Park
▭	Indian Reservation

SOUTHERN NEVADA

1 WHITE DOMES LOOP

This is a great little loop hike through the slickrock formations of the White Domes in the northern portion of Valley of Fire State Park. Highlights include an old movie set and a short sandstone narrows.

Start: 57.5 miles northeast of Las Vegas
Distance: 1.2-mile loop
Hiking time: About 2 hours
Difficulty: Easy due to little elevation change
Trail surface: Sand, dirt, and rocks
Best seasons: Fall through spring
Water: None
Other trail users: None

Canine compatibility: Leashed dogs permitted, maximum 6-foot leash
Fees and permits: Entrance fee
Schedule: Open all year
Maps: CalTopo.com MapBuilder Topo layer; Gaia GPS Trails Illustrated layer
Trail contacts: Valley of Fire State Park, 29450 Valley of Fire Rd., Overton NV 89040; (702) 397-2088; http://parks.nv.gov/parks/valley-of-fire

FINDING THE TRAILHEAD

 From the intersection of US 95 and I-15 in downtown Las Vegas, drive 32.8 miles north on I-15. Turn right on NV 169, the Valley of Fire Highway, and drive 19.0 miles. Turn left on the road to the visitor center and Fire Canyon/White Domes. Continue past the visitor center 2.0 miles, and then turn left on the White Domes Road. Drive 3.7 miles to the White Domes Trailhead at the end of the road. GPS: N36 29.151' / W114 31.980'

THE HIKE

Leave the White Domes Trailhead to the south and follow the White Domes Trail up and over a sandy pass between two of the many white domes of sandstone. On the far side the trail descends to a small flat with the remains of a Hollywood movie set, which was used in the 1965 filming of *The Professionals*. Now the trail turns to the right (west) and follows a drainage through a narrows, where the canyon walls squeeze in to a trail less than 5 feet wide. This narrows is short and you soon emerge into a more open area. Now the White Domes Trail turns right (north) and climbs gently to a pass between slickrock formations. It then crosses a gravelly flat and turns east and then south to return to the trailhead, meeting the parking lot at its northwest corner.

The origin of the term *slickrock* is unknown, although the word dates from 1925, according to Merriam-Webster. Slickrock means smooth, rounded sandstone formations, like those in the White Domes area. The official definition mentions wind polishing, though wind has little effect other than removing loose grains of sand. The main agent of erosion in slickrock country is running water. Rainfall splashes on the rock and runs off in sheets. Where water pockets form in depressions on the rock, the standing water slowly dissolves the calcite cement that holds the sand grains together. When the water pocket dries out, wind removes the loose sand, deepening the pocket.

White Domes Trail

Walking in loose sand can be tedious, especially if you try to force your pace. The key is to slow down and walk a bit flatfooted. A brisker pace causes you to dig your toes in and waste energy.

Sheets of rainwater (and melting snow in higher slickrock deserts, such as Utah's Canyonlands) run down the rock, dissolving the calcite and removing loose grains of sand. Rivulets coalesce into drainages, which tend to form along weaknesses in the rock such as joints and faults.

A *joint* is a crack in the rock without any movement of the rock on either side of the joint, other than to make the crack wider. A *fault* is a break in the rock caused by movement of one mass of rock relative to the other. Joints commonly form as erosion removes overlying layers of rock. The reduced pressure allows the formerly buried layers to expand, and the result is that the rock cracks apart.

In sandstone, joints are usually parallel to each other, so that as running water expands the joints, the remaining mass of rock tends to be roughly rectangular. Another erosion mechanism, spalling, occurs when water gets into a crack and freezes. The resulting expansion of ice widens the crack and eventually causes a slab of rock to break off. This creates a tendency toward rounded, dome shapes. As erosion continues, the sandstone domes become isolated with expanses of flat rock or sand in between.

Slickrock country can seem chaotic because of the joint canyons that seem to run every which way, but the fact that running water is the main agent of erosion imposes order on the landscape. Every tiny drainage leads to a larger one, which in turn leads to a larger one, and so on until (in this case) the runoff reaches the Overton Arm of Lake Mead, the former course of the Virgin River, which in turn flows into the Colorado River and to the sea.

White Domes Trail

Sometimes the effect of joints can be seen when they are still buried. Flat expanses of sandstone often have a thin layer of soil or sand. In such areas plants can be seen growing in straight lines as if manually planted there. What's happening is that the plants tend to grow along the slightly buried joints because moisture tends to collect along the hidden cracks.

Joint canyons can be truly impressive—straight as an arrow and sometimes hundreds of feet deep. Often the floor of the joint canyon is covered with loose sand so the fact that water widened the joint is not obvious. Many years may pass between major rainstorms in any given desert area, so that erosion proceeds at a very slow pace and drifting sand tends to obscure the fact that the joint is a watercourse. Also remember that the landscape evolves over geologic time, where a human lifetime is but an instant.

While most of the sandstone formations in the Valley of Fire are red, white sandstone is predominant in the White Domes area. Color variations in the sandstone are caused by slight mineral impurities that stain the fine grains of quartz. Red rocks are generally the result of trace amounts of iron oxide (rust), and white rocks lack coloration, letting the natural white color of the quartz grains show.

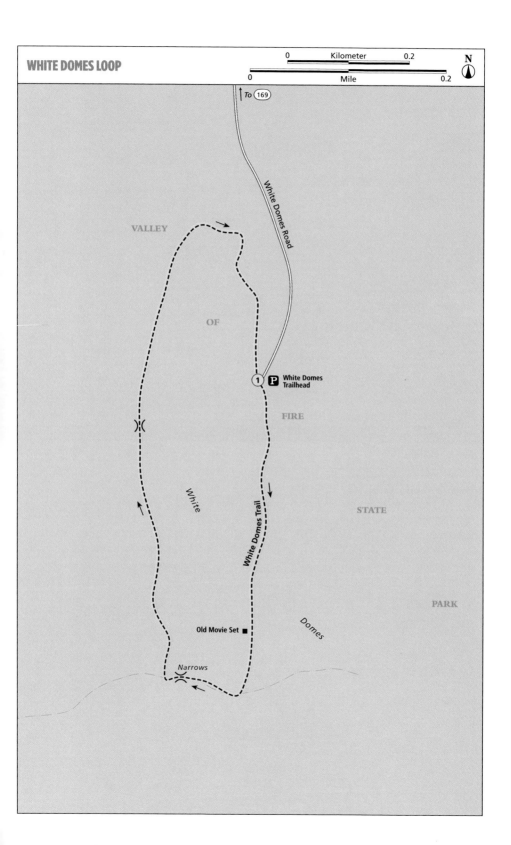

WHITE DOMES LOOP

0   Kilometer   0.2

0   Mile   0.2

N

To 169

White Domes Road

VALLEY

OF

1 P White Domes
      Trailhead

FIRE

White

White Domes Trail

STATE

PARK

Old Movie Set ■

Domes

Narrows

White Domes Trail

MILES AND DIRECTIONS

0.0 Start the loop clockwise by hiking south on the White Domes Trail from the trail sign at the south end of the parking lot.

0.4 Pass the old movie set, turn right, and follow the trail west down the wash.

0.7 At the end of the narrows, follow the trail north over a low pass.

1.0 The White Domes Trail turns right and heads east.

1.1 Follow the trail south.

1.2 Arrive back at the White Domes Trailhead.

2 SILICA DOME

This is a short but fine walk to the top of Silica Dome, a sandstone formation overlooking the head of Fire Canyon. It offers one of the best viewpoints in the park.

Start: 54.6 miles northeast of Las Vegas
Distance: 0.8-mile out-and-back
Hiking time: About 1 hour
Difficulty: Easy due to little elevation change
Trail surface: Sand and slickrock
Best seasons: Fall through spring
Water: None
Other trail users: None

Canine compatibility: Leashed dogs permitted, maximum 6-foot leash
Fees and permits: Entrance fee
Schedule: Open all year
Maps: CalTopo.com MapBuilder Topo layer; Gaia GPS Trails Illustrated layer
Trail contacts: Valley of Fire State Park, 29450 Valley of Fire Rd., Overton NV 89040; (702) 397-2088; http://parks.nv.gov/parks/valley-of-fire

FINDING THE TRAILHEAD

From the intersection of US 95 and I-15 in downtown Las Vegas, drive 32.8 miles north on I-15. Turn right on NV 169, the Valley of Fire Highway, and drive 19.0 miles. Turn left on the road to the visitor center and Fire Canyon /White Domes. Continue past the visitor center 2.8 miles to the Silica Domes Trailhead on the right. GPS: N36 27.324' / W114 30.143'

THE HIKE

From the parking lot follow the trail east across a ravine toward an old road. After a few feet on the road, the trail turns south and heads directly toward Silica Dome. A short climb leads to the summit and a panoramic view. Directly below you to the southwest lies the head of Fire Canyon, the major drainage for the area.

The summit of Silica Dome is an easy-to-reach vantage point from which you can get an idea of the topography of the park. Valley of Fire is in the Mojave Desert, which covers the southern tip of Nevada. Vast areas of the valleys around you are covered with creosote bush.

Silica Dome is the location where the fight scene from the movie *Star Trek: Generations* was filmed, probably the most famous movie of the many that have been shot at Valley of Fire.

A lot of park visitors wonder why they don't see any wildlife, but then they are constantly on the move or talking to each other. Any noise or movement tends to cause wildlife to move off. Using metal-tipped trekking poles virtually guarantees that you won't see any wildlife. Your best chance to see wildlife is to sit quietly in one place for a while, especially around sunset and sunrise.

Fire Canyon from Silica Dome

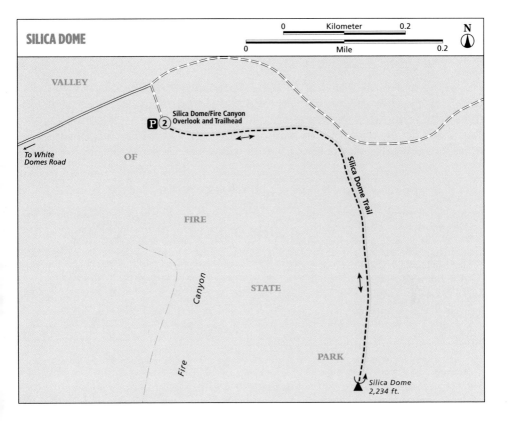

ORIGIN OF SILICA DOME

The name *Silica Dome* comes from the fact that sandstone is usually composed of tiny grains of quartz, a mineral primarily formed from silica. Quartz is a hard mineral and survives erosion that dissolves softer minerals. Sedimentary rocks such as those that make up Silica Dome are formed when silica sand grains are deposited in layers, usually underwater but occasionally in sand-dune fields. As more layers are deposited above and heat and pressure increases, the sand grains become cemented together with a mineral such as calcite and compressed into stone. Later, when the layers of sandstone are exposed by uplifting, water dissolves the calcite and carries away the sand grains, starting the process anew.

MILES AND DIRECTIONS

0.0   Leave the Silica Dome Trailhead and hike east across a ravine.

0.2   When the trail meets an old road, turn right and head south, directly toward Silica Dome.

0.3   Start the climb by walking up easy sandstone slabs toward the summit.

0.4   Arrive at Silica Dome. Return the way you came.

0.8   Arrive back at the Silica Dome Trailhead.

3 CATHEDRAL ROCK

The popular trail to the top of 8,261-foot Cathedral Rock is a great way to get a view of Kyle Canyon and the surrounding peaks without having to make the much longer climb to one of the high summits. Cathedral Rock got its name because of its cathedral-like prominence above upper Kyle Canyon.

Start: 37.5 miles northwest of Las Vegas
Distance: 2.8-mile out-and-back
Hiking time: About 2 hours
Difficulty: Moderate due to 1,090-foot elevation change
Trail surface: Dirt and rocks
Best seasons: Spring through fall
Water: Unnamed spring
Other trail users: Horses
Canine compatibility: Leashed dogs permitted

Fees and permits: None
Schedule: Open all year
Maps: CalTopo.com MapBuilder Topo layer; Gaia GPS Gaia Topo layer
Trail contacts: Spring Mountains National Recreation Area, Humboldt-Toiyabe National Forest, 4701 N. Torrey Pines Dr., Las Vegas NV 89130-2301; (702) 872-5486; https://www.fs.usda.gov/htnf

FINDING THE TRAILHEAD

From the intersection of US 95 and I-15 in downtown Las Vegas, drive 16.7 miles northwest on US 95. Turn left on NV 157, Kyle Canyon Road, and drive 20.8 miles to the Lower Cathedral Trailhead, on the right. Parking is limited, so it is best to arrive early, especially on weekends. There is additional parking in the Cathedral Rock Picnic Area just up the road. Entry to the picnic area requires a fee. GPS: N36 15.455' / W115 38.974'

THE HIKE

After climbing the stairs above the Lower Cathedral Trailhead parking area, turn left on the Cathedral Rock Trail. Initially the trail traverses above the highway below, but soon climbs away. It meets the main Cathedral Rock Trail, which comes in from the left from the Cathedral Rock Picnic Area. Stay right and continue the ascent. Broad switchbacks take the well-graded trail back and forth through a dense stand of young aspen trees. These aspens are a uniform height because the trail is climbing up a major avalanche path. Sometime in the recent past, probably in the last few decades, a major avalanche wiped out all the trees here. The aspens were the first trees to appear after the conifers were destroyed. Evidence of frequent large avalanches—in the form of snapped-off and damaged trees—is obvious when the trail switchbacks at the edges of the avalanche path.

As you climb, the towering limestone cliffs of Cathedral Rock loom above the trail to the west. Watch for a short unmarked spur trail to the left, at the end of one of the switchbacks. This trail leads to a small, pleasant, unnamed spring, one of the many hidden springs that gave the Spring Mountains their name. As the trail climbs to a point nearly level with the saddle south of Cathedral Rock, a final switchback leads to the right and

Cathedral Rock

traverses through a fine mixed stand of ponderosa pine, white fir, and Douglas fir. A second spring pours out of a culvert at the saddle.

Above the saddle the Cathedral Rock Trail makes its final ascent to the summit via a series of switchbacks. Because Cathedral Rock is at the end of a ridge projecting north, the views of Kyle Canyon are spectacular, extending the length of the canyon and far out into the desert to the east. To the south the long, high ridge that connects Griffith Peak and Charleston Peak, known locally as the South Rim, dominates the skyline high above you, with Charleston Peak visible to the southwest.

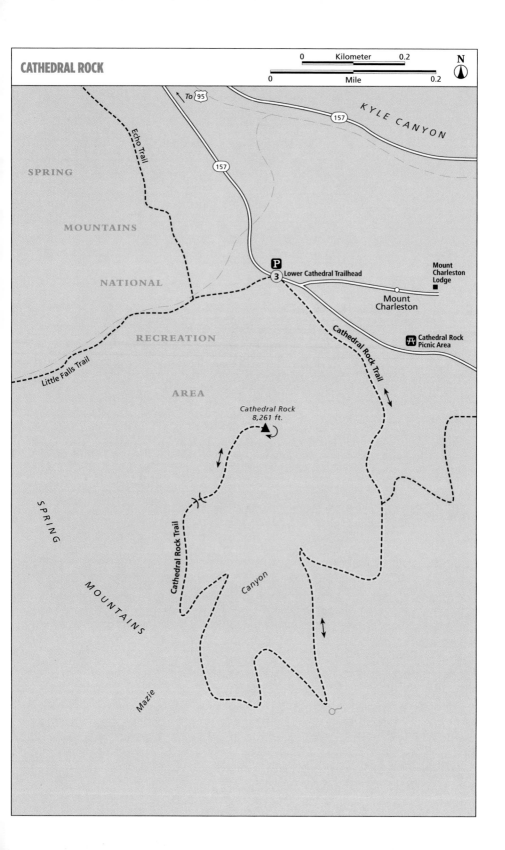

CATHEDRAL ROCK

Kyle Canyon from the Cathedral Rock Trail

Many people assume that Kyle Canyon was carved by glaciers because of the imposing limestone cliffs. Actually, there is no evidence of glacial activity in the Spring Mountains. This spectacular landscape was carved primarily by flowing water. Since most of the streams are seasonal, much of the erosion takes place during the occasional major storm. Summer thunderstorms are especially effective at eroding canyons because they commonly drop large amounts of rain into small areas in a short period of time. The resulting flash floods often contain more sand and rock than water and can cause dramatic changes in the landscape in a few hours.

The limestone formations in Kyle Canyon and the Spring Mountains are about the same age as the Redwall limestone in the Grand Canyon. Massive limestone cliffs are common throughout the Rocky Mountains and intermountain areas of North America. The nearly pure limestone was deposited in a deep ocean environment. Microscopic sea creatures swam in this ancient ocean, and when they died their shells fell to the sea floor in a steady rain. Over millions of years the shells built up layers of sediment hundreds or even thousands of feet thick. As additional sediment accumulated on top, the layers of shells were compressed into solid rock.

MILES AND DIRECTIONS

- 0.0 Climb the stairs above the parking lot and turn left onto the Cathedral Rock Trail.
- 0.3 The trail from the Cathedral Rock Picnic Area joins from the left; stay right.
- 0.7 The spur trail on the left leads to an unnamed spring. Stay right on the Cathedral Rock Trail.
- 1.3 Reach a saddle.
- 1.4 Reach the summit of Cathedral Rock. Return the way you came.
- 2.8 Arrive back at the trailhead.

4 CHARLESTON PEAK.

Charleston Peak, at 11,811 feet, is the highest point in the Spring Mountains as well as southern Nevada. There are two main trails to the summit: South Loop Trail and Trail Canyon–North Loop. Both offer about the same length and difficulty, but the scenery and the final approach to the summit are different. This approach, via the South Loop Trail, gets nearly all the climbing over early and then traverses the long, scenic South Rim ridge from Griffith Peak to Charleston Peak, passing through one of the most extensive bristlecone forests in Nevada.

Start: 37.5 miles northwest of Las Vegas
Distance: 16.4-mile out-and-back
Hiking time: About 10 hours
Difficulty: Strenuous due to 4,270-foot elevation change and high elevations
Trail surface: Dirt and rocks, short sections of old road near the start
Best seasons: Summer through fall
Water: None
Other trail users: Horses

Canine compatibility: Leashed dogs permitted
Fees and permits: None
Schedule: Open all year
Maps: CalTopo.com MapBuilder Topo layer; Gaia GPS Gaia Topo layer
Trail contacts: Spring Mountains National Recreation Area, Humboldt-Toiyabe National Forest, 4701 N. Torrey Pines Dr., Las Vegas NV 89130-2301; (702) 872-5486; https://www.fs.usda.gov/htnf

FINDING THE TRAILHEAD

From the intersection of US 95 and I-15 in downtown Las Vegas, drive 16.7 miles northwest on US 95. Turn left on NV 157, Kyle Canyon Road, and drive 20.8 miles to the Lower Cathedral Trailhead, on the right. Parking is limited, so it is best to arrive early, especially on weekends. There is additional parking in the Cathedral Rock Picnic Area just up the road. Entry to the picnic area requires a fee. GPS: N36 15.455' / W115 38.974'

THE HIKE

From the trailhead the South Loop Trail climbs above the picnic area, traversing through a mixed forest of mountain mahogany, ponderosa pine, and quaking aspen. Climbing steadily, the trail crosses the canyon above the picnic area, and then climbs steeply along the east side of the canyon, following an old road. The old road ends and the trail narrows where it crosses the canyon again, below towering limestone cliffs. The canyon is clearly a major avalanche path, as shown by the destroyed trees and small aspens growing in the canyon bottom.

Switchbacks lead up the north side of the canyon until the trail is above the cliffs. The South Loop Trail then climbs out of the canyon to the north and switchbacks up a broad ridge. The first limber and bristlecone pines appear at this point. A couple of the switchbacks provide views overlooking Charleston Peak miles to the north. The trail continues its well-graded but steady climb to the ridge south of Charleston Peak, known

Cathedral Rock

locally as the South Rim. A sign that you're nearing the South Rim is the disappearance of all trees except for bristlecone pines.

At the ridge a sign marks the junction with the Griffith Peak Trail, coming in from the left. Stay right on the South Loop Trail, and follow it north toward Charleston Peak. The trail skirts the edge of the South Rim and traverses beautiful alpine meadows and groves of bristlecone pines. Occasionally the trail passes through a saddle on the rim and lets you look down into Kyle Canyon, now more than 3,000 feet below.

As the trail gradually climbs, it begins skirting the edge of timberline as it traverses the western slopes of the South Rim. After the last trees are left behind, the trail begins the final ascent of the mountain. Watch for an unmarked spur trail on the right above a saddle, which leads to the scattered wreckage of a plane that crashed here in 1955.

Above the crash site the South Loop Trail swings around to the west and climbs to the summit of Charleston Peak via a final switchback up the western slopes. The windswept summit is marked by a couple of solar-powered radio repeaters, an aluminum benchmark disk, and a summit register mounted on a short pole. A rock shelter just to the north offers some protection from the wind.

Charleston Peak was named after the city of Charleston, South Carolina, by a topographic mapping group of the US Army Corps of Engineers in 1869. The native Southern Paiutes called the peak *Nuvant*, and it was the most famous place in the mythology of the Chemehuevi and the western bands of the Southern Paiute.

This hike showcases how life adapts to increasing elevation and harsher conditions. During the ascent from the trailhead to the South Rim and the junction with the Griffith Peak Trail, you are climbing through a forest that is protected from the prevailing southwest winds by the slope's northeast aspect. As a result the trees grow tall and slender as they compete with their fellow trees for sunlight. This tendency is especially apparent in the ponderosa pines that grow on the lower slopes just above the trailhead. Mature ponderosa pines drop their lower branches, so that the bottom 20 or 30 feet of the trunk is bare of limbs. Ponderosa pines are very heat-tolerant as long as they get enough water, so they are typically the lowest tall trees growing in the Nevada mountain ranges. Cold limits their upper range, so as you climb you'll see more cold-tolerant trees such as limber pine, Douglas fir, and white fir mixing in with the ponderosa pines, and finally replacing them.

One adaptation that evergreen trees make to cold is to grow denser foliage, which conserves heat. Limber pines have needles in tight bunches of five, as opposed to the looser bundles of three on ponderosa pines. This effect is even more pronounced in

PLANE CRASH SITE

On November 17, 1955, an Air Force C-54 transport plane crashed into the slopes of Charleston Peak just south of the summit, apparently during bad weather. The crash, the aircraft mission, and even the names of the fourteen men who died in the crash were kept secret until 2001. The plane was flying from Palmdale, California, to Groom Lake, the top-secret military test center north of Las Vegas. Aboard were some of the designers and engineers involved in the highly classified U2 spy plane, as well as the flight crew. Apparently the pilot was flying in and out of clouds and misjudged a turn, striking the mountain at the 11,400-foot level. Over the years much of the wreckage has been carried off by souvenir hunters.

Bristlecone pine, South Loop Trail, Mount Charleston

Engelmann spruce, whose single short needles are crowded together on the branches. Likewise, bristlecone pines, which you'll encounter as you near the top of the climb to the South Rim, have five short needles tightly bunched together.

Another adaptation to cold is huddling. As you continue northwest along the ridge toward Charleston Peak and approach timberline, you'll notice that the trees are shorter and tend to grow in small groves. By growing together in such clusters, trees give each other protection from the fiercely cold winter winds and blowing snow.

Krummholz is another adaptation and is common right at timberline. Because the icy wind and abrasive blowing snow tend to kill exposed tree limbs and needles, the only surviving trees are small and grow in dense mats behind a boulder or a rock ledge. The obstruction tends to protect the foliage from wind and driven snow as well as causing snowdrifts to form on their lee sides, providing further protection. Some krummholz appear to have no protection, but they are protected by snowdrifts that regularly form in the same place because of variations in the terrain.

When a tree does manage to send up a vertical trunk above the protective mat, the wind kills all the branches on the upwind side, so the remaining branches appear to be streaming downwind like a flag, which is why these trees are often referred to as "flag trees."

On the final climb of Charleston Peak, beyond the crash site, the only plants that can survive the arctic conditions grow low to the ground, often in mats. Seasonal wildflowers must flower and go to seed quickly in order to reproduce before the short growing season comes to an end.

Mount Charleston

Mount Charleston

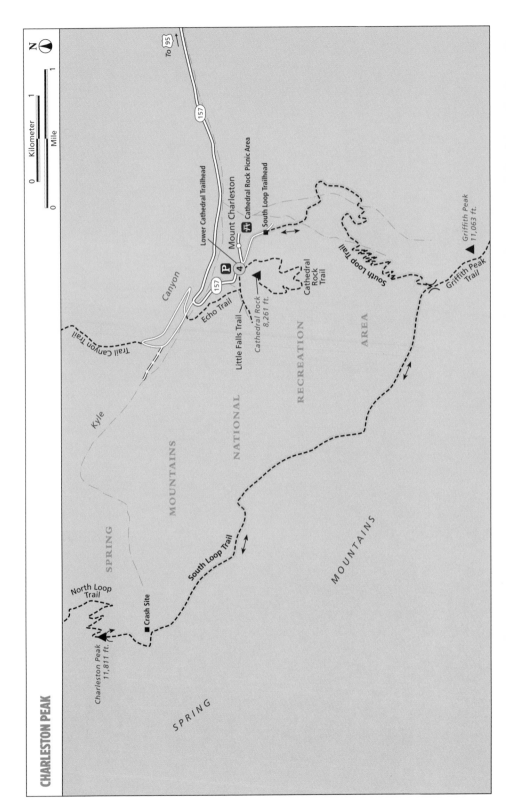

CHARLESTON PEAK

Notice how the bristlecones growing just below the South Rim are relatively tall and slender, at least for bristlecone pines, and the trees growing along the South Rim and its western slopes are short and squat. That's because the trees on the east slopes are more protected from prevailing winter storms, which come out of the west. The trees along the South Rim ridge must endure much harsher winter weather, but as a result they live much longer than the more sheltered trees.

MILES AND DIRECTIONS

0.0 From the Lower Cathedral Trailhead, walk up the road into the Cathedral Rock Picnic Area.

0.4 From the South Loop Trailhead, start on the South Loop Trail.

1.0 The South Loop Trail crosses the drainage in the avalanche path below Griffith Peak.

1.5 The trail crosses the drainage again and climbs the west slopes of the canyon.

2.0 Cross the ridge and follow the trail southwest across a minor avalanche path.

4.0 Reach a junction with the Griffith Peak Trail in a saddle on the South Rim. Stay right on the South Loop Trail.

7.7 An unmarked hiker trail turns right and leads to the wreckage from a 1955 plane crash.

7.8 Rejoin the South Loop Trail; stay right.

8.2 Reach Charleston Peak. Return the way you came.

16.4 Arrive back at Lower Cathedral Trailhead.

5 MARY JANE FALLS

Probably the most popular hike in the Spring Mountains, the reputation of this well-graded trail is deserved. The hike takes you through fine alpine forest into the cliff-bound head of Kyle Canyon and ends at a permanent waterfall.

Start: 37.8 miles northwest of Las Vegas
Distance: 3.0-mile out-and-back
Hiking time: 2–3 hours
Difficulty: Moderate due to 1,100-foot elevation change
Trail surface: Dirt and rocks
Best seasons: Spring through fall
Water: Mary Jane Falls
Other trail users: Horses
Canine compatibility: Leashed dogs permitted

Fees and permits: None
Schedule: Open all year
Maps: CalTopo.com MapBuilder Topo layer; Gaia GPS Gaia Topo layer
Trail contacts: Spring Mountains National Recreation Area, Humboldt-Toiyabe National Forest, 4701 N. Torrey Pines Dr., Las Vegas NV 89130-2301; (702) 872-5486; https://www .fs.usda.gov/htnf

FINDING THE TRAILHEAD

From the intersection of US 95 and I-15 in downtown Las Vegas, drive 16.7 miles northwest on US 95. Turn left on NV 157, Kyle Canyon Road, and drive 20.5 miles. Bear right onto Echo Road and continue 0.4 mile. Turn left at the Mary Jane Falls turnoff and drive 0.2 mile to the Mary Jane Falls Trailhead. GPS: N36 16.044' / W115 39.756'

Mary Jane Falls flows all year but is most spectacular in the spring after a snowy winter.

THE HIKE

From the trailhead the Mary Jane Falls Trail climbs west up the north side of the broad head of Kyle Canyon, climbing steadily but not too steeply through beautiful stands of quaking aspen, ponderosa pine, white fir, and Douglas fir. Watch for the point where the trail abruptly switchbacks to the right and leaves the canyon bottom. A series of well-graded switchbacks ascend to the north, finally leading to the base of an imposing limestone cliff. The trail then turns northwest and follows the base of the cliff to Mary Jane Falls. The falls are best in the spring after a snowy winter, but they run all year long. On a hot day it's pleasant to climb into the large cave at the base of the falls and cool off, but use care negotiating the mossy, slippery rocks. A short trail leads left from the falls to a small cave.

Rattlesnakes are present throughout North America into southern Canada from sea level to near timberline and are found as high as 10,000 feet right here in the Spring Mountains. In reality the tiny desert bark scorpion is far more dangerous, having killed ten times as many people as rattlesnakes in Arizona—a state with a lot of rattlesnakes. Rattlesnakes present a manageable hazard on the trail, and you are more likely to be injured on the way to the trailhead by a driver yakking on a cell phone than you are by a rattlesnake.

Mary Jane Falls Trail

The rattlesnake's unique rattle is defensive and serves to warn away large animals. Since rattlesnakes used to share habitats with large hoofed animals such as bison and elk, and still coexist with domestic cattle, the shrill, unmistakable sound of the rattle is a great defense. The rattle itself consists of hollow buttons, or segments, of kerotin (the same protein-based material that forms hair and fingernails), which grow on the tail. Although mature rattlesnakes usually give hikers plenty of warning by shaking their tails so fast that they are a blur, they don't always rattle—most snakes sense you before you're even aware of their presence and move quietly away. Young rattlesnakes have a single button and although they may shake their tail furiously, they don't produce a sound. They do have venom, though.

A member of the pit viper family, rattlesnakes hunt mice and other small rodents and mammals by sensing ground vibrations, by smell, and by infrared light. The "pits" that give pit vipers their name are actually organs sensitive to infrared light, which humans cannot see. Because infrared light is given off by warm objects, warm-blooded mammals stand out against their backgrounds when viewed in infrared.

When the rattlesnake strikes its prey, it injects poisonous venom through a pair of fangs that are hollow like a hypodermic needle. The fangs fold back against the roof of the snake's mouth when not in use. Rattlesnake venom is hemotoxic, or tissue-destructive. The venom has two functions: first, to immediately paralyze the snake's prey so it can't run off, and second, to start the digestive process. Rattlesnakes swallow their prey whole, so they can't handle prey that can run away or fight back.

Most human victims of rattlesnakes are snake collectors or people attempting to handle or tease rattlesnakes. And more bites take place around human habitation than in the wild. For the hiker, a little bit of knowledge can reduce the rattlesnake hazard to almost zero.

Contrary to the popular notion that rattlesnakes thrive in scorching heat, they are cold-blooded like all reptiles and take their body temperature from their environment. Since

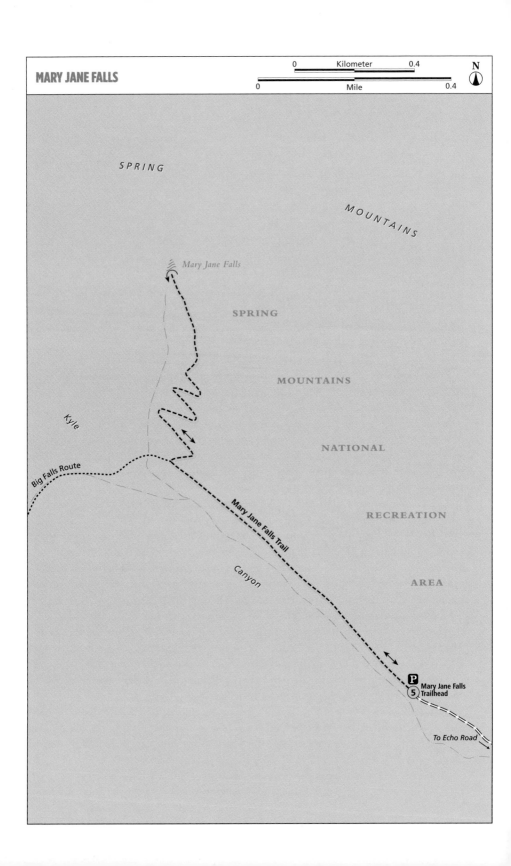

MARY JANE FALLS

0   Kilometer   0.4
0   Mile   0.4

N

SPRING

MOUNTAINS

Mary Jane Falls

SPRING

MOUNTAINS

Kyle

NATIONAL

Big Falls Route

Mary Jane Falls Trail

RECREATION

Canyon

AREA

P
5 Mary Jane Falls
   Trailhead

To Echo Road

Mary Jane Falls Trail

they prefer a body temperature of about 80 degrees Fahrenheit, they prefer soil or stone surfaces at about that temperature. Temperatures of 100 Fahrenheit will quickly kill a rattlesnake. When the weather is hot, rattlesnakes seek the coolness of burrows or the shade of bushes and rocks. During chilly weather, they'll emerge and sun themselves on rocks or bare dirt. And during the winter and prolonged cold spells, they'll hibernate in burrows. Rattlesnakes can only strike about half their length, although they can strike from any position, not just a defensive coil. The western diamondback, the most common rattlesnake species in Nevada, averages about 4 to 5 feet and occasionally reaches 7 feet in length. Another common rattlesnake, the Mohave, is usually smaller but its venom is more potent.

To avoid surprises, always watch the ground ahead of you as you walk. If you want to look at distant scenery, stop first. Avoid placing your hands or feet closer than 3 feet to any place you cannot see into, such as the underside of dense brush. Don't walk close to shady overhanging rocks or ledges. Look over logs before stepping over them, or better yet, go around. If camping in warm weather, when snakes are nocturnal due to the daytime heat, sleep in a closed tent.

If someone is bitten, keep the victim calm and seek medical attention as soon as possible. Many defensive bites are dry because the snake doesn't waste venom on animals that are too large to eat. The main danger from rattlesnake bites is infection from the deep puncture wounds. Even if venom is injected, modern medical treatment uses antivenin injections that neutralize the venom and minimize tissue damage.

MILES AND DIRECTIONS

0.0　From the Mary Jane Falls Trailhead, follow the Mary Jane Falls Trail northwest up the canyon.

0.7　The trail turns sharply right as the unsigned route to Big Falls continues straight ahead. After you bend to the north, follow the switchbacks up the northeast slopes of the canyon below Mary Jane Falls.

1.5　Arrive at Mary Jane Falls. Return the way you came.

3.0　Arrive back at the Mary Jane Falls Trailhead.

6 MUMMY SPRING

This trail is an alternative approach to Mummy Spring using the North Loop Trail. It is shorter than the hike via Trail Canyon and starts from a higher trailhead. As a bonus, there are some fine stands of exposed, gnarled bristlecone pines along the hike.

Start: 39.1 miles northwest of Las Vegas
Distance: 5.2-mile out-and-back
Hiking time: 3–4 hours
Difficulty: Strenuous due to 1,380-foot elevation change and high elevations
Trail surface: Dirt and rocks
Best seasons: Spring through fall
Water: Mummy Spring
Other trail users: Horses

Canine compatibility: Leashed dogs permitted
Fees and permits: None
Schedule: Open all year
Maps: CalTopo.com MapBuilder Topo layer; Gaia GPS Gaia Topo layer
Trail contacts: Spring Mountains National Recreation Area, Humboldt-Toiyabe National Forest, 4701 N. Torrey Pines Dr., Las Vegas NV 89130-2301; (702) 872-5486; https://www.fs.usda.gov/htnf

FINDING THE TRAILHEAD

From the intersection of US 95 and I-15 in downtown Las Vegas, drive 16.7 miles northwest on US 95. Turn left on NV 157, Kyle Canyon Road, and drive 17.5 miles. Turn right on NV 158 and drive 4.9 miles to the North Loop Trailhead, on the left. GPS: N36 18.528' / W115 36.691'

THE HIKE

The North Loop Trail first skirts the edge of the road cut above the highway, then turns south and climbs steadily through stands of mountain mahogany, ponderosa pine, piñon pine, and juniper. As the slope steepens, the trail begins to switchback, and soon the first limber pine, white fir, and bristlecone pines appear. As the North Loop Trail comes out onto a windswept point, bristlecone pines begin to dominate the forest. A switchback on the end of the ridge offers a sweeping view of the Las Vegas Valley. After leaving this open area behind, the trail climbs through denser forest, and finally tops out on the end of another ridge. Now the trail descends gradually, passing through two saddles before arriving at a third, where there is an unsigned trail junction.

In the saddle a huge bristlecone pine, dubbed the Rain Tree, has been estimated to be more than 3,000 years old, which would make it the oldest bristlecone pine in the Spring Range. Trees can be dated precisely by taking core samples with a tree-boring tool, which does not harm the tree, but this has apparently not been done with Rain Tree.

Leave the saddle by turning right onto a distinct but unmarked trail. This trail descends gradually to end at Mummy Spring, which drips over a limestone ledge. The gully containing the spring is also an avalanche path, judging by the small, young aspen trees below the spring. The open ravine below the spring also gives you a view out to the north, toward the Sheep Range.

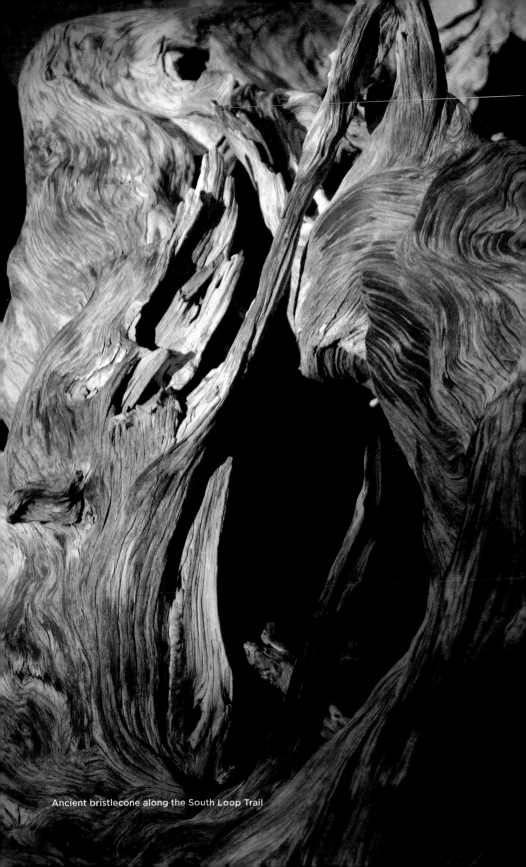

Ancient bristlecone along the South Loop Trail

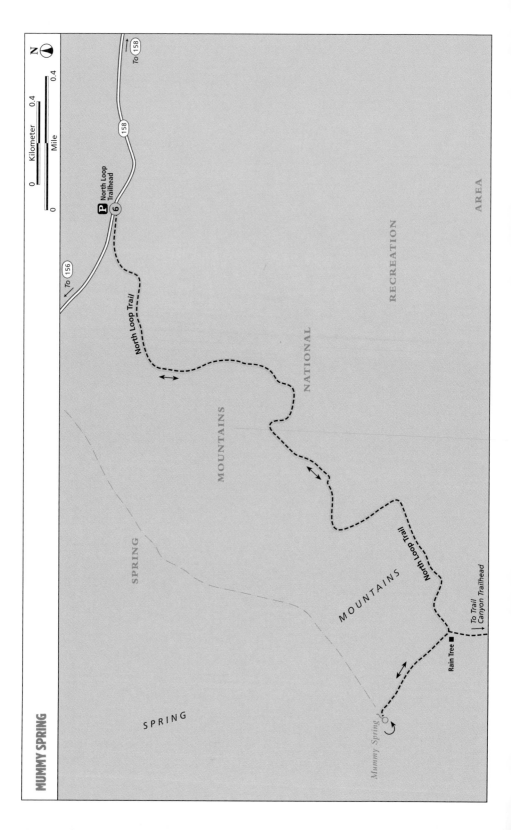

Another animal that provokes unreasonable fear in many desert dwellers is the the tarantula, which may measure 4 or more inches across the legs. This fear is unfounded—tarantulas, though fearsome-looking, are not aggressive and their bite is no worse than a bee or wasp sting.

Tarantulas are found throughout the western United States but are especially common in the Southwest. They live in burrows, emerging at night to hunt insects, other spiders, and lizards, which they attack by abruptly jumping or pouncing on. Venom injected by the spider's fangs serves to subdue their prey. Normally, they stay within a few dozen feet of their burrows, and retreat underground if threatened. Tarantulas are long-lived and may survive up to 15 years if not killed by predators such as rodents, birds, snakes, skunks, and javelinas. They are often seen crossing paved roads at night or even during the day, and many tarantulas are killed by cars and occasionally by misinformed people who think they are dangerous.

In the wild the nastiest enemy of the tarantula is the tarantula hawk, a large, dark blue wasp with red or orange wings. The female tarantula hawk attacks and paralyzes its hapless victim with multiple stings. It then drags the spider, which is many times the weight of the attacker, to its burrow. The tarantula hawk then lays its eggs on the back of the live but paralyzed tarantula, and exits, sealing the burrow behind it. When the young hatch, they feed on the spider.

Despite their gentle nature, never handle a tarantula. The fine hair on their undersides is very irritating, especially if it gets in your eyes, nose, or mouth. Avoid tarantula hawks also. While they are not aggressive toward humans or large animals, their sting is far worse than a tarantula's bite.

MILES AND DIRECTIONS

0.0 Leave the North Loop Trailhead and start on the North Loop Trail.

1.2 The North Loop Trail reaches a ridge with windblown bristlecone pines and a view to the northeast.

2.0 At the first saddle, continue on the North Loop Trail.

2.1 At the second saddle, continue on the North Loop Trail.

2.2 Arrive at the third saddle, the site of the Rain Tree, and turn right on an unmarked trail.

2.6 Arrive at Mummy Spring. Return the way you came.

5.2 Arrive back at the North Loop Trailhead.

7 BRISTLECONE LOOP

This trail circles an unnamed hill at the head of Lee Canyon and passes through an extensive stand of ancient bristlecone pines. This is one of the few trails in the Spring Mountains that is open to mountain bikers and it makes a fine ride.

Start: 47.9 miles northwest of Las Vegas

Distance: 5.6-mile loop

Hiking time: About 4 hours

Difficulty: Moderate due to 1,100-foot elevation gain

Trail surface: Dirt and rocks, old roads, 0.4-mile section of paved highway to close the loop

Best seasons: Spring through fall

Water: None

Other trail users: Horses and mountain bikes

Canine compatibility: Leashed dogs permitted

Fees and permits: None

Schedule: All year

Maps: CalTopo.com MapBuilder Topo layer; Gaia GPS Gaia Topo layer

Trail contacts: Spring Mountains National Recreation Area, Humboldt-Toiyabe National Forest, 4701 N. Torrey Pines Dr., Las Vegas NV 89130-2301; (702) 872-5486; https://www.fs.usda.gov/htnf

FINDING THE TRAILHEAD

From the intersection of US 95 and I-15 in downtown Las Vegas, drive 30.2 miles northwest on US 95. Turn left on NV 156, Lee Canyon Road. Continue 17.7 miles to the Upper Bristlecone Trailhead at the end of the highway, across from the Las Vegas Ski and Snowboard Resort. GPS: N36 18.407' / W115 40.687'

THE HIKE

At first the trail heads southwest along a ridge above the ski area. A fence on both sides of the trail was erected to protect some of the fragile, endemic plants that grow here. Soon the trail drops into a canyon bottom filled with an alpine forest of white fir, Douglas fir, bristlecone pines, and aspen. After the Bristlecone Trail makes a sharp right turn and climbs out of the canyon to the north, it crosses a more exposed slope where living conditions are much tougher than the canyon bottom you just left. These are exactly the conditions that bristlecone pines favor. In fact the Spring Mountains have extensive stands of bristlecones—at some 18,000 acres, the largest stand of bristlecones anywhere. Bristlecone pines are easy to identify by their needles, which grow in tight groups of five, giving the branches a "bottlebrush" appearance.

Bristlecone pines actually do grow well below timberline, where they are taller and more slender than their gnarled timberline counterparts. But the easy living exacts a price: "Low elevation" bristlecone pines rarely live 1,000 years before succumbing to disease, rot, or insects.

Descending slightly to a saddle, the trail reaches the end of a now-abandoned road built by the Works Progress Administration during the 1930s. The WPA and its sister "alphabet agencies" provided employment for thousands of people during the Great Depression and constructed roads, trails, bridges, and campgrounds throughout the national forests.

At a saddle the Bristlecone Trail meets the Bonanza Trail; stay right on the Bristlecone Trail. The trail continues to descend and the broad roadbed allows for some fine views.

Continue on the Bristlecone Trail as it heads east along the south slopes of a ridge. The trail swings around the east end of this ridge and descends into Scout Canyon in one long switchback to the west. The trail then turns east, and then south to end at the Lower Bristlecone Trailhead. Walk a short distance down the dirt road to NV 156, then follow the highway south to the Upper Bristlecone Trailhead.

Bristlecone pines are the patriarchs of the southwestern forests and their gnarled appearance reinforces that impression. Bristlecone pines are the oldest living trees anywhere and among the oldest living things on earth. Currently, the oldest known bristlecone pine is the Methuselah Tree in the White Mountains on the Nevada-California border, dated at 4,789 years old. An older tree was found in the Snake Range in east-central Nevada, but its age—over 4,900 years old—was only discovered after it had been cut down for research purposes. Normally, trees are dated by taking core samples with a special coring tool that leaves the tree undamaged, but in this case the researcher's tree-coring tool broke before he could finish his summer research project. Not suspecting that the tree he was about to study was so old, he asked permission from the managing agency to cut down just this one tree with a chainsaw.

The age of such a tree boggles the imagination. The oldest bristlecone pines started their lives at the dawn of recorded human history, thousands of miles away in the Middle

Ski area in Lee Canyon from the Bristlecone Loop Trail

Bristlecone Trail

East, and have lived through all the events since then. Wars have raged and civilizations have fallen while the trees clung to life in some of the most inhospitable places on earth—timberline on isolated mountain ranges in the middle of a desert.

Young bristlecone pines, those that have only reached 1,500 years or so in age, grow in the same fashion as other conifers, with a single, roundish central trunk covered with bark and living cambium. Bristlecone pines growing in sheltered forests below timberline grow straight and tall but rarely live more than 1,000 years before succumbing to heart rot. Timberline trees are short and gnarled, and older trees may be 5 feet thick and only 10 or 15 feet tall. As the tree ages, the roots become exposed by erosion and dry out, leaving the tree with less ability to support a full crown of branches. The tree's tactic is strip growth, where much of the cambium dies and the bark falls away, leaving most of the circumference of the trunk bare wood. Only a strip of bark may run up the trunk, providing nutrients to a few living branches. Under that living strip, new wood is added very slowly, and the new wood is exceptionally dense and resinous. The bristlecone not only needs very little water and soil to survive, but also creates wood that is very resistant to decay and attack by insects.

The type of soil makes a difference also. Bristlecone pines grow well on granite and quartzite-derived soils, but the oldest trees grow on dolomite, as found in the White Mountains of California and Nevada. The limestone and dolomites found on the high

Bristlecone Trail

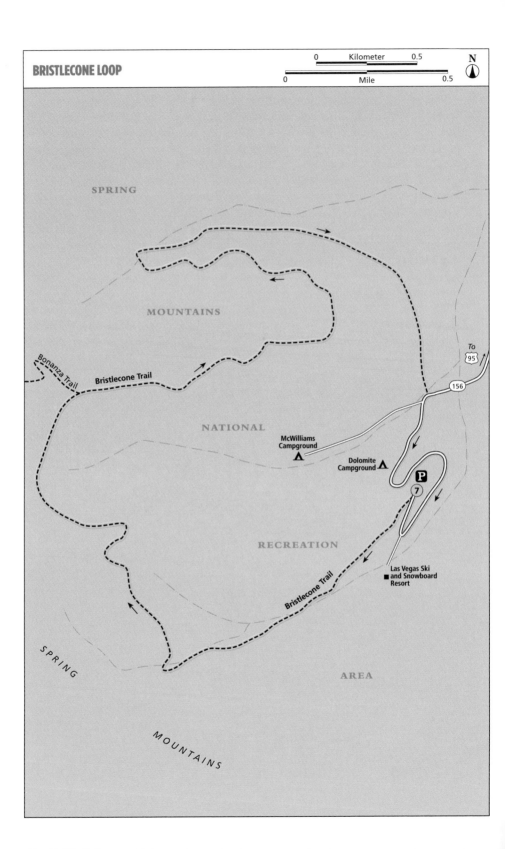

BRISTLECONE LOOP

0   Kilometer   0.5

0   Mile   0.5

N

SPRING

MOUNTAINS

Bonanza Trail

Bristlecone Trail

NATIONAL

McWilliams
Campground

Dolomite
Campground

To
95

156

P
7

Las Vegas Ski
and Snowboard
Resort

RECREATION

Bristlecone Trail

SPRING

AREA

MOUNTAINS

ridges of the Spring Mountains are also a favorable environment, which is one reason the bristlecone stands are so extensive here.

There appear to be several reasons that dolomite and limestone are such favorable environments for bristlecone pines. These calcite rocks form poor soil and plants are widely spaced. Young bristlecone pines need a lot of light to support their early fast growth, so they may favor dolomite and limestone because of the lack of competition. Also, light-colored dolomite and limestone reflect more light than darker rocks, which provides more light for the tree's photosynthesis, as well as keeping soil moisture and temperatures up. Slight increases in soil moisture make a large difference in the young bristlecone's rate of growth.

Because it is so resistant to decay, dead bristlecone wood lasts a long time—one piece more than 9,000 years old has been found (one good reason why you should never build campfires at timberline). By correlating tree rings between living and dead bristlecone wood, the tree ring record can be extended thousands of years into the past, giving researchers a window into past environments and climate.

MILES AND DIRECTIONS

0.0 Leave the Upper Bristlecone Trailhead on the Bristlecone Trail.

1.0 The Bristlecone Trail turns abruptly right (north) and leaves the canyon.

1.8 Cross the high point of the loop.

2.0 The singletrack trail becomes an old, closed road.

2.3 You'll reach the junction with the Bonanza Trail in a saddle; stay right to remain on the Bristlecone Trail.

3.2 The Bristlecone Trail crosses a ridge and starts to descend into Scout Canyon.

4.0 The trail arrives in the bottom of Scout Canyon and turns sharply right.

5.2 Arrive at Lower Bristlecone Trailhead. Follow the dirt road a few yards to NV 156, then follow the highway south to the Upper Bristlecone Trailhead.

5.6 Return to Upper Bristlecone Trailhead.

8 BONANZA PEAK

This hike ascends 10,380-foot Bonanza Peak using the Bonanza Trail and a short, easy cross-country hike. Bonanza Peak is the northernmost 10,000-foot peak in the Spring Mountains and has a commanding view of the Spring Mountains from an unusual perspective. Though not much farther from the city than the popular Lee and Kyle Canyon areas, you'll see far fewer people in this remote portion of the national recreation area.

Start: 52.0 miles northwest of Las Vegas
Distance: 7.8-mile out-and-back
Hiking time: About 6 hours
Difficulty: Strenuous due to 2,900-foot elevation change and high elevations
Trail surface: Dirt and rocks, cross-country
Best seasons: Spring through fall
Water: None
Other trail users: Horses

Canine compatibility: Leashed dogs permitted
Fees and permits: None
Schedule: Open all year
Maps: CalTopo.com MapBuilder Topo layer; Gaia GPS Gaia Topo layer
Trail contacts: Spring Mountains National Recreation Area, Humboldt-Toiyabe National Forest, 4701 N. Torrey Pines Dr., Las Vegas NV 89130-2301; (702) 872-5486; https://www.fs.usda.gov/htnf

FINDING THE TRAILHEAD

From the intersection of US 95 and I-15 in downtown Las Vegas, drive 35.9 miles northwest on US 95. Turn right on Cold Creek Road and continue 16.1 miles to the end of the road at the Bonanza Trailhead. Toward the end you'll pass through a subdivision; stay on Cold Creek Road. After passing the subdivision the road becomes gravel for the last 2.0 miles and is passable by ordinary cars with care. GPS: N36 22.945' / W115 44.441'

THE HIKE

The Bonanza Trail climbs away from the trailhead to the southwest, passing through stands of mountain mahogany and ponderosa pine. It soon begins to switchback up a broad ridge at an easy but relentless grade. As the trail continues to climb, the magnificent old-growth ponderosa pines are joined by white and Douglas firs. About halfway up the ascent, the north end of a switchback comes to the edge of the old fire that burned over the top of Willow Peak, giving views of the limestone cliffs of Willow Peak itself and the desert far beyond to the north.

As you climb, watch for the first appearance of bristlecone pines. This five-needled pine is joined by another, limber pine, which has longer needles in more open bunches. As the name implies, limber pine has flexible branches that allow it to shed heavy snow loads. More switchbacks finally lead to a saddle on the edge of the burn, on the ridge between Willow and Bonanza Peaks.

Bonanza Peak

From the summit of Bonanza Peak, the northernmost 10,000-foot peak in the Spring Mountains, you can get a different perspective of Charleston Peak and the central part of the range.

Continue on the Bonanza Trail to the south as it climbs the ridge above the saddle, soon entering an unburned forest of bristlecone pines. Switchbacks lead up the west side of the ridge, and when the trail levels out and starts to descend along the slopes of Bonanza Peak, leave the trail and walk directly up to the peak. The summit itself is a small rocky knob with views to the north, east, and south. Charleston Peak is visible to the southeast at the head of Kyle Canyon, as are the summits at the head of Lee Canyon.

CROWN FIRES

The old burn on the east side of Willow Peak is an example of a crown fire. These fires occur in dry, windy conditions and are aggravated by unnatural forest conditions such as heavy accumulations of dead plant material on the forest floor. If enough heat is generated, the fire may change from a low-intensity ground fire, which is generally beneficial to the forest, to a high-intensity crown fire where the fire moves rapidly through the treetops, killing the trees and almost every living thing in its path. Such fires in heavy timber can release the same energy as a nuclear explosion every few minutes.

The burn on the northeast slopes of Willow Peak is in the early stages of forest succession. When a forest is destroyed by a natural or man-made disaster such as a snow

Bonanza Peak

Bonanza Peak

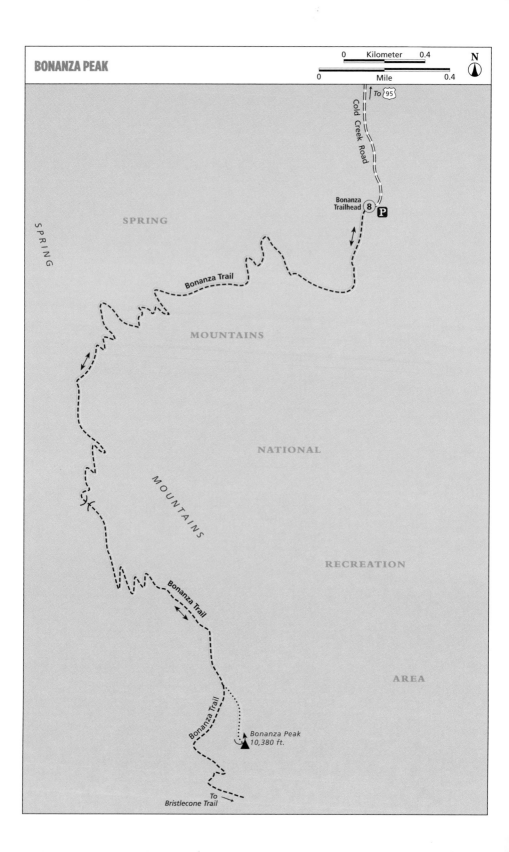

BONANZA PEAK

0   Kilometer   0.4

0   Mile   0.4

N

To 95

Cold Creek Road

Bonanza
Trailhead   8   P

SPRING

Bonanza Trail

MOUNTAINS

SPRING

NATIONAL

MOUNTAINS

RECREATION

Bonanza Trail

AREA

Bonanza Trail

Bonanza Peak
10,380 ft.

To
Bristlecone Trail

avalanche, landslide, windstorm, flood, or wild fire, the forest immediately begins to restore itself.

Forest succession varies with the forest type and the climate, but the same general process is always followed. The first step is soil recovery, in the case of a flood or forest fire where the soil may be covered or destroyed. A lot of changes take place that are hidden within the soil, caused by beneficial microbes, fungus, and burrowing creatures such as earthworms. That sets the stage for the first visible plants to take hold. Grass and brush are usually the first plants to grow on the diminished soil left in the wake of the event. As more plants grow, they enrich the soil and eventually the soil is good enough to support the first trees.

On higher slopes quaking aspen is usually the first tree to become established. Aspen requires a lot of sunlight and open burned slopes are ideal sites, once the soil is thick enough and rich enough to support tree roots. Aspen grows quickly, and old burns are often covered with 10-foot-tall young aspen trees within a few years.

As the aspens mature, they provide shade for evergreens such as Douglas and white fir, whose seedlings can't withstand intense sunlight. It may take 100 years or more, but eventually the evergreens grow taller than the aspens and begin to deprive them of the sunlight they need. At the same time, the aspens are dying of old age—aspens don't live much longer than 100 years. The end result is a new evergreen mountain forest.

Such a forest was once referred to as a "climax forest," meaning the final and stable forest type. Today it's recognized that forests are always in flux, and there isn't necessarily a final stage.

MILES AND DIRECTIONS

0.0   Leave the Bonanza Trailhead on the Bonanza Trail.

1.7   View the burn on Willow Peak; continue on the Bonanza Trail.

2.7   Reach a saddle on the ridge between Willow and Bonanza Peaks; continue south on the Bonanza Trail.

3.7   Leave the trail and follow a faint hiker trail up the south ridge of Bonanza Peak, keeping just to the right of the rocky ridge crest until just below the summit.

3.9   Bonanza Peak; return the way you came.

7.8   Arrive back at the Bonanza Trailhead.

9 CALICO TANKS

This is an easy day hike to natural water tanks in the red rock Calico Hills. Such water tanks are vital for wildlife, and they were also important for natives and settlers.

Start: 20.2 miles west of Las Vegas
Distance: 2.0-mile out-and-back
Hiking time: About 1 hour
Difficulty: Easy due to minor elevation change
Trail surface: Dirt and rocks
Best seasons: All year
Water: None
Other trail users: None
Canine compatibility: Leashed dogs permitted
Fees and permits: Entrance fee
Schedule: Access is via the Scenic Drive, which is open daily Nov 1–Feb 28/29, 6 a.m.–5 p.m.; Mar 1–Mar 31, 7 a.m.–7 p.m.; Apr 1–Sept 30, 6 a.m.–8 p.m.; Oct 1–Oct 31, 6 a.m.–7 p.m.
Maps: CalTopo.com MapBuilder Topo layer; Gaia GPS Gaia Topo layer
Trail contacts: Bureau of Land Management, Red Rock/Sloan Canyon Field Office, 1000 Scenic Loop Dr., Las Vegas, NV 89161; (702) 515-5350; https://www.blm.gov/visit/red-rock-canyon-national-conservation-area

FINDING THE TRAILHEAD

From the intersection of US 95 and I-15 in downtown Las Vegas, drive 5.1 miles west on US 95. Exit onto Summerlin Parkway and drive 3.8 miles west. Exit onto Town Center Drive and turn left. Continue 2.3 miles, and then turn right onto West Charleston Boulevard, NV 159. Continue 6.2 miles, and then turn right (north) on the Red Rock Canyon Scenic Drive. Drive 2.8 miles to the Calico Hills 1 Viewpoint and Trailhead, on the right. GPS: N36 9.718' / W115 27.008'

THE HIKE

Follow the wash north 0.25 mile, then turn right (east) at the third canyon and continue up a side canyon through the red slickrock to a large natural water tank (tinaja). When they have water, this and other tinajas in the Calico Hills are important sources of water for the area's wildlife.

Animals have many other survival strategies to help them cope with the heat and dryness of the desert. Many desert animals are nocturnal, at least in the summer. They avoid the extreme heat of day by nesting or denning up until the coolness and higher humidity of evening set in. Burrowing animals have a major advantage in that their occupied burrows are at about 80 degrees Fahrenheit year-round, and the humidity remains at a comfortably high level due to ground moisture and moisture given off by the animal. On the desert surface, summer humidity often drops to just a few percent during the day, which quickly dehydrates any animal without a source of water.

Many birds stay in their nests in trees, where the temperature is 10 or 20 degrees cooler than that near the ground. Soaring birds climb to great heights with little expenditure of energy, rising on the strong updrafts created by the sun beating on expanses of bare rock and open areas. Since the temperature of dry air falls at 5.5 degrees Fahrenheit for every 1,000 feet of elevation gained, those buzzards, ravens, and hawks that are tiny specks high

Calico Tanks Trail

DESERT WATER ETIQUETTE

Tinaja is Spanish for *tank*. Most natural desert water tanks are smaller than the Calico Tanks and tend to form where cascading floodwaters have scoured out deep basins in the bedrock underlying normally dry washes. They tend to occur in deep canyons where the additional shade helps keep the water from evaporating. In many desert ranges, tinajas are the only year-round source of water for wildlife. Hikers can use the water as well, but should observe a few commonsense courtesies. Take only the water you need, and use it sparingly for all purposes except drinking. Never bathe in a tinaja or pollute it with soap or food scraps. Others will need the water. Avoid camping nearby, as your presence will scare away the animals that normally come to drink during the night. Finally, water from a tinaja should always be purified before drinking or cooking with it.

Calico Tanks Trail

in the summer sky really are laughing at you—they are sailing around in cool air while you fry in the ground heat.

Animals such as desert bighorn sheep can go days without water, but eventually they do need a drink. Others, such as the kangaroo rat, never drink liquid water. They extract all the water they need from their food.

Insects and spiders would be quickly broiled by the extreme desert heat found within a few inches of the ground, which often exceeds 150 degrees Fahrenheit during the day. Some insects, such as ants, take advantage of burrows during summer days, while in the winter they forage in broad daylight, taking advantage of the ground warmed to a comfortable temperature by the winter sun. Other insects and spiders use the cool and moist microclimates found under rocks, logs, and bark. The common bark scorpion gets its

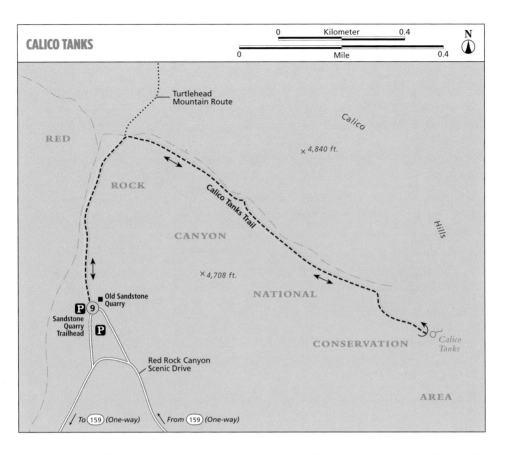

name from the fact that it spends its days clinging upside down to the underside of rocks and wood, emerging at night to hunt insects.

One of the most remarkable desert adaptations is that of the spadefoot toad. This desert toad is found in seasonal desert pools that may be dry for years at a time, until a lucky rainstorm temporarily fills the pool. The mature spadefoots survive extended dry periods by burrowing into the mud at the bottom of the drying pools and creating a moisture-conserving cocoon from layers of old skin. When rain finally comes, the spade-foots appear within hours and the desert night is filled with their low calls. Spadefoots reproduce very quickly. Eggs hatch within 9 to 72 hours, and the entire life cycle, from egg to adult, is completed in 9 to 14 days, so that the adults can burrow in before the pond dries up once again.

MILES AND DIRECTIONS

0.0 Leave the Sandstone Quarry Trailhead and follow the Calico Tanks Trail up the wash.

0.3 Turtlehead Mountain Route, an unsigned user trail goes left; stay right on the Calico Tanks Trail and follow it southeast into the Calico Hills.

1.0 Arrive at Calico Tanks. Return the way you came.

2.0 Arrive back at the Sandstone Quarry Trailhead.

10 TURTLEHEAD MOUNTAIN

A cross-country day hike to a 6,089-foot summit offering spectacular views of the red rocks, the Spring Mountains, and the Keystone Thrust fault system.

Start: 20.2 miles west of Las Vegas
Distance: 4.0-mile out-and-back
Hiking time: About 3 hours
Difficulty: Strenuous due to cross-country hiking and elevation gain
Trail surface: Trail, cross-country, and some rock scrambling
Best seasons: All year
Water: None
Other trail users: None
Canine compatibility: Leashed dogs permitted
Fees and permits: Entrance fee

Schedule: Access is via the Scenic Drive, which is open daily Nov 1–Feb 28/29, 6 a.m.–5 p.m.; Mar 1–Mar 31, 7 a.m.–7 p.m.; Apr 1–Sept 30, 6 a.m.–8 p.m.; Oct 1–Oct 31, 6 a.m.–7 p.m.
Maps: CalTopo.com MapBuilder Topo layer; Gaia GPS Gaia Topo layer
Trail contacts: Bureau of Land Management, Red Rock/Sloan Canyon Field Office, 1000 Scenic Loop Dr., Las Vegas, NV 89161; (702) 515-5350; https://www.blm.gov/visit/red-rock-canyon-national-conservation-area

FINDING THE TRAILHEAD

From the intersection of US 95 and I-15 in downtown Las Vegas, drive 5.1 miles west on US 95. Exit onto Summerlin Parkway and drive 3.8 miles west. Exit onto Town Center Drive and turn left. Continue 2.3 miles, and then turn right onto West Charleston Boulevard, NV 159. Continue 6.2 miles, and then turn right (north) on the Red Rock Canyon Scenic Drive. Drive 2.8 miles to the Calico Hills 1 Viewpoint and Trailhead, on the right. GPS: N36 9.718' / W115 27.008'

THE HIKE

Follow the Calico Tanks Trail until the trail turns east, then leave the trail and hike north up the wash. Once north of the Calico Hills with a clear view of Turtlehead Mountain to the north, head up the ravine left (west) of the peak. Although there is no constructed trail, enough hikers follow this route to create informal trails. Ascend this ravine to its head, which will require some rock scrambling in places. At the top of the ravine, turn right and follow the ridge a short distance to the summit. The spectacular views of La Madre Mountain and the Calico Hills are well worth the climb.

The type of soil present on a mountain slope strongly affects the plants that grow on it. Sandstone-derived soils, as found near the start of the hike up Turtlehead Mountain, are better at supporting sagebrush than limestone, as found above the Keystone Thrust Fault on the upper part of this hike. That explains why the slopes below the Scenic Drive are so densely covered in sage while the slopes behind the Calico Hills and White Rock Hills are sparsely vegetated.

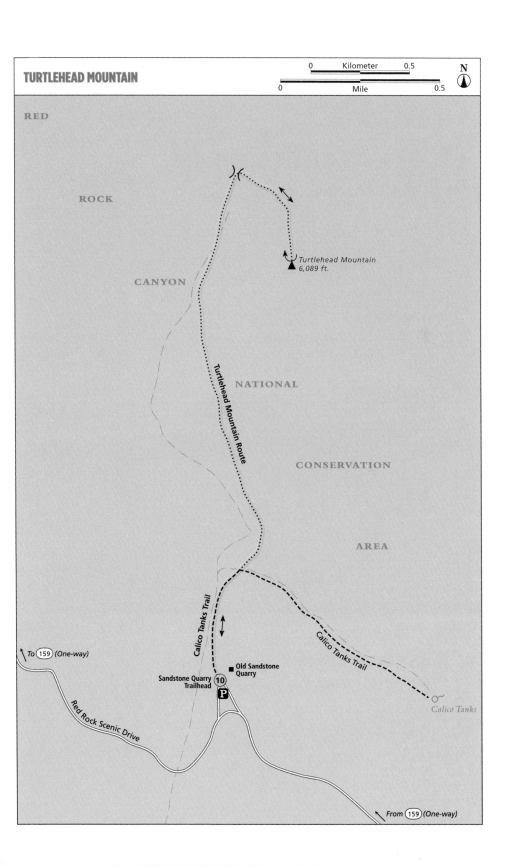

TURTLEHEAD MOUNTAIN

0   Kilometer   0.5

0   Mile   0.5

N

RED

ROCK

CANYON

NATIONAL

CONSERVATION

AREA

Turtlehead Mountain
6,089 ft.

Turtlehead Mountain Route

Calico Tanks Trail

Calico Tanks Trail

To 159 (One-way)

Sandstone Quarry
Trailhead

10
P

Old Sandstone
Quarry

Calico Tanks

Red Rock Scenic Drive

From 159 (One-way)

Turtlehead Mountain

MILES AND DIRECTIONS

0.0 From the Sandstone Quarry Trailhead, start on the Calico Tanks Trail.

0.3 Leave the Calico Tanks Trail and hike north up the wash.

1.2 Enter the ravine west of Turtlehead Mountain.

1.6 At the head of the ravine, turn right and hike southeast to the summit.

2.0 Arrive at Turtlehead Mountain. Return the way you came.

4.0 Arrive back at the Sandstone Quarry Trailhead.

11 WILLOW SPRING LOOP

This hike features a variety of plant communities including riparian, pines, oaks, and sagebrush desert. You can also see prehistoric pits that were used by natives to roast food.

Start: 25.4 miles west of Las Vegas
Distance: 1.0-mile loop
Hiking time: About 1 hour
Difficulty: Easy
Trail surface: Dirt and rocks, sand and gravel
Best seasons: All year
Water: None
Other trail users: None
Canine compatibility: Leashed dogs permitted
Fees and permits: Entrance fee
Schedule: Access is via the Scenic Drive, which is open daily Nov 1– Feb 28/29, 6 a.m.–5 p.m.; Mar 1– Mar 31, 7 a.m.–7 p.m.; Apr 1–Sept 30, 6 a.m.–8 p.m.; Oct 1–Oct 31, 6 a.m.–7 p.m.
Maps: CalTopo.com MapBuilder Topo layer; Gaia GPS Gaia Topo layer
Trail contacts: Bureau of Land Management, Red Rock/Sloan Canyon Field Office, 1000 Scenic Loop Dr., Las Vegas, NV 89161; (702) 515-5350; https://www.blm.gov/visit/red-rock-canyon-national-conservation-area

FINDING THE TRAILHEAD

From the intersection of US 95 and I-15 in downtown Las Vegas, drive 5.1 miles west on US 95. Exit onto Summerlin Parkway and drive 3.8 miles west. Exit onto Town Center Drive and turn left. Continue 2.3 miles, and then turn right onto West Charleston Boulevard, NV 159. Continue 6.2 miles, and then turn right (north) on the Red Rock Canyon Scenic Drive. Drive 7.1 miles, then turn right onto the Willow Spring Picnic Area road. Continue 0.9 mile to the Willow Spring Picnic Area, on the right. GPS: N36 9.611' / W115 29.879'

THE HIKE

From the Willow Spring Picnic Area, walk to the right and follow the Willow Spring Trail along the base of the White Rock Hills. You'll pass several Native American roasting pits (sometimes called mescal pits) and then cross the road to the Lost Creek parking area. Now, follow the right fork of the Lost Creek Trail across the wash. Turn right at a junction on the southwest side of the wash to stay on the Willow Spring Trail. After a short distance the trail turns right and crosses the wash to the Willow Spring Picnic Area.

Desert plants have a number of ways of adapting to the dry, hot conditions of the desert. Regardless of the means, all plants need water—about 80 to 90 percent of most plant tissue is water. Water is required to support the chemical reactions that sustain the plant, including the vital process of photosynthesis (using sunlight to make food), and it provides a transport mechanism for minerals and other chemicals within the plant. Plant cells are full of water under slight pressure, which provides support for most plants. Transpiration of water from the leaves of plants cools the plant.

Rock climbers along the Willow Spring Loop

A VARIED NATIVE MENU

Ancient inhabitants slow-cooked agave plants, other vegetables, and meats in roasting pits. The food was placed in a bed of hot coals mixed with cobbles and covered with plant materials and earth. After enough time had passed, the cooked food, ash, and fire-cracked rock were dug out. The discarded rock and ash forms a doughnut-shaped ring often several feet high and containing thousands of heating rocks. The vast quantity of rocks shows how long some of these pits were in use. Also known as mescal pits, these cooking sites are common in the Southwest.

Another important food source for natives and wildlife alike is the singleleaf piñon pine. The singleleaf piñon is easily recognized since it is the only pine with needles growing singly, as the name implies, rather than in bunches of two or more. Like its cousin the Colorado piñon, the seeds are edible and used to be an important food source for the native inhabitants, who would gather in temporary villages in places where the pine nut harvest was good. Pine nuts are a human delicacy often used in southwestern-style cooking and are still an important food source for birds and small mammals.

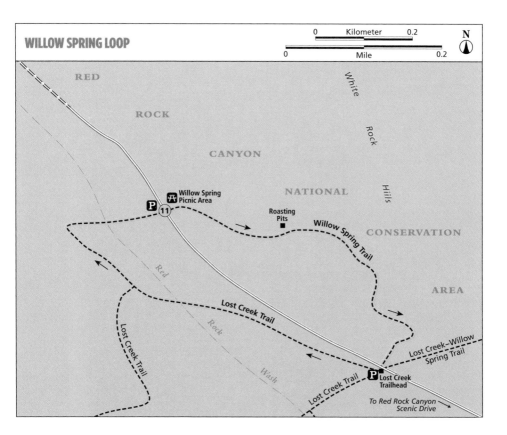

MILES AND DIRECTIONS

0.0 Leave Willow Spring Picnic Area on the Willow Spring Trail at the right side of the parking area.

0.5 Cross the highway to the Lost Creek Trailhead and then follow the right fork of the Lost Creek Trail across Rock Wash.

0.8 Turn right on the Willow Spring Trail.

1.0 Cross the road and arrive at Willow Spring Trailhead.

12 BRIDGE MOUNTAIN

This is a challenging cross-country day hike to a natural bridge and great views of Red Rock Canyon, in the Red Rock Canyon National Conservation Area.

Start: 29.2 miles west of Las Vegas
Distance: 6.0-mile out-and-back
Hiking time: About 4 hours
Difficulty: Strenuous due to elevation gain and cross-country, faint trails
Trail surface: Cross-country, steep exposed system of joints and ledges near hike's end. This section does not require technical climbing equipment or skills, but does require extreme care. Only hikers experienced in cross-country travel should attempt this hike.
Best seasons: Fall through spring
Water: None
Other trail users: None
Canine compatibility: Leashed dogs permitted

Fees and permits: Entrance fee
Schedule: Access is via the Scenic Drive, which is open daily Nov 1–Feb 28/29, 6 a.m.–5 p.m.; Mar 1–Mar 31, 7 a.m.–7 p.m.; Apr 1–Sept 30, 6 a.m.–8 p.m.; Oct 1–Oct 31, 6 a.m.–7 p.m. The western access from Mountain Springs is open all year, road conditions permitting.
Maps: CalTopo.com MapBuilder Topo layer; Gaia GPS Gaia Topo layer
Trail contacts: Bureau of Land Management, Red Rock/Sloan Canyon Field Office, 1000 Scenic Loop Dr., Las Vegas, NV 89161; (702) 515-5350; https://www.blm.gov/visit/red-rock-canyon-national-conservation-area

FINDING THE TRAILHEAD

From the intersection of US 95 and I-15 in downtown Las Vegas, drive 5.1 miles west on US 95. Exit onto Summerlin Parkway and drive 3.8 miles west. Exit onto Town Center Drive and turn left. Continue 2.3 miles, and then turn right onto West Charleston Boulevard, NV 159. Continue 6.2 miles, and then turn right (north) on the Red Rock Canyon Scenic Drive. Drive 7.1 miles, then turn right onto the Willow Spring Picnic Area road. Continue 1.2 miles to the end of the paved road and the start of the unmaintained Rocky Gap Road. You'll need a high-clearance, four-wheel-drive vehicle to continue beyond this point. Drive 3.5 miles farther to Red Rock Summit. GPS: N36 7.822' / W115 32.005'

THE HIKE

Although this is a day hike of moderate length, the trail is minimal, and the last 400-foot climb to the natural bridge on Bridge Mountain is along a steep exposed system of joints and ledges. This section does not require technical climbing equipment or skills, but does require extreme care. Only hikers experienced in cross–country travel should attempt this hike.

The trail begins at Red Rock Summit and leaves the road to the east. It follows a hiker trail, then winds up around the head of a basin that drains to the west and follows a ridge northeast to the crest of the escarpment.

Now the trail turns south along the crest to a point directly west of the head of the north fork of Pine Canyon. It descends around the heads of two small drainages to the east then climbs a steep side hill to the top of a long narrow ridge that runs off to the east

Bridge Mountain at the right end of the escarpment

into Pine Creek. No trail exists in the resistant sandstone, but the route is intermittently marked by two black parallel lines of paint.

The trail becomes poorly defined as it snakes down the crest of the ridge to the east. Hikers should stay on the crest as much as possible as the going is easier there than it is on the side hill. Soon after the limestone rock disappears and exposes the sandstone, the route drops off the ridge to the north into a small basin that empties into Pine Creek. At the lower edge of the basin, a sheer cliff descends into the depths of Pine Creek 1,500 feet below. Rising air currents are attractive to soaring birds that ride along the cliffs, and the rising air also carries flying insects to the higher elevations. Small insect-eating birds such as the white-throated swift and violet green swallow swoop along the edge, buzzing hikers and snapping up bugs on the wing.

From the head of Pine Creek, the route winds off through a slickrock bench studded with numerous small catch basins that hold water after a rain. Some of these basins are quite large; the largest is located in the extreme southeast corner of section 8, near the edge of the Mountain Springs topographic map. Water trapped in these tanks, or tinajas as the Spanish termed them, supports a diverse and fragile community of plants and animals. Ponderosa pines, junipers, piñon pines, and smaller bushes provide shelter for bird life. Amphibians such as frogs and toads breed in the ponds, and ravens, hawks, deer, bighorn sheep, and hundreds of other animals rely on the tinajas for water. People should never camp within 0.25 mile of such water sources as the presence of humans will scare the wildlife away. Since there is no outlet from the tanks, pollutants from soap, human waste, or litter will remain in the basins indefinitely, poisoning the creatures that depend on these natural reservoirs.

From the large tank mentioned above, the trail becomes a mere route across the slick-rock bench. The correct route is marked intermittently with small patches of orange paint in the shape of bighorn sheep tracks. If the correct route is not followed carefully, hikers will find themselves perched on the edge of a sheer drop with no way down. In

BRIDGE MOUNTAIN

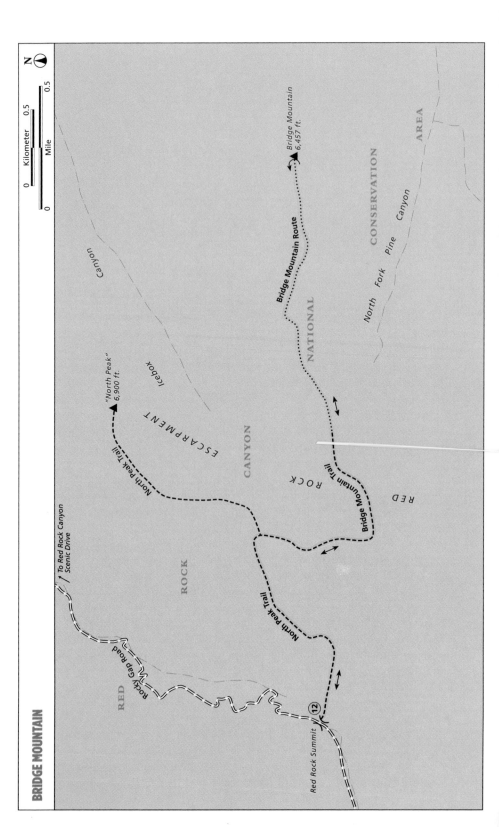

N

0   Kilometer   0.5

0   Mile   0.5

To Red Rock Canyon
Scenic Drive

RED

Rocky Gap Road

Red Rock Summit

12

North Peak Trail

ROCK

"North Peak"
6,900 ft.

North Peak Trail

ESCARPMENT

Icebox

Canyon

CANYON

Bridge Mountain Trail

RED   ROCK   NATIONAL

Bridge Mountain Route

CONSERVATION

North   Fork   Pine   Canyon

AREA

Bridge Mountain
6,457 ft.

many areas the route is broken by short vertical pitches that must be carefully negotiated. It is approximately 0.5 mile from the big tank to the bottom of the saddle that leads up to Bridge Mountain, with a drop of 350 feet.

To reach the bridge near the summit of Bridge Mountain, the route leads straight up a system of joints and ledges for a distance of 400 feet. The path is not as sheer as it appears during the approach, and there are plenty of holds for hands and feet. However, the climb is relatively exposed, and extreme care should be exercised during the climb. Hikers not comfortable with rock scrambling should turn back here. A misstep could plunge a hiker hundreds of feet into Pine Creek. Climbing within the joints offers more security, but climbing the faces alongside is slightly easier.

Once the bridge has been reached and explored, a further route leads up onto the bench above, from inside the alcove near the pine tree. Just 100 yards north of the bridge is a large, deep, nearly circular tinaja nearly 80 feet across and 60 feet deep. Over the bench to the east is a large alcove that shelters a hidden forest of ponderosa pines. Trees grow very slowly in this area because of the dry conditions. Wood is relatively scarce, slowly replaced, and absolutely should not be used to build fires. A fire in the hidden forest could cause damage that would not heal in a thousand years. Note that all wood gathering and ground fires are prohibited in the Red Rock backcountry.

Return to Red Rock Summit by retracing your route. Do not attempt to take short-cuts or alternate routes.

Note: This hike description was provided by the Bureau of Land Management.

THE KEYSTONE THRUST FAULT ZONE

This hike offers an excellent view of the Keystone Thrust Fault Zone. Tremendous forces associated with the movement of the Earth's crustal plates have forced the dark gray limestones to ride up over the red and white sandstones that were formed later, and were originally positioned above the limestone. The limestone weathers into fairly large blocks that remain in place, trapping sand, silt, and plant debris, which develops into soil that supports a heavy cover of shrubs and small trees. The sandstone weathers differently, breaking down into sand grains that are easily washed and blown away, constantly exposing a new surface of solid rock that is bare of all plants except lichens and a few shrubs growing in cracks. The contrast between the brush-covered limestone and the bare sandstone beneath it clearly delineates the Keystone Thrust Fault Zone.

MILES AND DIRECTIONS

- **0.0** Leave Red Rock Summit and follow the informal trail to the east.
- **0.3** The trail swings north through a small basin and then climbs onto a ridge to the north.
- **0.4** Follow the trail up the ridge to the northeast.
- **1.1** Reach the crest of the escarpment. Turn right and follow the informal trail along the ridge to the south.
- **2.3** Arrive at the saddle below Bridge Mountain. Hikers not comfortable with rock scrambling should turn back here.
- **3.0** Arrive at Bridge Mountain. Return the way you came.
- **6.0** Arrive back at Red Rock Summit.

13 ICEBOX CANYON

Featuring a seasonal waterfall and box canyon, this short hike nevertheless takes you deep into the towering cliffs of the Red Rock Escarpment.

Start: 25.4 miles west of Las Vegas
Distance: 2.2-mile out-and-back
Hiking time: About 2 hours
Difficulty: Easy
Trail surface: Dirt and rocks, boulder-hopping
Best seasons: All year
Water: None
Other trail users: None
Canine compatibility: Leashed dogs permitted
Fees and permits: Entrance fee
Schedule: Access is via the Scenic Drive, which is open daily Nov 1–Feb 28/29, 6 a.m.–5 p.m.; Mar 1–Mar 31, 7 a.m.–7 p.m.; Apr 1–Sept 30, 6 a.m.–8 p.m.; Oct 1–Oct 31, 6 a.m.–7 p.m.
Maps: CalTopo.com MapBuilder Topo layer; Gaia GPS Gaia Topo layer
Trail contacts: Bureau of Land Management, Red Rock/Sloan Canyon Field Office, 1000 Scenic Loop Dr., Las Vegas, NV 89161; (702) 515-5350; https://www.blm.gov/visit/red-rock-canyon-national-conservation-areaml

FINDING THE TRAILHEAD

From the intersection of US 95 and I-15 in downtown Las Vegas, drive 5.1 miles west on US 95. Exit onto Summerlin Parkway and drive 3.8 miles west. Exit onto Town Center Drive and turn left. Continue 2.3 miles, and then turn right onto West Charleston Boulevard, NV 159. Continue 6.2 miles, and then turn right (north) on the Red Rock Canyon Scenic Drive. Drive 8.0 miles to the Icebox Canyon Trailhead, on the right. GPS: N36 9.017' / W115 29.049'

THE HIKE

From the trailhead, the Icebox Canyon Trail descends to cross Red Rock Wash and follows the Icebox Canyon drainage upstream, generally staying on the north side of the bed. When the canyon narrows, the trail drops into the wash. Boulder-hop up the wash to a seasonal waterfall and box canyon. Icebox Canyon derives its name from the cooler temperatures in this narrow canyon.

The main reason Icebox Canyon is so much cooler and lusher than the open desert below is due to the effect of microclimates. A microclimate is a small area, such as a canyon, valley, or slope aspect, that has a different climate than the surrounding area. Microclimates are often present in canyons such as Icebox Canyon because of cold air flowing down the canyon.

During calm periods and especially at night, heavier, denser cold air flows down mountain canyons. These cooler temperatures create microclimates, small areas where the year-round climate differs enough from the surrounding area to support a plant and animal community normally found at higher elevations. An example is the presence of ponderosa pines along the canyon, trees that are heat- and drought-resistant but do require a certain amount of water to survive. The shady depths of Icebox Canyon retard evaporation and provide a moister climate than the surrounding open desert.

Falls, Icebox Canyon

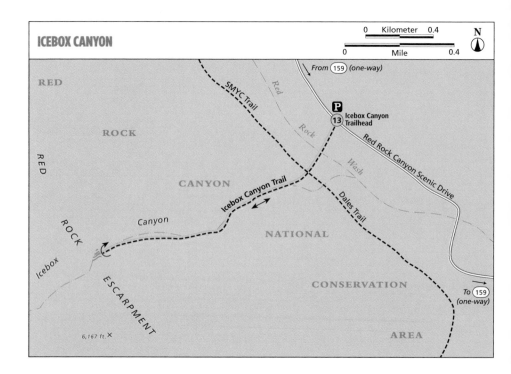

MILES AND DIRECTIONS

0.0 Leave the Icebox Canyon Trailhead on the Icebox Canyon Trail.

0.2 Cross the SMYC and Dales Trails; continue straight ahead on the Icebox Canyon Trail.

1.1 Arrive at the seasonal waterfall. Return the way you came.

2.2 Arrive back at the Icebox Canyon Trailhead.

14 LOST CREEK LOOP–CHILDREN'S DISCOVERY TRAIL

This loop hike to a box canyon features a seasonal waterfall and a panel of prehistoric pictographs. The waterfall is best in the spring after a snowy winter provides plenty of snowmelt.

Start: 25.0 miles west of Las Vegas
Distance: 1.2-mile loop
Hiking time: About 1 hour
Difficulty: Easy
Trail surface: Dirt and rocks
Best seasons: All year
Water: None
Other trail users: None
Canine compatibility: Leashed dogs permitted
Fees and permits: Entrance fee
Schedule: Access is via the Scenic Drive, which is open daily Nov 1–Feb 28/29, 6 a.m.–5 p.m.; Mar 1–Mar 31, 7 a.m.–7 p.m.; Apr 1–Sept 30, 6 a.m.–8 p.m.; Oct 1–Oct 31, 6 a.m.–7 p.m.
Maps: CalTopo.com MapBuilder Topo layer; Gaia GPS Gaia Topo layer
Trail contacts: Bureau of Land Management, Red Rock/Sloan Canyon Field Office, 1000 Scenic Loop Dr., Las Vegas, NV 89161; (702) 515-5350; https://www.blm.gov/visit/red-rock-canyon-national-conservation-area

FINDING THE TRAILHEAD

From the intersection of US 95 and I-15 in downtown Las Vegas, drive 5.1 miles west on US 95. Exit onto Summerlin Parkway and drive 3.8 miles west. Exit onto Town Center Drive and turn left. Continue 2.3 miles, and then turn right onto West Charleston Boulevard, NV 159. Continue 6.2 miles, and then turn right (north) on the Red Rock Canyon Scenic Drive. Drive 7.1 miles, then turn right onto the Willow Spring Picnic Area road. Continue 0.5 mile to the Lost Creek Trailhead, on the left. GPS: N36 9.445' / W115 29.593'

THE HIKE

From the trailhead, start on the Lost Creek Trail by crossing the wash to the west. After the wash the trail climbs into an unnamed canyon and soon reaches a seasonal waterfall at the head of a box canyon. The loop continues along the north side of the canyon, where the trail passes a panel of pictographs. The Children's Discovery Trail ends at the junction with the Willow Spring Loop Trail; turn right to return to the trailhead.

All children and many adults love a treasure hunt. A high-tech form of treasure hunting, geocaching, has caught on in a big way, using Global Positioning System (GPS) receivers to hunt for hidden caches left by other people. Although the sport of geocaching predates the availability of GPS to civilians, GPS has made geocaching a lot more fun and appealing to a large number of people. Geocaches can be placed by anyone and located anywhere, from city to countryside, where their presence is legal. (FYI: National parks prohibit the placement of geocaches, as do National Wilderness Areas.)

Every year, people die in flash floods in the desert. This seems ironic, until you look at a narrow, flood-sculpted canyon and start to imagine the power of the floods that carve such places.

Falls, Lost Creek

BOX CANYONS

A box canyon is a canyon with no outlet at its upper end. Sometimes the obstacle is a jumble of boulders blocking the canyon floor, or, as is the case here, a seasonal waterfall. Smaller canyons are more likely than larger ones to "box up." The reason is that canyons erode headward, toward the steeper slopes. Rain falling on steep slopes runs downhill at a much higher speed than water running down gentler gradients. The ability of water to transport silt, sand, pebbles, and rocks increases rapidly as the speed of flow increases, so erosion proceeds much faster at the head of canyons than it does lower down. As the canyon head erodes, it undermines the slopes above, causing them to collapse—much like a child digging into a sandpile until it collapses. If the headward erosion of the canyon encounters a harder layer of rock, a dropoff or pour-off often forms, resulting in a box canyon.

Storm water pouring off a seasonal waterfall often erodes a "plunge pool" out of the bedrock at the base of the fall. Some plunge pools may be quite deep, and since plunge pools tend to form at the base of falls in deep, narrow canyons, where they are shaded from the sun much of the time, some larger plunge pools contain water year-round. Others are seasonal, holding water for a short time in the winter and spring.

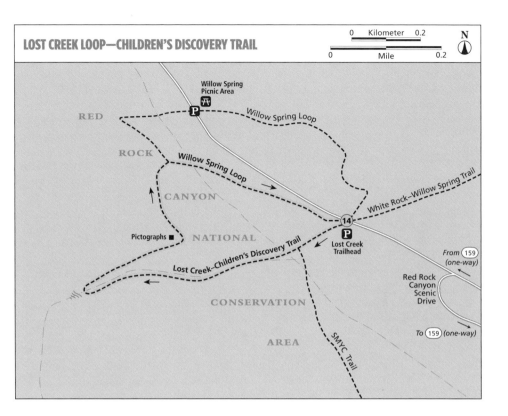

MILES AND DIRECTIONS

0.0 From the Lost Creek Trailhead, follow the left branch of the Lost Creek Trail across the wash.

0.1 At the junction with the SMYC Trail, stay right on the Lost Creek Trail.

0.5 Arrive at a seasonal waterfall.

0.7 View a pictograph panel on the left.

0.9 At the junction with the Willow Spring Loop Trail on the left, turn right to return to the Lost Creek Trailhead.

1.2 Arrive back at the Lost Creek Trailhead.

15 BASE OF THE ESCARPMENT

This trail winds along the base of the Red Rock Escarpment from Lost Creek to Oak Creek Canyon using a series of interconnecting trails. It offers excellent views of the rock faces of the escarpment as well as distant views of La Madre Mountain, the White Rock Hills, Turtlehead Peak, and the Calico Hills.

Start: 25.0 miles west of Las Vegas
Distance: 9.6-mile out-and-back
Hiking time: About 5 hours
Difficulty: Moderate due to length
Trail surface: Dirt and rocks
Best seasons: All year
Water: None
Other trail users: None
Canine compatibility: Leashed dogs permitted
Fees and permits: Entrance fee
Schedule: Access is via the Scenic Drive, which is open daily Nov 1–Feb 28/29, 6 a.m.–5 p.m.; Mar 1–Mar 31, 7 a.m.–7 p.m.; Apr 1–Sept 30, 6 a.m.–8 p.m.; Oct 1–Oct 31, 6 a.m.–7 p.m.
Maps: CalTopo.com MapBuilder Topo layer; Gaia GPS Gaia Topo layer
Trail contacts: Bureau of Land Management, Red Rock/Sloan Canyon Field Office, 1000 Scenic Loop Dr., Las Vegas, NV 89161; (702) 515-5350; https://www.blm.gov/visit/red-rock-canyon-national-conservation-area

FINDING THE TRAILHEAD

From the intersection of US 95 and I-15 in downtown Las Vegas, drive 5.1 miles west on US 95. Exit onto Summerlin Parkway and drive 3.8 miles west. Exit onto Town Center Drive and turn left. Continue 2.3 miles, and then turn right onto West Charleston Boulevard, NV 159. Continue 6.2 miles, and then turn right (north) on the Red Rock Canyon Scenic Drive. Drive 7.1 miles, then turn right onto the Willow Spring Picnic Area road. Continue 0.5 mile to the Lost Creek Trailhead, on the left. GPS: N36 9.445' / W115 29.593'

THE HIKE

Start on the left-hand branch of the Lost Creek Trail, and then turn left on the SMYC Trail, which crosses Red Rock Wash and heads south toward the base of the Red Rock Escarpment. Once on the slopes below the escarpment, the SMYC Trail turns southeast and wanders along the base of the escarpment to end at the Icebox Canyon Trail.

Cross the Icebox Canyon Trail and start on the Dales Trail, which continues to skirt the base of the escarpment in a southeasterly direction. Old roads confuse this section; when in doubt, stay close to the base of the escarpment. The Dales Trail turns more to the south as it approaches the mouth of Pine Creek Canyon. The trail ends at the Pine Creek Trail; turn right and follow the Pine Creek Trail west toward the mouth of Pine Creek Canyon.

At the ruins of the old homestead, the Pine Creek Trail splits to form a loop. Turn left on the Pine Creek Trail and cross Pine Creek, where you'll meet the Arnight Trail. Turn left on the Arnight Trail to continue the hike along the base of the escarpment.

Pine Canyon, base of the escarpment trail

The Arnight Trail crosses a drainage below an unnamed canyon cutting west into the escarpment, and turns southeast away from the escarpment. As the terrain levels out into a sage flat, the Arnight Trail reaches the Oak Creek Trailhead. Retrace your steps to the Lost Creek Trailhead.

Although Red Rock Canyon is not in the hydrographic Great Basin, the area where rivers have no outlet to the sea and all drainage ends in valleys and sinks, they are part of another Great Basin—the physiographic one, which is more commonly known as the Basin and Range geological province. Looking at the area from the point of view of a geologist, or more precisely, a physiographer, what links the area together is not the drainage pattern but the similarities of the mountains and valleys.

The Basin and Range province is a large area of the intermountain West where the topography consists of parallel, generally north–south-trending mountain ranges and broad intervening valleys. Southern and western Arizona, part of southeastern California, nearly all of Nevada, part of southeastern Oregon, southern Idaho, and western Utah are Basin and Range. Although the borders are not as clearly defined as that of the hydrographic Great Basin, they are generally accepted as the Sierra Nevada and the Cascade Mountains on the west, the Columbia Plateau to the north, and the Rocky Mountains to the east. It is on the southern boundary that the difficulties begin. Most physiographers include southeastern California in the Basin and Range, but not everyone agrees that western and southern Arizona should be included. One reason for this is that the generally north–south orientation of the mountains and valleys breaks down in Arizona, where some ranges run east–west.

Bridge Mountain and the escarpment

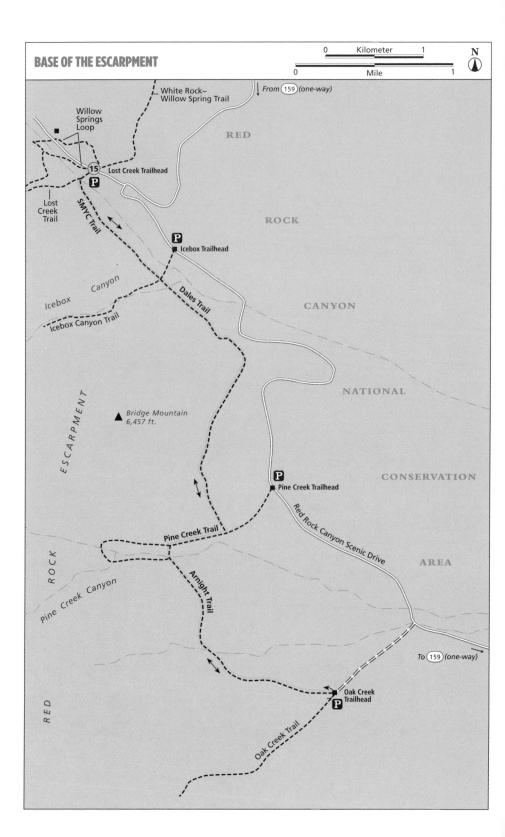

BASE OF THE ESCARPMENT

0   Kilometer   1
0   Mile   1

N

White Rock–
Willow Spring Trail

From ⑮⑨ *(one-way)*

Willow
Springs
Loop

RED

⑮ Lost Creek Trailhead

P

Lost
Creek
Trail

SMYC Trail

ROCK

P Icebox Trailhead

Dales Trail

Canyon

Icebox

Icebox Canyon Trail

CANYON

▲ Bridge Mountain
6,457 ft.

ESCARPMENT

NATIONAL

P Pine Creek Trailhead

CONSERVATION

Pine Creek Trail

Red Rock Canyon Scenic Drive

ROCK

Pine Creek Canyon

Arnight Trail

AREA

To ⑮⑨ *(one-way)*

Oak Creek
Trailhead
P

RED

Oak Creek Trail

The parallel, long mountain ranges and valleys were formed by faulting during the collision of the Pacific and North American plates. During this collision the Basin and Range country was stretched from east to west, and the crust broke along north–south fault lines. Some blocks sank to form valleys, while others rose and tilted to form fault-block mountains.

MILES AND DIRECTIONS

0.0 From the Lost Creek Trailhead, start on the left fork of the Lost Creek Trail.

0.1 Turn left on the SMYC Trail and follow it south toward the base of the Red Rock Escarpment.

0.9 Cross the Icebox Canyon Trail and start on the Dales Trail, which crosses the Icebox Canyon drainage and continues along the base of the Red Rock Escarpment.

2.8 Turn right on the Pine Creek Trail.

3.2 At the ruins of the old homestead, turn right on the left fork of the Pine Creek Trail and cross Pine Creek.

3.3 On the south side of Pine Creek, turn left on the Arnight Trail and follow it along the base of the Red Rock Escarpment.

3.9 The Arnight Trail turns southeast away from the base of the escarpment.

4.8 Arrive at the Oak Creek Trailhead. Return the way you came.

9.6 Arrive back at the Lost Creek Trailhead.

SOUTHEASTERN CALIFORNIA

16 TELESCOPE PEAK

This is a rugged but very rewarding hike to the highest summit in Death Valley National Park and the Panamint Mountains. There is a small campground at the trailhead that makes a good base camp for the hike.

Start: 63.6 miles west of Furnace Creek
Distance: 12.0-mile out-and-back
Hiking time: About 7 hours or 2 days
Difficulty: Strenuous
Trail surface: Dirt and rocks
Best seasons: Spring, summer, and fall
Water: None
Other trail users: None
Canine compatibility: Dogs not permitted
Fees and permits: Entrance fee
Schedule: Open all year
Maps: CalTopo.com MapBuilder Topo layer; Gaia GPS Trails Illustrated layer
Trail contacts: Death Valley National Park, PO Box 579, Death Valley, CA 92328; (760) 786-3200; https://www.nps.gov/deva

FINDING THE TRAILHEAD

Before visiting Death Valley, make certain you top off your gas tank and carry plenty of water and extra food. The park is extremely remote.

From Furnace Creek, drive 33.7 miles north and west on CA 190, then turn left on the Emigrant Canyon Road. Continue 30.1 miles to the end of the road at Mahogany Flat Campground. The last 1.5 miles of the road may require a high-clearance vehicle. GPS: N36 13.794' / W117 4.092'

THE HIKE

Follow the trail as it climbs gradually south along the eastern slopes of the Panamint Mountains, passing through an open forest of piñon pine and mountain mahogany. The view begins to open up as the trail turns west and climbs to the crest south of Rogers Peak. Death Valley is visible to the east, more than 9,000 feet below this lofty trail.

Now the trail passes through a broad saddle—this is a possible campsite for those who wish to do the hike as a 2-day backpack trip. Leaving the saddle, the trail climbs south around the west slopes of Bennett Peak, now offering views of Panamint Valley 8,000 feet below to the west. South of Bennett Peak, the trail regains the crest and stays there. You'll pass the occasional limber pine, and then, as the climb becomes steeper on the north ridge of Telescope Peak, the long-lived bristlecone pine. The last 0.2 mile to Telescope Peak is a rugged scramble.

Badwater Basin, at 282 feet the lowest point in North America, lies 11,331 feet below you to the east as you stand on the 11,049-foot summit. On a clear day, you can see

LIMBER PINE

Limber pines, as the name implies, have flexible branches that shed snow well, and so are well-adapted to living in this harsh alpine environment. Though not nearly as long-lived as bristlecone pines, limber pines can still reach 2,000 years.

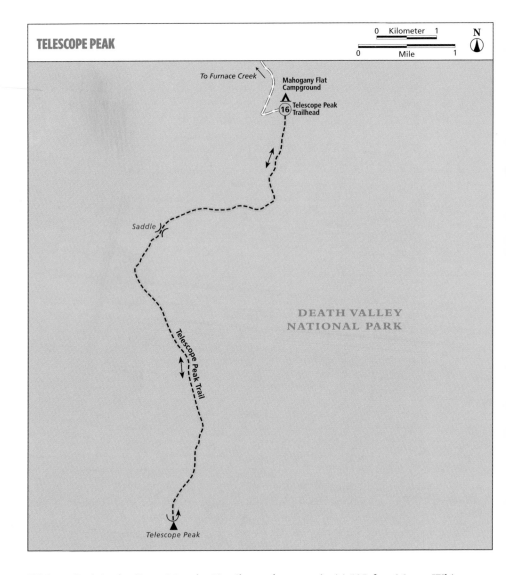

Whitney Peak in the Sierra Nevada, 40 miles to the west. At 14,505 feet, Mount Whitney is the highest point in the United States outside of Alaska.

MILES AND DIRECTIONS

0.0   Trailhead at Mahogany Flat Campground—hike south on the Telescope Peak Trail.

2.1   Pass through a broad saddle and optional campsite.

5.8   Final scramble to summit.

6.0   Telescope Peak; return the way you came.

12.0 Trailhead.

17 EUREKA DUNES

These tall dunes are in the far northwest corner of Death Valley National Park. Over 700 feet high, they are the highest sand dunes in California.

Start: 48.9 miles east of Big Pine
Distance: 1–3 miles depending on route
Hiking time: 2–3 hours
Difficulty: Moderate
Trail surface: Cross-country on sand
Best seasons: Late fall to early spring
Water: None
Other trail users: None

Canine compatibility: Dogs not permitted
Fees and permits: Entrance fee
Schedule: Open all year
Maps: CalTopo.com MapBuilder Topo layer; Gaia GPS Trails Illustrated layer
Trail contacts: Death Valley National Park, PO Box 579, Death Valley, CA 92328; (760) 786-3200; https://www.nps.gov/deva

FINDING THE TRAILHEAD

From Big Pine, drive east on CA 168. After about 2.4 miles, turn right onto Death Valley Road. Follow this paved road about 30 miles past the boundary of Death Valley National Park. The pavement ends in about 3 miles; continue on the graded road 3.5 miles, then turn right on the graded Eureka Dunes Road and continue 10 miles to the Eureka Dunes Dry Camp on the north side of the dunes. GPS: N37 6.731' / W117 40.811'

THE HIKE

Since all of the walking on the dunes is cross-country and there is no particular route, you can spend an hour just walking to the base of the dunes, or several hours walking along the crest and exploring the slopes. Some of the plants found on the dunes are endangered, so avoid walking on any vegetation.

The dunes are a photographer's delight, especially in the hours just after sunrise and before sunset, when the slanting light gives an otherworldly dimension to the shifting sands.

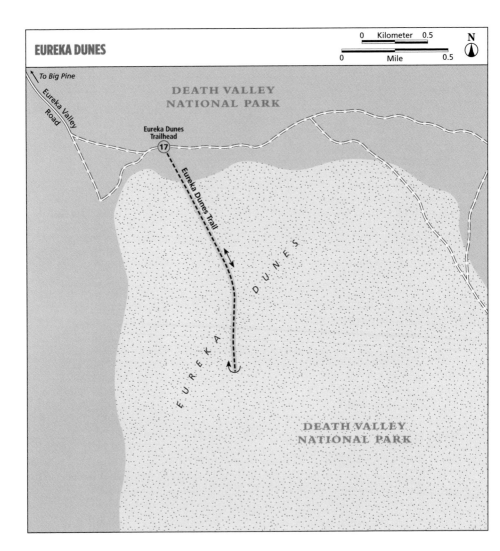

MILES AND DIRECTIONS

0.0 Hike southeast toward the crest of the dunes.

1.0 Top of the dune closest to the trailhead; continue your exploration of the dunes, then return directly to the trailhead, which will be generally north of you and visible from the northwest slopes of the dunes.

18 **FALL CANYON**

Located in eastern Death Valley National Park, this hike ascends a colorful canyon through a spectacular narrows.

Start: 34.4 miles north of Furnace Creek
Distance: 6.2-mile out-and-back
Hiking time: About 4 hours
Difficulty: Moderate
Trail surface: Rocky trail and gravel dry wash
Best seasons: Late fall to early spring
Water: None
Other trail users: None

Canine compatibility: Dogs not permitted
Fees and permits: Entrance fee
Schedule: Open all year
Maps: CalTopo.com MapBuilder Topo layer; Gaia GPS Trails Illustrated layer
Trail contacts: Death Valley National Park, PO Box 579, Death Valley, CA 92328; (760) 786-3200; https://www .nps.gov/deva

FINDING THE TRAILHEAD

 From Furnace Creek, drive 17 miles northwest on CA 190, then turn right on Death Valley Road. Continue 14.9 miles, then turn right on Titus Canyon Road. Follow this graded road 2.5 miles to the East Canyon Traihead. GPS: N36 49.315' / W117 10.442'

THE HIKE

The unmarked trail leaves the parking area behind the primitive restroom and follows the base of the Grapevine Mountains northwest and then northeast to the mouth of Fall Canyon. It drops into a wash; head upstream here and you'll soon enter the mouth of Fall Canyon.

This is bighorn sheep country—keep an eye out for these graceful animals. They'll always be above you, keeping you in sight as they make their away across steep slopes and cliffs. As the canyon narrows, you'll pass the colorful, warped dolomite and limestone of the Bonanza King Formation.

You'll pass through a short but spectacular narrows, then reach a dry fall. This is the end of the hike—return the way you came.

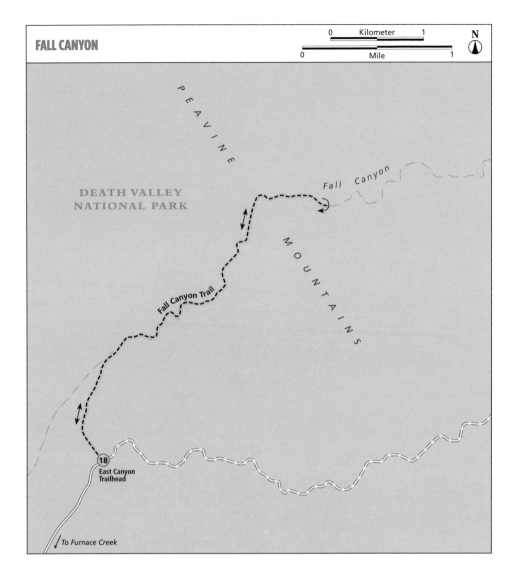

MILES AND DIRECTIONS

0.0 Leave the parking area and follow the trail north along the base of the mountains; stay right at trail junctions.

0.7 Enter the mouth of Fall Canyon and hike upstream.

3.1 Dry fall; return the way you came.

6.2 Trailhead.

19 UBEHEBE CRATER

This easy day hike takes you around an easily accessible volcanic crater in the northern part of Death Valley National Park.

Start: 56 miles northwest of Furnace Creek

Distance: 1.7-mile loop

Hiking time: About 1 hour

Trail surface: Dirt and rocks

Best seasons: Late fall to early spring

Water: None

Other trail users: None

Canine compatibility: Dogs not permitted

Fees and permits: Entrance fee

Schedule: Open all year

Maps: CalTopo.com MapBuilder Topo layer; Gaia GPS Trails Illustrated layer

Trail contacts: Death Valley National Park, PO Box 579, Death Valley, CA 92328; (760) 786-3200; https://www.nps.gov/deva

FINDING THE TRAILHEAD

 From Furnace Creek, drive 17 miles northwest on CA 190, then turn right on North Highway. Continue 39 miles to the parking lot overlooking Ubehebe Crater. GPS: N17 0.709' / W117 27.293'

THE HIKE

Start by hiking south from the parking lot, following the trail along the crater rim. In 0.5 mile, Little Hebe Crater comes into view. This is a good destination for those wanting a very short hike; in that case, return the way you came.

Otherwise, continue the loop along the south rim of the crater. The trail turns north, then west, and returns to the parking lot.

MAAR VOLCANO

Ubehebe Crater is a Maar volcano, formed when a steam explosion blew out a crater 600 feet deep and half a mile across. It is the largest of many Maar volcanoes in the area, and the youngest, possibly as young as 2,100 years. These volcanoes erupted when hot magma rose from the Earth's depths and came into contact with groundwater. The water flashed into steam and blew out the craters in tremendous explosions. Cinders from the eruptions cover the crater rims and part of the surrounding area.

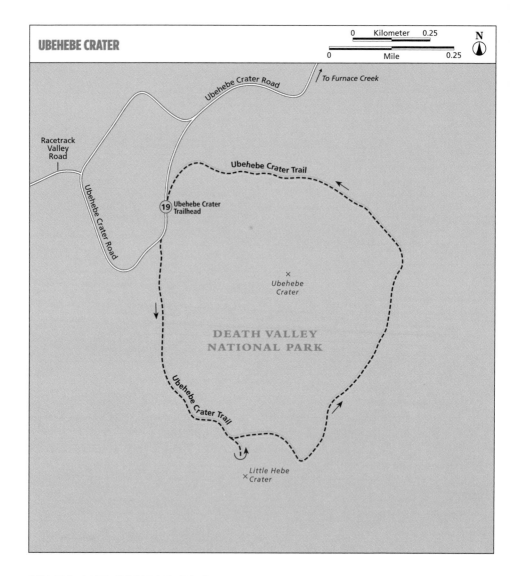

MILES AND DIRECTIONS

0.0   From the parking lot, hike south along the crater rim.

0.5   Little Ubehebe Crater; this is a good destination for those wanting a shorter trip.

0.7   High point on rim.

1.7   Complete the loop at the parking lot.

20 DESOLATION CANYON

A cross-country route up a colorful and less-traveled canyon in the western Black Mountains, in Death Valley National Park.

Start: 6.5 miles south of Furnace Creek
Distance: 3.2-mile out-and-back
Hiking time: About 3 hours
Difficulty: Easy
Trail surface: Cross-country in a dry wash
Best seasons: Late fall to early spring
Water: None
Other trail users: None

Canine compatibility: Dogs not permitted
Fees and permits: Entrance fee
Schedule: Open all year
Maps: CalTopo.com MapBuilder Topo layer; Gaia GPS Trails Illustrated layer
Trail contacts: Death Valley National Park, PO Box 579, Death Valley, CA 92328; (760) 786-3200; https://www.nps.gov/deva

FINDING THE TRAILHEAD

 From Furnace Creek, drive 1.4 miles south, then turn right on Badwater Road. Continue 4.6 miles, then turn left on Desolation Canyon Road. Drive 0.5 mile to the trailhead at the end of the road. GPS: N36 23.749' / W116 50.324'

THE HIKE

A minor canyon lies south of the trailhead; ignore this canyon and walk cross-country east toward the mouth of the east fork of Desolation Canyon (the main fork lies farther north, but the east fork is the more interesting of the two). The wash climbs gradually southeast as the canyon grows deeper and the colorful walls rise around you.

There are several side drainages that you can explore for short distances. If you do so, remember that all side canyons drain downhill to the main canyon. There are a couple of easy dry falls to climb up in the main canyon.

After 1.6 miles, the easy walking ends at an impassable dry waterfall; return the way you came.

COLORS IN THE ROCKS

Rocks derive their color from concentrations of minerals. Red, orange, and purple shades are commonly caused by hematite, yellow by limonite, and green and blue by chlorite and nontronite. All are iron-rich minerals, except for chlorite, which is a magnesium-iron silicate.

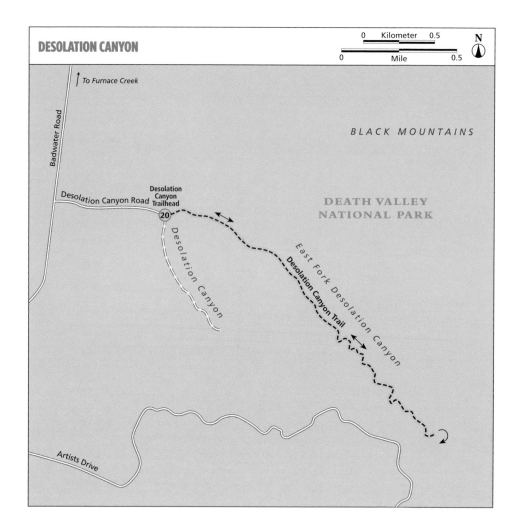

DESOLATION CANYON

0 Kilometer 0.5
0 Mile 0.5
N

To Furnace Creek

Badwater Road

BLACK MOUNTAINS

Desolation Canyon Road

Desolation Canyon Trailhead

20

DEATH VALLEY NATIONAL PARK

Desolation Canyon

East Fork Desolation Canyon

Desolation Canyon Trail

Artists Drive

MILES AND DIRECTIONS

0.0   Hike east toward the mouth of the East Fork of Desolation Canyon.

1.6   Impassable dry fall; return the way you came.

3.2   Trailhead.

21 NATURAL BRIDGE CANYON

This short and easy hike leads to a rare natural bridge.

Start: 17.2 miles south of Furnace Creek
Distance: 2.0-mile out-and-back
Hiking time: About 2 hours
Difficulty: Easy
Trail surface: Cross-country in a dry wash
Best seasons: Late fall to early spring
Water: None
Other trail users: None

Canine compatibility: Dogs not permitted
Fees and permits: Entrance fee
Schedule: Open all year
Maps: CalTopo.com MapBuilder Topo layer; Gaia GPS Trails Illustrated layer
Trail contacts: Death Valley National Park, PO Box 579, Death Valley, CA 92328; (760) 786-3200; https://www.nps.gov/deva

FINDING THE TRAILHEAD

 From Furnace Creek, drive 1.4 miles south, then turn right on Badwater Road. Continue 12.9 miles, then turn left on graded Natural Bridge Road. Drive 2.9 miles to the trailhead at the end of the road. GPS: N36 16.871' / W116 46.212'

THE HIKE

Follow the obvious trail east into the mouth of Natural Bridge Canyon, then follow the gravel wash upstream. You'll soon spot the bridge spanning the canyon about 40 feet above the bed. Continue up the canyon, where you'll encounter some easy dry falls. A mile from the trailhead, you'll reach an impassable 20-foot fall. This point is worth the short extra hike from the bridge because of the views of the Funeral Mountains, and Death Valley as you return to the trailhead.

POWER OF WATER

Some people mistakenly refer to dry washes such as this one as "ancient rivers," and think that wind is the major erosive force in desert landscapes. There's nothing ancient about them, as anyone who's witnessed a flash flood in a desert canyon will testify. Natural Bridge Canyon, the stone bridge itself, and the stark terrain of Death Valley were all carved by water during rare but powerful flash floods. Wind plays a very minor role, mainly moving around and polishing rocks.

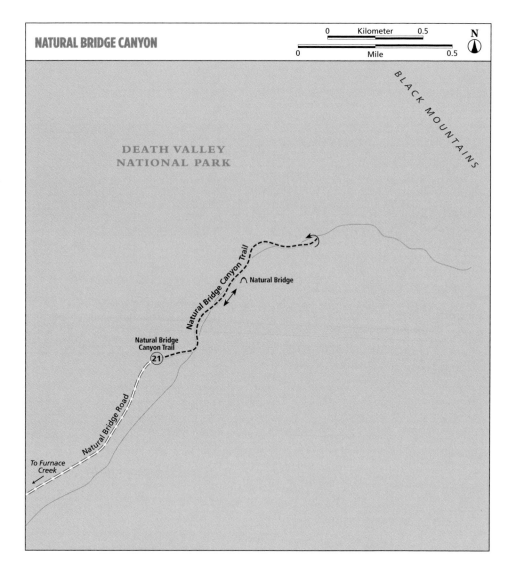

0   Kilometer   0.5

N

0   Mile   0.5

BLACK MOUNTAINS

DEATH VALLEY
NATIONAL PARK

Natural Bridge Canyon Trail

⌒ Natural Bridge

Natural Bridge
Canyon Trail

(21)

Natural Bridge Road

To Furnace
Creek

MILES AND DIRECTIONS

0.0   Natural Bridge Trailhead; hike east into the mouth of Natural Bridge Canyon.

0.7   Natural bridge; return the way you came.

1.0   Impassable dry fall; return the way you came.

2.0   Trailhead.

22 FORT PAIUTE

This hike in the Mojave National Preserve features the only perennial stream in the eastern Mojave National Preserve, as well as a pioneer wagon road. This is a very remote area; make sure you fill your tank at Needles or Barstow and carry extra water and food.

Start: 40 miles northwest of Needles
Distance: 5.2-mile loop with a cherry stem
Hiking time: About 3 hours
Difficulty: Moderate
Trail surface: Dirt and rocks, dry wash
Best seasons: Late fall to early spring
Water: Paiute Spring
Other trail users: None

Canine compatibility: Leashed dogs permitted
Fees and permits: None
Schedule: Open all year
Maps: CalTopo.com MapBuilder Topo layer; Gaia GPS Trails Illustrated layer
Trail contacts: Mojave National Preserve, 2701 Barstow Rd., Barstow, CA 92311; (760) 252-6100; https://www.nps.gov/moja

FINDING THE TRAILHEAD

From Needles, drive 34 miles west, then take exit 115 toward Goffs. At Goffs, after 6.2 miles, turn left on CR 66. After 0.2 mile, turn right on Lanfair Road, which becomes a graded road after about 10 miles. Cedar Canyon Road goes left 16.3 miles from Goffs; continue 0.8 mile and turn right on a graded road. (GPS: N35 8.308' / W115 11.211') This road follows a buried telephone cable and you should see an occasional marker sign. There are numerous minor roads branching off; stay on the main road heading east toward the south end of the Paiute Range. Continue 10.0 miles from Lanfair Road, then turn left on a two-track road at the foot of the Paiute Range. Continue 1.2 miles, passing the historic Mohave Road, and park at a large turnout on the east side of the road that overlooks Paiute Gorge. GPS: N35 6.695' / W115 0.616'

THE HIKE

The trail descends steeply east then north into the bed of Paiute Canyon. Follow the dry wash generally eastward as it twists and turns through the folded rock strata created by the geologic forces that uplifted the range. When the canyon turns southeast, the wash becomes filled with tamarisk and willows, a sure sign that groundwater is near the surface. Sure enough, you'll soon reach Paiute Spring, where water surges to the surface and forms a permanent stream. After a bit more dense vegetation, the canyon opens up and a side canyon enters from the southwest. This point marks the start of the out-and-back hike to Fort Paiute.

Follow the trail east along the slopes north of the canyon bottom. As the canyon opens up, you'll reach the ruins of Fort Paiute. After exploring the ruins, return the way you came to reach the southwest-trending side canyon.

Follow the old Mohave Road up this side canyon. There are several petroglyphs in this area, proving that the area was inhabited long before the first European explorers arrived. The trail climbs over a low pass in the Paiute Range, known as Paiute Hill, then descends to meet the trailhead access road. Turn right to return to your vehicle.

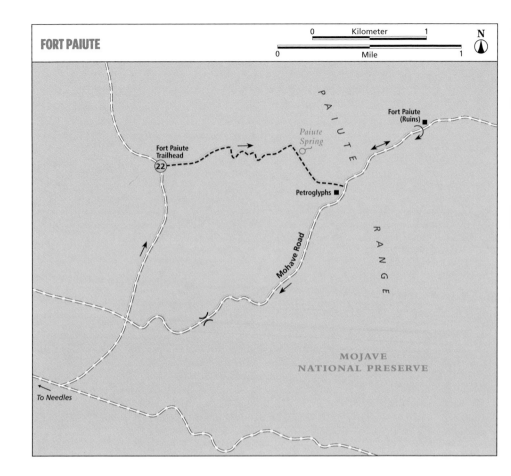

MILES AND DIRECTIONS

0.0   Follow the trail east into Paiute Gorge.

0.9   Paiute Spring.

1.3   Turn left on historic Mohave Road, starting the out-and-back hike.

1.9   Ruins of Fort Paiute; retrace your steps.

2.6   Turn left to follow Mohave Road southwest.

3.7   Cross a low pass (Paiute Hill) on the crest of the Paiute Range.

4.3   Turn right on the trailhead access road.

5.2   Trailhead.

23 NEW YORK PEAK

This cross-country day hike in the Mojave National Preserve takes you to a remote summit in the New York Mountains with outstanding views. Although the hike is relatively short, it is strenuous due to the elevation gain. Hikers should be experienced in desert hiking and carry a map, compass, and GPS.

Start: 77.9 miles southwest of Las Vegas
Distance: 4.4-mile out-and-back
Hiking time: About 4 hours
Difficulty: Strenuous
Trail surface: Old doubletrack roads, cross-country
Best seasons: Late fall to early spring
Water: None
Other trail users: None

Canine compatibility: Leashed dogs permitted
Fees and permits: None
Schedule: Open all year
Maps: CalTopo.com MapBuilder Topo layer; Gaia GPS Trails Illustrated layer
Trail contacts: Mojave National Preserve, 2701 Barstow Rd., Barstow, CA 92311; (760) 252-6100; https://www.nps.gov/moja

FINDING THE TRAILHEAD

 From I-15, 54 miles southwest of Las Vegas, take the Nipton Road 3.4 miles east, then turn right on Ivanpah Road. Continue 18.0 miles, then turn right (west) on a two-track road. This junction is just where Ivanpah Road turns southeast. Numerous mining roads branch off—stay on the main road 2.5 miles to the trailhead, 0.3 mile from the wilderness boundary. A high-clearance vehicle is recommended. GPS: N35 16.302' / W115 17.186'

THE HIKE

From the trailhead, follow the old road west, upstream, along Keystone Canyon past the wilderness boundary. Just after the boundary, the canyon and old road swing south, and you'll pass the old road to Live Oak Canyon. Stay on the main trail up Keystone Canyon. Just before Keystone Canyon turns back to the west, another old road branches left, this one to Keystone Spring. Again, stay on the old road and continue up Keystone Canyon, which soon turns west once again. After turning southwest, the old road ends at a mining site.

Hike south cross-country up the slope to the crest of the ridge, then turn right and climb the ridge west to the main crest of the New York Mountains. Here, turn left and follow the main ridge to the base of New York Peak. The summit itself is a rugged scramble—if this doesn't appeal, the view is still excellent from the base.

As you make the final ascent along the main ridge, watch for patches of white firs growing among the piñon pines on the highest north-facing slopes. These alpine trees are normally found at much higher altitudes, and these remnants are left over from the last glacial period 10,000 years ago.

In the clear desert air, the view extends for more than 100 miles in all directions, from the Panamint Range in Death Valley National Park in the northwest, to the San Jacinto and San Bernardino Mountains to the southwest, and the Hualapai Mountains of Arizona to the southeast.

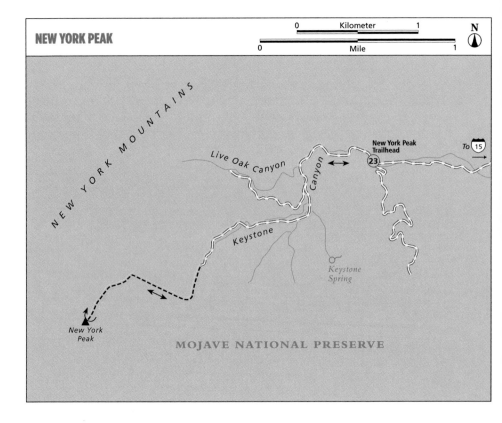

MILES AND DIRECTIONS

0.0 Follow the old road west, up Keystone Canyon.

0.3 Wilderness boundary.

0.6 Old road to Live Oak Canyon forks right; stay left in Keystone Canyon.

0.7 Old road to Keystone Spring goes left; stay right in Keystone Canyon.

1.4 End of the old road at an old mine; hike cross-country up the slope to the south to the crest of the ridge.

1.6 Ridge crest—turn west and follow the ridge uphill.

1.9 Main crest of New York Mountains—turn left and hike southwest toward New York Peak.

2.2 New York Peak; return the way you came.

4.4 Trailhead.

24 **KELSO DUNES**

Although this is a short and easy cross-country hike, it takes you to some tall sand dunes in a beautiful setting within the Mojave National Preserve. Kelso Dunes are the second tallest but most extensive in California.

Start: 78 miles northwest of Needles
Distance: About 3 miles cross-country out-and-back
Hiking time: About 2 hours
Difficulty: Moderate
Trail surface: Sand
Best seasons: Late fall to early spring
Water: None
Other trail users: None

Canine compatibility: Leashed dogs permitted
Fees and permits: None
Schedule: Open all year
Maps: CalTopo.com MapBuilder Topo layer; Gaia GPS Trails Illustrated layer
Trail contacts: Mojave National Preserve, 2701 Barstow Rd., Barstow, CA 92311; (760) 252-6100; https://www.nps.gov/moja

FINDING THE TRAILHEAD

 From Needles, drive 61 miles west on I-40, then take exit 78 and turn right on Kelbaker Road. Continue 14.1 miles, then turn left on Kelso Dunes Road. Drive 2.9 miles to the parking area and trailhead. GPS: N34 53.524' / W115 41.923'

THE HIKE

From the trailhead, hike toward the highest point of the dunes, a distance of about 1.5 miles. Then return the way you came—if you wish.

The simplicity of the hike is misleading. You can easily spend hours wandering the dunes, especially if you are a photographer or wildlife watcher. The best time to walk the dunes is around sunrise, when the slanting light brings out the contours of the sand. This is also the time to see animal and plant tracks, before the wind and human activity erase them. Plant tracks? Yes, plants, especially grasses, make tracks in the sand when the wind blows their stems or branches back and forth.

Kelso Dunes formed about 9,000 years ago, after the climate grew drier and warmer, and several large post-glacial lakes dried up. The exposed lake bottom sediments were blown by the wind and funneled into the Kelso Dunes area by the surrounding mountains.

Kelso Dunes

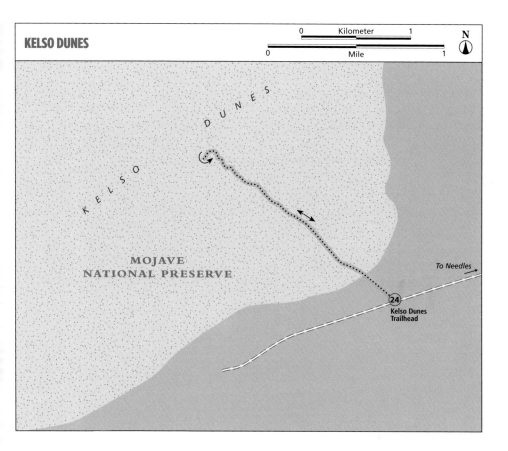

MILES AND DIRECTIONS

0.0 Leave the trailhead and hike northwest toward the highest point of the dunes.

1.5 High point of the dunes; return the way you came.

3.0 Trailhead.

25 MID HILLS TRAIL

This hike uses the north half of the Mid Hills Trail, one of the few constructed trails in the Mojave National Preserve, to reach a scenic high point with a great view.

Start: 73.4 miles northwest of Needles
Distance: 7.0-mile out-and-back
Hiking time: About 4 hours
Difficulty: Moderate
Trail surface: Dirt and rocks
Best seasons: Late fall to early spring
Water: None
Other trail users: None
Canine compatibility: Leashed dogs permitted
Fees and permits: None
Schedule: Open all year
Maps: CalTopo.com MapBuilder Topo layer; Gaia GPS Trails Illustrated layer
Trail contacts: Mojave National Preserve, 2701 Barstow Rd., Barstow, CA 92311; (760) 252-6100; https://www.nps.gov/moja

FINDING THE TRAILHEAD

From I-40 46 miles west of Needles, take exit 100 and turn right (northwest) on Essex Road. Continue 9.7 miles, then turn right on Black Canyon Road. Drive 15.8 miles north, then turn left on Wild Horse Canyon Road and continue 1.9 miles to the trailhead opposite the Mid Hills Campground entrance. GPS: N35 7.394' / W115 25.986'

THE HIKE

Follow the Mid Hills Trail as it climbs steadily southeast into low hills. After crossing a saddle, the trail descends south through two more saddles and then comes out onto an open plain. A steady descent leads to a two-track road and Black Canyon Wash. After crossing the road, follow the trail southeast, downstream, along the wash.

The trail soon leaves the wash and heads southwest, climbing up the slope to cross another doubletrack road, where it contours south before making a final short climb to a saddle.

This broad saddle is a fine viewpoint and it is set almost in the center of the vast Mojave National Preserve, giving you panoramic views of the desert plains and mountains.

MILES AND DIRECTIONS

- **0.0** Hike southeast on the Mid Hills Trail.
- **1.7** Cross a doubletrack road.
- **3.0** Cross another doubletrack.
- **3.5** Reach a saddle on the ridge overlooking Gold Valley and Wild Horse Canyon; return the way you came.
- **7.0** Trailhead.

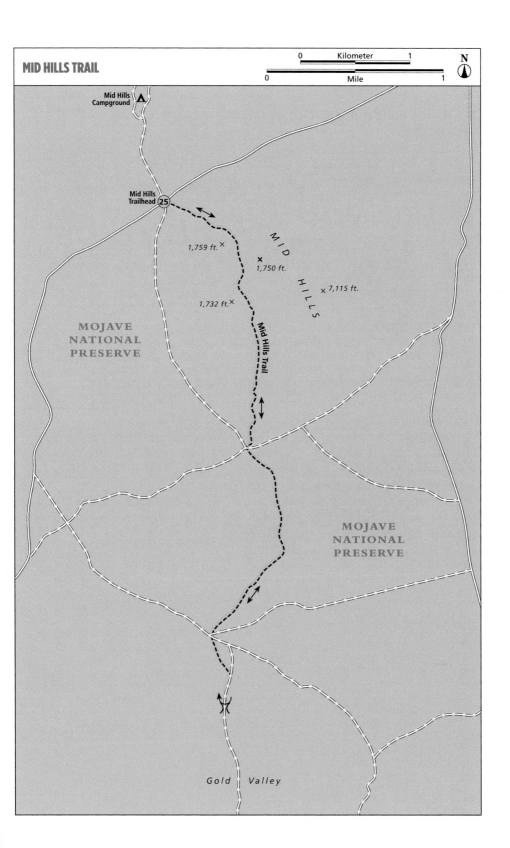

MID HILLS TRAIL

0 — Kilometer — 1

0 — Mile — 1

N

Mid Hills
Campground

Mid Hills
Trailhead 25

1,759 ft. ×

× 1,750 ft.

M I D   H I L L S

× 7,115 ft.

1,732 ft. ×

MOJAVE
NATIONAL
PRESERVE

Mid Hills Trail

MOJAVE
NATIONAL
PRESERVE

Gold   Valley

26 HOLE-IN-THE-WALL

This hike is short but spectacular. It leads through a narrow slot in a volcanic cliff.

Start: 66 miles west of Needles
Distance: 1.8-mile out-and-back
Hiking time: About 3 hours
Difficulty: Easy
Trail surface: Slot canyon, sand, and rocks
Best seasons: Late fall to early spring
Water: None
Other trail users: None

Canine compatibility: Leashed dogs permitted
Fees and permits: None
Schedule: Open all year
Maps: CalTopo.com MapBuilder Topo layer; Gaia GPS Trails Illustrated layer
Trail contacts: Mojave National Preserve, 2701 Barstow Rd., Barstow, CA 92311; (760) 252-6100; https://www.nps.gov/moja

FINDING THE TRAILHEAD

From I-40 46 miles west of Needles, take exit 100 and turn right (northwest) on Essex Road. Continue 9.7 miles, then turn right on Black Canyon Road. Drive 9.8 miles, then turn left and drive 0.5 mile, past the Hole-in-the-Wall Visitor Center to the road's end at the Hole-in-the-Wall Trailhead. GPS: N35 2.650' / W115 23.878'

THE HIKE

Head west on the trail a short distance to a narrow slot in the cliffs. Rings bolted to the walls help you descend this narrow slot canyon, which is sometimes only wide enough for one person. A second, longer descent soon brings you out into Banshee Canyon, surrounded by boulders and colorful cliffs.

Follow the trail southwest to the Mid Hills Trail, then turn right and head west. The hike ends where the trail meets the main Mid Hills Trail at a T junction just before a sandy wash. Retrace your steps to the trailhead.

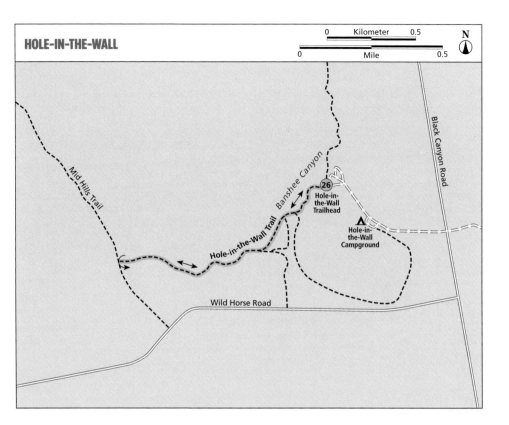

MILES AND DIRECTIONS

0.0 Head west on the Hole-in-the-Wall Trail.

0.2 Banshee Canyon.

0.9 Junction with the Mid Hills Trail; retrace your steps.

1.8 Hole-in-the-Wall Trailhead.

27 QUAIL SPRING BASIN

This day hike follows an old road into the remote Quail Spring area in the Providence Mountains section of the Mojave National Preserve.

Start: 62.6 miles west of Needles
Distance: 5.7-mile out-and-back with a loop section
Hiking time: About 4 hours
Difficulty: Moderate
Trail surface: Old, closed two-track road
Best seasons: Late fall to early spring
Water: None
Other trail users: None

Canine compatibility: Leashed dogs permitted
Fees and permits: None
Schedule: Open all year
Maps: CalTopo.com MapBuilder Topo layer; Gaia GPS Trails Illustrated layer
Trail contacts: Mojave National Preserve, 2701 Barstow Rd., Barstow, CA 92311; (760) 252-6100; https://www.nps.gov/moja

FINDING THE TRAILHEAD

From I-40 52 miles west of Needles, take exit 78 and turn right (northeast) on Kelbaker Road. Continue 9.7 miles, then turn right (northeast) on a two-track road. A high-clearance vehicle is recommended; drive 0.9 mile to the wilderness boundary. GPS: N34 50.572' / W115 36.724'

THE HIKE

Follow the old road south and then southeast as the terrain rises gradually below the foothills of the southern Providence Mountains. The ascent levels out as you reach the saddle between the Horse Hills and the Providence Mountains. Quail Spring Basin lies below this saddle to the east. Continue east to a fork; turn left and walk north to start the loop portion of the hike. (The right fork is your return.)

When the old road reaches the main wash at the north side of the basin, ignore an old road going north and turn right (east). This old road soon turns south and follows the main wash downhill. When you reach another road junction, turn sharply right and

DESERT BUSHES

Creosote bush is the most common plant of the Mojave Desert as well as the Sonoran and Chihuahuan Deserts. Creosote grows up to 6 feet tall and has many small stems that rise at an angle from the base of the plant. The small dark green leaves are evergreen, and during moist periods creosote bears small yellow flowers. It is extremely drought-tolerant and survives extended dry periods by dropping all of its mature leaves and many of its twigs. The newest leaves are retained during dry periods and can survive a loss of 50 percent of their moisture. Photosynthesis continues during droughts so that the plant can immediately use any rain that arrives. Creosote's root system is shallow but extensive so that the plant can take advantage of fleeting soil moisture. The roots produce a germination inhibitor that prevents any creosote seedlings from growing within the root area. The inhibitor also prevents other plants from taking root and competing with the creosote for scarce water.

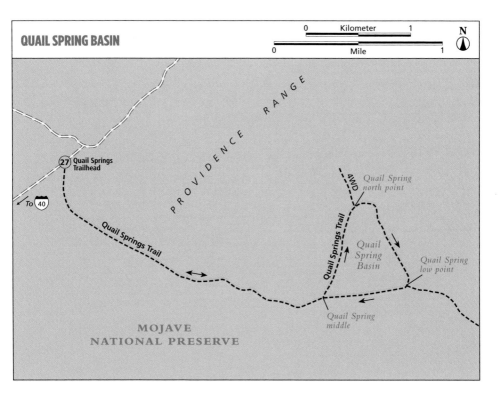

QUAIL SPRING BASIN

hike west toward the saddle between the Horse Hills and the Providence Mountains. You'll pass the junction where you started the loop; continue west and northwest to return to the trailhead.

MILES AND DIRECTIONS

0.0 Hike south and then southeast on the old road.

1.8 Cross a saddle into Quail Spring Basin.

2.0 Start of the loop hike—turn left (north) on the old road—the right fork will be your return route. GPS: N34 49.901' / W115 35.078'

2.5 An old road forks north; stay right and follow the old road east and then south, descending gradually through Quail Spring Basin. GPS: N34 50.359' / W115 34.882'

3.2 Low point in Quail Spring Basin; stay right and hike west toward the saddle. GPS: N34 49.958' / W115 34.553'

3.7 Close the loop at the above junction; continue west over the saddle and return to the trailhead.

5.7 Trailhead.

28 PANORAMA LOOP

This aptly named loop takes you over several peaks with views of the west end of Joshua Tree National Park as well as the Salton Sea, Mount San Jacinto, and Mount San Gorgonio.

Start: 5.1 miles south of Yucca
Distance: 6.3-mile loop with an out-and-back section
Hiking time: About 4 hours
Difficulty: Moderate
Trail surface: Dirt and rocks
Best seasons: Fall through spring
Water: None
Other trail users: None

Canine compatibility: Dogs not allowed
Fees and permits: Park entrance fee
Maps: CalTopo.com MapBuilder Topo layer; Gaia GPS Trails Illustrated layer
Trail contacts: Joshua Tree National Park, 74485 National Park Dr., Twentynine Palms, CA 92277-3597; (760) 367-5500; https://www.nps.gov/jotr/

FINDING THE TRAILHEAD

From the intersection of CA 62 and Joshua Lane in Yucca Valley, go south on Joshua Lane 5.1 miles to the Black Rock Backcountry Board. GPS: N34 4.505' / W11 23.275'

THE HIKE

From the Black Rock Backcountry Board, follow the trail up Black Rock Wash. This broad, sandy wash is popular with horses and the going may be slow in soft sand. Stay right at the junction with the California Hiking and Riding Trail, remaining in Black Rock Wash. A trail forking right leads to the south end of Black Rock Campground and is a good alternative start and finish for those hikers staying in the campground. (Use care at a water tank to stay on the trail.)

As you continue up Black Rock Wash, the trail reaches the base of the foothills and you'll pass Black Rock Spring, which is usually dry. Just 0.1 mile beyond the spring, the wash forks; turn left to start the loop portion of the hike. Continue east-southeast up this wash to its head, where a trail leads south to Peak 5,195.

From the summit, the trail heads southwest down a ridge, then turns west to return to Black Rock Wash. Follow the wash downstream, past the loop junction and Black Rock Spring, to the Black Rock Trailhead.

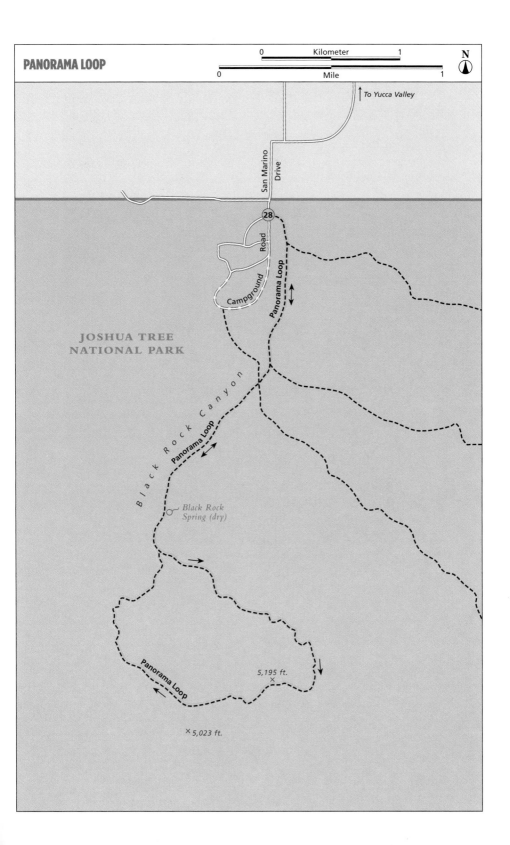

PANORAMA LOOP

0 — Kilometer — 1
0 — Mile — 1

N

To Yucca Valley

San Marino Drive

28

Campground Road

Panorama Loop

JOSHUA TREE
NATIONAL PARK

Black Rock Canyon

Panorama Loop

Black Rock
Spring (dry)

Panorama Loop

5,195 ft.
×

× 5,023 ft.

Joshua Tree along the Panorama Loop

MILES AND DIRECTIONS

0.0 Black Rock Trailhead.

0.1 California Hiking and Riding Trail; stay right.

0.6 Short Loop Trail; stay right.

0.8 Burnt Hill Trail on left and Spur Trail to Black Rock Campground on right; continue straight ahead.

1.6 Black Rock Spring (normally dry).

1.7 Fork in Black Rock Wash and start of clockwise loop.

3.0 Peak 5,195.

4.5 End of loop section, stay left and return the way you came.

6.3 Arrive back at Black Rock Trailhead.

29 WONDERLAND WASH

This is a delightful and easy cross-country walk into the heart of the Wonderland of Rocks.

Start: 15.5 miles south of Joshua Tree
Distance: 3.6-mile out-and-back
Hiking time: About 2 hours
Difficulty: Easy
Trail surface: Dirt and rocks
Best seasons: Fall through spring
Water: None
Other trail users: None
Canine compatibility: Dogs not permitted

Fees and permits: Entrance fee
Schedule: Open all year
Maps: CalTopo.com MapBuilder Topo layer; Gaia GPS Trails Illustrated layer
Trail contacts: Joshua Tree National Park, 74485 National Park Dr., Twentynine Palms, CA 92277-3597; (760) 367-5500; https://www.nps .gov/jotr/

FINDING THE TRAILHEAD

 From CA 62 in Joshua Tree, drive 14.0 miles south and southeast on Quail Spring Road/Park Boulevard, and then turn left on the Queen Valley Road. Continue 1.5 miles to the Wall Street Mill Trailhead, on the left. GPS: N34 1.490' / W116 8.493'

THE HIKE

Starting at the Wall Street Mill Trailhead, walk the Wall Street Mill Trail 0.2 mile to the unsigned Wonderland Ranch Trail, an old road. Turn left, and follow the trail 0.1 mile to the ruins of the pink ranch building. Walk a few yards northwest of the old ranch house to Wonderland Wash, and follow the wash upstream to the north approximately 1.4 miles to an area of large granite domes, some of which are 300 feet high. This area is popular with rock climbers.

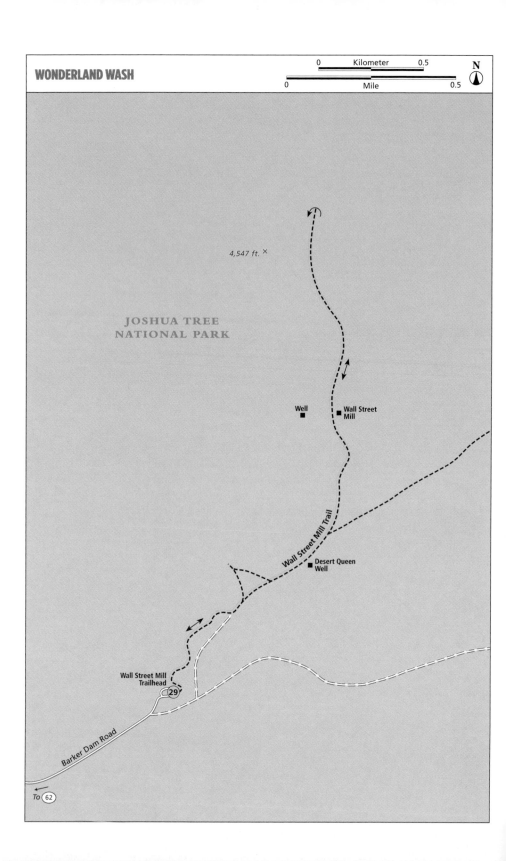

0   Kilometer   0.5

0   Mile   0.5

N

4,547 ft. ×

JOSHUA TREE
NATIONAL PARK

Well

Wall Street
Mill

Wall Street Mill Trail

Desert Queen
Well

Wall Street Mill
Trailhead

29

Barker Dam Road

To 62

Pool, Wonderland of Rocks

MILES AND DIRECTIONS

0.0 Wall Street Mill Trailhead.

0.3 Wonderland Ranch Trail; turn left.

0.4 Wonderland Ranch ruins.

1.8 Domes area; return the way you came.

3.6 Trailhead.

Granite formations, Joshua Tree National Park

30 MASTODON PEAK LOOP

This fine loop hike combines part of the Cottonwood Nature Trail with a trail past Mastodon Peak and a historic mining site, as well as Cottonwood Springs Oasis.

Start: 8.1 miles north of I-10 and Pinto Basin Road exit
Distance: 2.2-mile loop
Hiking time: About 1 hour
Difficulty: Easy
Trail surface: Dirt and rocks
Best seasons: Fall through spring
Water: None
Other trail users: None
Canine compatibility: Dogs not allowed

Fees and permits: Entrance fee
Schedule: Open all year
Maps: CalTopo.com MapBuilder Topo layer; Gaia GPS Trails Illustrated layer
Trail contacts: Joshua Tree National Park, 74485 National Park Dr., Twentynine Palms, CA 92277-3597; (760) 367-5500; https://www.nps.gov/jotr/

FINDING THE TRAILHEAD

From I-10 at the Pinto Basin Road exit, drive north 7.0 miles to the Cottonwood Visitor Center, and turn right. Drive 1.1 miles to the end of the road at Cottonwood Spring Backcountry Board and Trailhead. (You can also access the trail from the Cottonwood Group Campground.) GPS: N33 44.212' / W115 48.632'

THE HIKE

From the Cottonwood Spring Trailhead, walk a few yards west up the road to the Cottonwood Spring Nature Trail. Walk this trail northwest and north up a wash to the Mastodon Peak Trail. Informative signs on the nature trail explain the native Cahuilla Indians use of Sonoran Desert plants for medicine, food, and tools and materials.

Turn right onto the Mastodon Peak Trail, which immediately passes the site of the old Winona Mill. Little remains of the mill except concrete foundations. Built by George Hulsey in the 1920s, the mill was used to crush ore from the Mastodon Mine as well as claims in the Dale Mining District to the north. Hulsey and other residents planted non-native trees and shrubs, which still grow in the mill area.

The trail heads northeast and climbs up to the Mastodon Mine, just below the top of Mastodon Peak. A slanting mine shaft, sealed with a locked grate, and some mining machinery mark the spot. Hulsey operated the mine from 1919 to 1932, and its gold ore was assayed at $744 per ton. Unfortunately, the miners, following the main gold vein, eventually discovered that the rich ore ended at a fault, and the mine was abandoned.

From just south of the mine, it is possible to make the short scramble to the top of Mastodon Peak, an optional side hike that adds only 0.1 mile to the hike. For such an easy-to-reach summit, the views are outstanding, including the southern portions of the park, as well as the Coachella Valley and Salton Sea to the south.

The trail now descends south into a wash, where it meets the Lost Palms Trail. Turn right and follow the Lost Palms Trail northwest to Cottonwood Spring, marked by a stand of California fan palms. Between 1870 and 1910 the spring was a critical watering

Cottonwood Spring, Mastodon Peak Trail

point in the otherwise arid desert. Because it was one of only two watering places between Mecca and the Dale Mining District, Cottonwood Spring was a popular and necessary stopping point for freight haulers, prospectors, and other desert travelers. These travelers planted the California fan palms and Fremont cottonwoods that shade the canyon bottom. For a time, water was pumped 18 miles from the spring to the Iron Chief Mine in the Eagle Mountains.

Bedrock mortars, marked by a sign, are the only remaining evidence that natives used Cottonwood Spring for many years before the white people came. These small basins in the rock were carved out by the grinding of grain and seeds with a rounded stone, called a pestle.

Output from the spring has varied widely. Around 1900, the spring apparently delivered around 3,000 gallons per day, but by 1970 the flow had dropped to a few gallons per

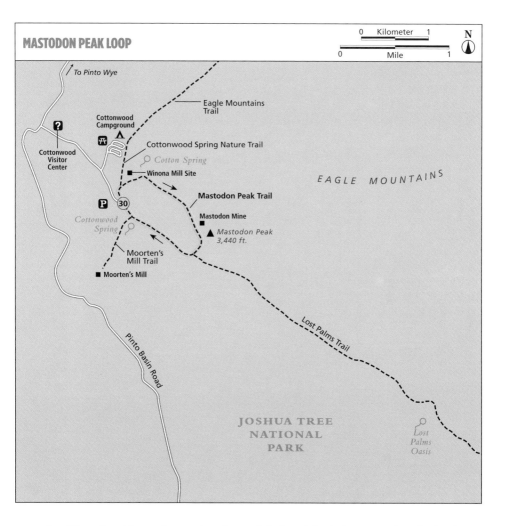

0   Kilometer   1

0   Mile   1

N

To Pinto Wye

Eagle Mountains
Trail

Cottonwood
Campground

Cottonwood Spring Nature Trail

Cottonwood
Visitor
Center

Cotton Spring

Winona Mill Site

EAGLE MOUNTAINS

Mastodon Peak Trail

P 30

Mastodon Mine

Cottonwood
Spring

▲ Mastodon Peak
3,440 ft.

Moorten's
Mill Trail

■ Moorten's Mill

Lost Palms Trail

Pinto Basin Road

JOSHUA TREE
NATIONAL
PARK

Lost
Palms
Oasis

day. There is evidence that earthquakes and fault activity influence springs in the desert, and this is borne out by the 1971 San Fernando Valley earthquake. After the earthquake, the output of Cottonwood Spring increased somewhat, to about 30 gallons per day.

From the spring, walk less than 0.1 mile west to the trailhead.

MILES AND DIRECTIONS

0.0   Cottonwood Spring Trailhead.

0.4   Winona Mill site and Mastodon Peak Trail; turn right.

1.3   Mastodon Mine.

1.5   Lost Palms Trail; turn right.

2.1   Cottonwood Spring.

2.2   Cottonwood Spring Trailhead.

ARIZONA

31 NORTH KAIBAB TRAIL

This is a strenuous but rewarding backpack to the Colorado River at the bottom of the Grand Canyon, following the famous transcanyon Kaibab Trail. This route is also used by the Arizona Trail.

Start: 2 miles north of Grand Canyon Lodge, North Rim Village
Distance: 28.4-mile out-and-back
Hiking time: 2–3 days
Difficulty: Strenuous
Trail surface: Dirt trails
Best seasons: Fall and late spring
Water: Roaring Springs, Cottonwood Camp, Phantom Ranch, and Bright Angel Campground
Other trail users: Mule pack trains

Canine compatibility: Dogs prohibited on trails in Grand Canyon National Park
Fees and permits: Permit required for camping in the canyon
Schedule: Open May 15 through Oct 15
Maps: CalTopo.com MapBuilder Topo layer; Gaia GPS Trails Illustrated layer
Trail contacts: Grand Canyon National Park, PO Box 129, Grand Canyon, AZ 86023; (928) 638-7888; www.nps.gov/grca

FINDING THE TRAILHEAD

From the Grand Canyon Lodge on the North Rim, drive about 2 miles north on the main entrance road (AZ 67) to the trailhead parking area on the right. GPS: N36 13.03' / W112 3.40'

THE HIKE

The first 4.7 miles of the North Kaibab Trail quickly descend into Roaring Springs Canyon to meet Bright Angel Creek. Roaring Springs, as the name suggests, can be heard long before it is seen. Water gushes out of a cave in the Redwall limestone and cascades down to Bright Angel Creek. Water from the springs is pumped to both the North and South Rims to serve tourists and residents.

About 2 miles down the creek is Cottonwood Campground, a good destination for first-time canyon hikers. Fremont cottonwood, box elders, pale hoptree, Knowlton hop, and coyote willows line the creek banks. American dippers may be seen doing their "kneebends" on boulders in the stream or "flying" underwater in search of aquatic invertebrates to eat.

Back on the main trail, travel another 3 miles to reach the entrance of the Box, where vertical walls of black Precambrian schist tower 1,000 feet above the creek. After 3 miles more you reach Phantom Ranch, built in 1922 and the only lodge within the Grand Canyon. Mail sent out from the ranch will be postmarked "Mailed from the bottom of the Canyon." The delightful booklet *Recollections of Phantom Ranch* by Elizabeth Simpson delves into the fascinating history of this isolated guest ranch.

Bright Angel Campground and the Colorado River are about a mile beyond Phantom Ranch.

Strong hikers could do this as a 2-day backpack, but breaking it up into 3 or 4 days will give you more time to enjoy this remarkable place.

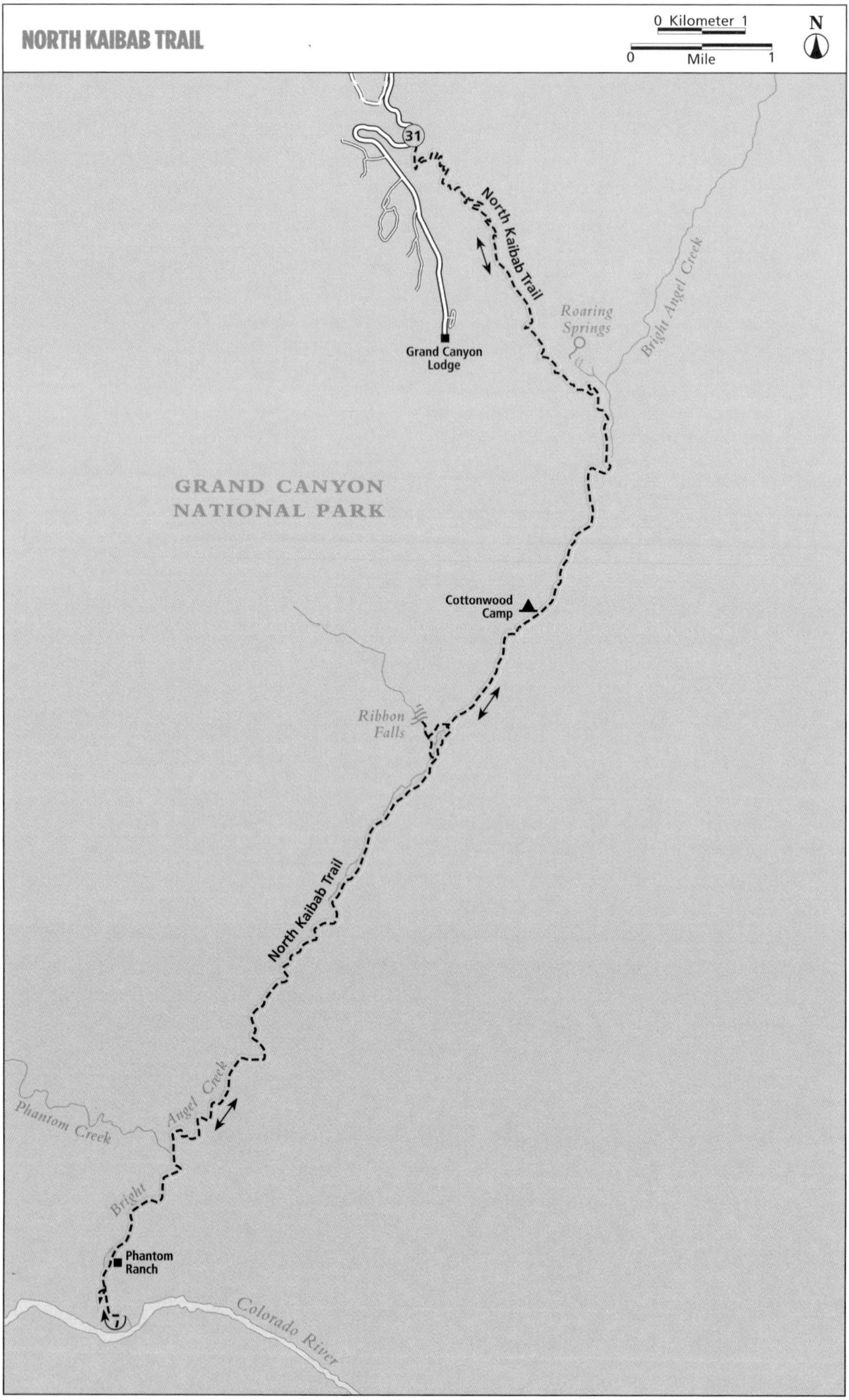
NORTH KAIBAB TRAIL
0 Kilometer 1
0 Mile 1
N
31
North Kaibab Trail
Grand Canyon Lodge
Roaring Springs
Bright Angel Creek
GRAND CANYON NATIONAL PARK
Cottonwood Camp
Ribbon Falls
North Kaibab Trail
Phantom Creek
Bright Angel Creek
Phantom Ranch
Colorado River

Hiking the North Kaibab Trail

MILES AND DIRECTIONS

0.0 Start at the North Kaibab Trailhead.

4.7 Reach Roaring Springs.

6.8 Pass Cottonwood Campground.

14.2 Reach the Colorado River, your turnaround point.

28.4 Arrive back at the trailhead.

> **Option:** About 1.5 miles downstream from Cottonwood Campground is a short side trip to Ribbon Falls. The waters of Ribbon Creek are highly mineralized with calcium carbonate derived from the limestone formations above. As the mineral slowly precipitates out of the creek water, an apron of calcium carbonate, or travertine, is formed behind the falls. Moss, maidenhair ferns, yellow columbine, and scarlet monkey flowers thrive in the spray from the falls.

Hikers on the Kaibab Trail, Grand Canyon

32 TANNER-GRANDVIEW

Using two of the most scenic trails in the Grand Canyon, this hike features some of the canyon's most interesting geology.

Start: 21 miles east of Grand Canyon Village
Distance: 24.8-mile one way with shuttle
Hiking time: About 4 days
Difficulty: Strenuous
Trail surface: Dirt and rocks
Best seasons: Fall through spring
Water: Colorado River, Hance Creek, Page Spring (shown as Miners Spring on some maps)
Other trail users: None

Canine compatibility: Dogs prohibited on trails in Grand Canyon National Park
Fees and permits: Entrance fee; permit and fee required for backcountry camping
Schedule: Open all year
Maps: CalTopo.com MapBuilder Topo layer; Gaia GPS Trails Illustrated layer
Trail contacts: Grand Canyon National Park, PO Box 129, Grand Canyon, AZ 86023; (928) 638-7888; www.nps.gov/grca

FINDING THE TRAILHEAD

This one-way hike requires a car shuttle. To reach the end of the hike from Grand Canyon Village, drive south on the main park road, then turn east onto Desert View Drive. Eleven miles from the village, turn left (north) onto the signed Grandview Point Road; park in the signed trailhead parking area. GPS: N35 59.87' / W111 59.26'

To reach the start of the hike from Grandview Point, turn left (east) onto Desert View Drive. Go about 11 miles to Lipan Point, and turn left into the parking area. GPS: N36 1.95' / W111 51.13'

THE HIKE

The Tanner Trailhead is signed and starts on the east side of the parking lot to the south of the viewpoint. A steep series of switchbacks descend rapidly through the rim formations to the saddle at the head of Seventyfive Mile Creek. After the confinement of the upper section of the trail, the sudden view to the west is startling. The trail now contours around Escalante and Cardenas Buttes on the gentle slopes of the red Supai sandstone. At the north end of Cardenas Butte, the trail descends abruptly through the Redwall limestone in a series of switchbacks, then works its way through the greenish Muav limestone and greenish-purple Bright Angel shale slopes.

There are a few small campsites scattered around the mouth of Tanner Canyon at the Colorado River. Tanner Canyon is normally dry, but water can be obtained from the river. The route now turns south and follows the bench just above the river. Although there has never been a formal trail between Tanner and Red Canyons, enough hikers have traveled the route to create a trail. Tanner Rapids, visible below, is shallow and rocky and creates more of a problem for riverboats than some of the larger rapids. After skirting a narrow section where the river presses against its left bank, the trail moves inland and follows the foot of the shale slopes to the mouth of Cardenas Creek. Campsites are more plentiful here than back at the mouth of Tanner Canyon.

Grandview Trail

The trail crosses Cardenas Creek but dead-ends with a view of Unkar Creek Rapids, which makes it a worthwhile side trip of about a mile round-trip. Your route goes up the dry bed of Cardenas Creek about 0.2 mile and then climbs onto the ridge above the river. Walk to the west edge for a spectacular view of Unkar Creek Rapids, 200 feet straight down. Now turn south and climb the gentle red-shale ridge directly toward Escalante Butte. Stay on the crest of the ridge to pick up the trail again as the ridge narrows. The trail turns west and heads into the nameless canyon west of Cardenas Creek at about the 3,800-foot level. After rounding the west end of the point, the trail turns back to the east to descend into Escalante Creek. Walk down the bed of Escalante Creek, and then leave the bed at about the 3,200-foot level (there is an impassable fall farther downstream) and climb through a low saddle to the south. Descend into the unnamed south fork of Escalante Creek and follow it to the Colorado River (a barrier fall has an obvious bypass on the left). Nevills Rapids is a minor one, but as the river enters Granite Gorge ahead, it crashes through some of the hardest rapids in the canyon.

Turn left along the river's left bank. Notice how a rising ramp of hard rock forms a cliff right into the river and forces our route to climb. The bench is Shinumo quartzite, a layer of resistant rock near the bottom of the Grand Canyon series. As the river rolls downstream through this section, the rocks at river level become harder and the gorge becomes steeper-walled and deeper. The contrast between this section and the river valley at the foot of the Tanner Trail is already impressive, but the narrowest section is still downstream. After about 0.5 mile the route reaches the rim of Seventyfive Mile Canyon and turns east along the edge of the narrow, impassable gorge. About 0.4 mile up this side canyon, the route drops into the bed and follows it back to the river, passing almost directly underneath the trail 200 feet above. At the river turn left (downstream) again, and walk about 0.6 mile along the easy beach to the mouth of Papago Creek. There are several good campsites here for small groups.

Just downstream of Papago Creek, a cliff falls directly into the river and appears to block the route. Go up Papago Creek a few yards and climb up a steep gully, which will require some scrambling. Work your way up easier ledges above to a point about 300 feet above the river, and then traverse east. If you are on the correct level, you will be able to reach the head of a steep gully that can be used to descend back to river level. The usual error is to traverse too low. If this happens, retrace your steps until you can climb to a higher level. Once you reach the river, a good trail follows the bank to the mouth of Red Canyon.

There is limited, sandy camping at Red Canyon. The Red Canyon Trail goes up the bed here and could be used for an early exit if necessary, but it is steeper and harder to follow than the Grandview Trail. At this point, start on the Tonto Trail, which climbs the slopes to the west. The view of mile-long Hance Rapids is great. Hance is one of the hardest Grand Canyon rapids to navigate due to the numerous rocks. As you continue to climb above the river on the Tonto Trail, note the trail climbing the slope on the opposite side of the river. This trail goes to Asbestos Canyon and was used to reach the asbestos mines on the north side of the river.

Colorado River from the Tanner Trail

About a mile from Red Canyon, the Tonto Trail turns south. After crossing dry Mineral Canyon, the trail turns west again and climbs a bit more to reach the greenish-gray shale slopes below Ayer Point. This terrace is called the Tonto Plateau and forms a prominent shelf about 1,200 feet above the Colorado River. The rim of the Tonto Plateau is formed from the hard Tapeats sandstone and overlooks dark, narrow Granite Gorge, already impressive in this area. The Tonto Trail follows the Tonto Plateau for about 60 miles. After Ayer Point the Tonto Trail turns south into Hance Canyon along the Tapeats sandstone rim. Hance Creek may be dry where the trail crosses, but there is always water a short distance downstream. There is also camping downstream, below the impressive Tapeats narrows.

After crossing Hance Creek the Tonto Trail continues northwest about 0.5 mile to a side canyon coming from the east side of Horseshoe Mesa. Turn west here onto the East Grandview Trail. Page Spring (shown as Miners Spring on some maps) is reliable. It is reached from a spur trail about a mile from the Tonto Trail junction. The final section of the trail climbs the high Redwall limestone cliff at the canyon head to reach Horseshoe Mesa and the junction with the main Grandview Trail. There is a Park Service campground on Horseshoe Mesa, but water will have to be carried from Hance Creek or Page Spring.

Turn left onto the Grandview Trail and climb 2 miles to the rim at Grandview Point.

MILES AND DIRECTIONS

0.0 Start at the Tanner Trailhead at Lipan Point.

1.2 Reach the head of Seventyfive Mile Creek.

3.4 Begin the Redwall descent.

4.3 Start down the ridge above Tanner Canyon.

6.5 Reach the Colorado River at Tanner Canyon. (FYI: A few small campsites are scattered around the mouth of the canyon.)

8.9 Reach and cross Cardenas Creek. (FYI: Campsites are available.)

10.7 Begin the traverse into Escalante Creek.

12.8 Descend to Escalante Creek.

14.6 Pass Nevills Rapids.

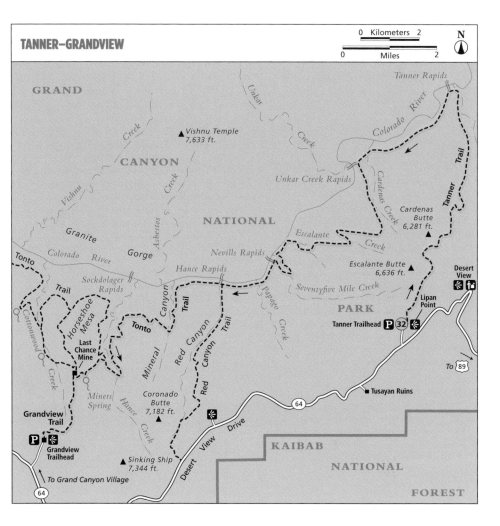

TANNER–GRANDVIEW

GRAND

CANYON

NATIONAL

PARK

KAIBAB

NATIONAL

FOREST

Vishnu Temple
7,633 ft.

Colorado River

Tanner Rapids

Unkar Creek Rapids

Cardenas
Butte
6,281 ft.

Escalante Butte
6,636 ft.

Desert
View

Lipan
Point

Tanner Trailhead P 32

Tanner Trail

Vishnu Creek

Granite

Colorado River

Gorge

Asbestos Creek

Nevills Rapids

Hance Rapids

Escalante Creek

Seventyfive Mile Creek

Sockdolager
Rapids

Tonto

Trail

Horseshoe
Mesa

Last
Chance
Mine

Tonto

Mineral Canyon

Red Canyon

Red Canyon Trail

Papago Creek

Tusayan Ruins

64

Miners
Spring

Coronado
Butte
7,182 ft.

Hance Creek

Cottonwood Creek

Grandview
Trail

P

Grandview
Trailhead

Sinking Ship
7,344 ft.

Desert View Drive

To 89

To Grand Canyon Village

64

15.3 Reach the mouth of Papago Creek. (FYI: Campsites for small groups are available.)

16.1 Reach the mouth of Red Canyon. (FYI: Limited, sandy camping is available.)

18.3 Cross Mineral Canyon.

21.5 Cross Hance Creek.

22.8 Pass side canyon coming from the east side of Horseshoe Mesa and turn west onto East Grandview Trail.

24.8 Reach the Grandview Trailhead and your shuttle.

33 **KEET SEEL**

This overnight backpack trip features one of the largest and best-preserved cliff houses in Arizona.

Start: 30 miles northwest of Kayenta
Distance: 14.0-mile out-and-back
Hiking time: About 8 hours or 2 days
Difficulty: Strenuous
Trail surface: Sand and rocks
Best seasons: Spring through fall
Water: Seasonal in creek
Other trail users: None
Canine compatibility: Dogs prohibited in Navajo National Monument
Fees and permits: Permit required; reservations can be made up to 60 days in advance. Visits to Keet Seel are closely regulated to preserve the ruin and prevent vandalism. The Park Service will give you directions to the trailhead when you pick up your hiking permit at the visitor center. Before receiving your permit, you must attend a trail orientation meeting either at 4 p.m. the day before your hike or at 8:15 a.m. the day of your hike. You must be on the trail no later than 9:15 a.m.
Schedule: Open Memorial Day to Labor Day
Maps: CalTopo.com MapBuilder Topo layer
Trail contacts: Navajo National Monument, PO Box 7717, Shonto, AZ 86045; (928) 672-2700; www.nps.gov /nava/index.htm

FINDING THE TRAILHEAD

From Kayenta drive about 20 miles southwest on US 160. Turn right (north) onto AZ 564 and drive another 10 miles to Navajo National Monument. GPS: N36 40.67' / W110 32.445'

THE HIKE

This trail takes you to one of the largest and most spectacular prehistoric cliff houses in Arizona—the 160-room Keet Seel, tucked under a huge overhang in a remote canyon. People of the Anasazi culture lived for more than a thousand years in the Four Corners region—the area where Utah, Colorado, New Mexico, and Arizona join at a common point.

The trail begins with a short but steep sandy descent to Laguna Creek in Tsegi Canyon. The trail then crosses the creek and heads up Keet Seel Canyon, passing the mouth of Dowozhiebito Canyon, which enters from the right. Most of the route traverses reservation land, and it's not uncommon to encounter Navajos on horseback or foot tending flocks of sheep or goats. Remember that the Park Service permit does not give you permission to deviate from the trail onto other Navajo land.

The route up Keet Seel Canyon is between towering walls of Navajo sandstone stained with long, dark stripes of desert varnish. The ledge-forming Kayenta Formation underlies the Navajo. Rainwater easily soaks into the porous sandstone and is pulled downward by gravity. When this groundwater encounters the shales and clay beds in the Kayenta, its downward journey is interrupted. The water then begins to migrate horizontally and, if it comes to a cliff face, emerges as a seep or spring. Look

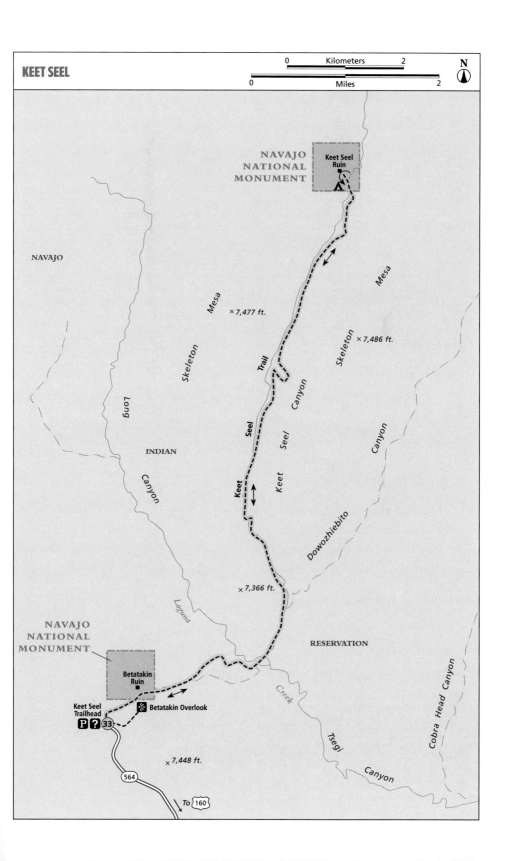

KEET SEEL

0 — Kilometers — 2
0 — Miles — 2

N

NAVAJO
NATIONAL
MONUMENT

Keet Seel
Ruin

NAVAJO

Mesa

×7,477 ft.

Mesa

Skeleton

×7,486 ft.

Skeleton

Canyon

Trail

Seel

Long

Seel

Keet

INDIAN

Keet

Canyon

Canyon

Dowozhiebito

×7,366 ft.

Laguna

RESERVATION

NAVAJO
NATIONAL
MONUMENT

Betatakin
Ruin

Keet Seel
Trailhead

P ? 33

Betatakin Overlook

Creek

Cobra Head Canyon

Tsegi

×7,448 ft.

Canyon

564

To 160

Along the trail grow high desert plants typical of the Colorado Plateau country—four-wing saltbush, big sage, virgin's bower, Mormon tea, rabbitbrush, snakeweed, skunkbush, juniper, and piñon. You may be lucky and spot a rock squirrel or chipmunk-like antelope squirrel, although most of the canyon country's mammals tend to be nocturnal. Common ravens, turkey vultures, scrub jays, canyon wrens, rock wrens, red-tailed hawks, and other birds may be seen or heard.

Keet Seel is a Navajo phrase meaning "broken pottery," and along the trail you may see pottery shards and other artifacts eroding out of the sand. Admire and photograph them, but please return them to exactly where you found them. Visitors sometimes pile artifacts on a rock for a picture and then leave them there. These "museum rocks" do not reveal as much information to archaeologists as leaving artifacts where they are discovered. All prehistoric artifacts are protected by federal, state, and tribal laws and should not be collected. Besides, the canyon spirits will haunt you.

From the mid-10th century to the late 13th, several hundred Ancient Puebloan people occupied Tsegi Canyon and its tributary, Keet Seel. Here they grew corn and several kinds of beans and squash, tended turkeys, and created exquisite pottery painted with geometric and animal designs. Then in the late 1200s, the Anasazi began to abandon the area. The exact cause is uncertain but is likely a combination of drought, disease, warfare, overpopulation, and the attraction of an emerging new religion at the time over in New Mexico.

for these seeps at the contact between the Navajo and Kayenta Formations. Remember, too, to treat all water before drinking.

About 0.5 mile from Keet Seel, there is a primitive campground but no purified water. You may enter the cliff house only with the ranger on duty.

MILES AND DIRECTIONS

0.0 Start at the trailhead by the visitor center and begin to descend.

0.9 Reach and then cross Laguna Creek.

1.3 Pass the mouth of Dowozhiebito Canyon on the right.

7.0 Arrive at Keet Seel ruin, your turnaround point. (FYI: There is a primitive campground about 0.5 mile from the ruin.)

14.0 Arrive back at the visitor center.

34 INNER BASIN TRAIL

This hike follows the path of an ancient glacier through very scenic alpine forests and meadows to the dramatic southeast face of Humphreys Peak.

Start: 21.6 miles northeast of Flagstaff
Distance: 7.5-mile loop with one cherry stem section
Hiking time: About 5 hours
Difficulty: Moderate
Trail surface: Dirt and rocks
Best seasons: Summer through fall
Water: None
Other trail users: Mountain bikes

Canine compatibility: Leashed dogs permitted
Fees and permits: None
Schedule: Open all year
Maps: CalTopo.com MapBuilder Topo layer; Gaia GPS Trails Illustrated layer
Trail contacts: Coconino National Forest, 1824 S. Thompson St., Flagstaff, AZ 86001; (928) 527-3600; www.fs.usda.gov/coconino

FINDING THE TRAILHEAD

From Flagstaff drive north on US 89, the main street through town, and continue about 17 miles to Schultz Pass Road (FR 420); turn left (west). This maintained dirt road is opposite the Sunset Crater National Monument turnoff. Drive 0.4 mile, then turn right at a T intersection. Continue 0.8 mile to another T intersection, and then turn left. About 0.6 mile farther, just before a locked gate at a cinder pit, turn right onto Lockett Meadow Road. Continue 2.8 miles to the Lockett Trailhead at the southwest corner of the loop road around Lockett Meadow. GPS: N35 21.415' / W111 37.375'

THE HIKE

Start on Inner Basin Trail, and hike southwest up the Interior Valley. The trail switchbacks up a steep, aspen-covered slope to meet the Pipeline Road. Turn right and walk this road to the watershed cabins.

From the cabins take Inner Basin Trail, the road that continues west-southwest up the Interior Valley. (This road is not open to the public and is used only by occasional official vehicles.) One hundred yards beyond the cabins, the road forks. Take the right fork, which goes to Bear Paw and Flagstaff Springs. The road climbs steadily through the dense alpine forest, which sometimes opens up for glimpses of the high peaks. Along the way you will see old signs of construction dating from the beginnings of the watershed project.

About 0.8 mile from the watershed cabins, a road forks left. This will be the return loop. For now continue on the main road (right), which ends in another 0.8 mile below Flagstaff Spring. The most notable feature here is the incredible swath of destruction in the 200-year-old fir and spruce forest. The winter of 1972-73 was the snowiest winter on record in Flagstaff—the airport received 210 inches, more than twice the normal depth. The San Francisco Peaks received far more snow than the city, and sometime during that winter a large avalanche came down the southeast face of Humphreys Peak and destroyed the trees.

To continue on the main hike, retrace your steps east down the road 0.8 mile to the junction mentioned above, and then turn right. This road goes south 0.5 mile to the

INNER BASIN TRAIL

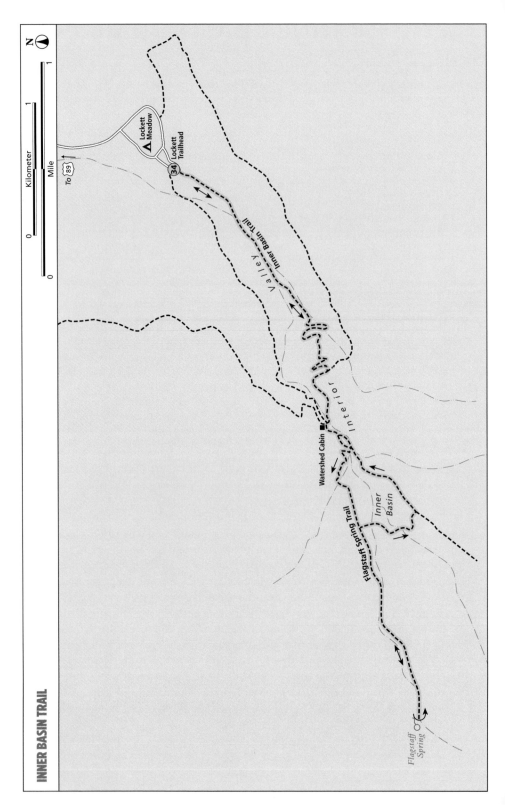

FLAGSTAFF'S WATER PROBLEM

Flagstaff has outgrown its water supply repeatedly over the years. In the early part of the 20th century, only a couple of decades after the city's founding, someone had an idea: tap the springs in the Interior Valley of the San Francisco Peaks. In an area with very few springs, this water was worth considerable effort to reach. A pipeline was built up Schultz Creek, west of the Dry Lake Hills, to Schultz Pass, then around the east slopes of Doyle Peak and into the Interior Valley. From the present site of the watershed cabins, branch pipelines were built to all the springs in the valley. An attempt was even made to tap a spring in Aubineau Canyon on the northeast side of Humphreys Peak.

In the 1950s, in an effort to find more water, the city drilled a number of exploratory wells in the Interior Valley. A few were successful and diesel-powered pumps were installed. Most of the old roads dating from the exploration period are overgrown now, but the valley still lacks a truly wild feeling. Until the mid-1970s, the entire watershed was closed to all public access, including hiking, snowshoeing, and cross-country skiing. Increasing public interest in outdoor activities finally caused the Forest Service to open the area to day recreation—camping is not allowed. Locked steel covers protect the springs, so there are no publicly accessible water sources in the Interior Valley.

south branch of the Interior Valley, passing through some fine aspen stands before reaching a broad open meadow just west of one of the city well sites. This meadow has the best views in the Interior Valley. From left to right the summits are Doyle, Fremont, Agassiz, and Humphreys Peaks. From this vantage point Fremont Peak is the most striking, with its pyramidal northeast face.

Turn left at the road junction in the meadow, and descend to the east–northeast, following the road back to the watershed cabins. Return to the trailhead via Inner Basin Trail, the way you came.

MILES AND DIRECTIONS

0.0   Start at the Lockett Trailhead, at the southwest corner of the Lockett Meadow loop road.

1.6   Turn right on the Pipeline Road.

1.9   Watershed cabins; turn left to continue on the Inner Basin Trail.

2.0   Go right at the fork onto the Flagstaff Spring Trail.

2.7   The road forks again; stay right. (FYI: The left fork will be your return loop.)

3.5   Reach Flagstaff Spring. Retrace your steps to the loop you passed earlier.

4.4   Turn right at the loop fork.

4.8   Turn left onto Inner Basin Trail.

5.6   Watershed cabins; turn right on the Pipeline Road.

5.9   Turn left on the Inner Basin Trail.

7.5   Arrive back at the Lockett Trailhead.

Options: From Flagstaff Spring continue cross-country up the forested slope, proceeding southwest from the spring, to reach the rim of Humphreys Cirque at 11,200 feet. You are near timberline, and there are excellent views of the stark alpine ridges above.

Humphreys Peak from the Inner Basin Trail

Fremont Peak from the Inner Basin Trail

Inner Basin, San Francisco Peaks

35 PARSONS TRAIL

This is a challenging trail and cross-country hike through the remote red-rock country in Sycamore Canyon Wilderness.

Start: 10.2 miles northwest of Cottonwood
Distance: 21.4-mile loop
Hiking time: About 2 days
Difficulty: Strenuous
Trail surface: Dirt trails, cross-country along dry washes on sand and boulders
Best seasons: Spring and fall
Water: Sycamore Creek downstream from Parsons Spring; seasonal pools upstream

Other trail users: None
Canine compatibility: Leashed dogs permitted
Fees and permits: None
Schedule: Open all year
Maps: CalTopo.com MapBuilder Topo layer; Gaia GPS Trails Illustrated layer
Trail contacts: Coconino National Forest, 1824 S. Thompson St., Flagstaff, AZ 86001; (928) 527-3600; www.fs.usda.gov/coconino

FINDING THE TRAILHEAD

From Cottonwood drive to the north end of town on AZ 89A and into the town of Clarkdale, then turn right (east) onto the road to Tuzigoot National Monument. After 0.2 mile, just after crossing the Verde River bridge, turn left (north) onto CR 139 (it becomes FR 131), a maintained dirt road. Drive 10 miles to the end of the road at the Sycamore Canyon Trailhead. GPS: N34 51.848' / W112 4.165'

THE HIKE

Sycamore Creek is normally dry above Parsons Spring. In the spring, seasonal pools above this point often make it possible to do this loop without carrying water. During summer and fall, though, you'll have to pick up enough water at Parsons Spring for your camp farther up the canyon. The catch is that during early spring, Sycamore Creek may be flooding from snowmelt in the high country, making this loop trip impossible. If the creek is running muddy at the trailhead, content yourself with a short day hike to Summers or Parsons Spring. Do not attempt to cross the creek when it is flooding. In summer this loop is recommended only for hikers experienced at dry camping in hot weather.

From the trailhead follow the good trail 0.2 mile north into Sycamore Creek. On the left the Packard Trail crosses the creek; this is our return trail. (**Note:** Sycamore Canyon is closed to camping between the trailhead and Parsons Spring.) Continue following Sycamore Creek on the broad, easy trail along the east bank. Sycamore Creek flows year-round and supports a rich variety of riparian trees, including the Arizona sycamore for which the canyon is named. About 1.5 miles from the trailhead, the canyon swings sharply left, then right. During the winters of 1993 and 1994, massive flooding completely rearranged the creekbed. Evidence of the flooding is everywhere: saplings leaning downstream, piles of driftwood and even huge logs far above normal stream level, and collapsed streambanks. But flooding is a normal occurrence in these deep canyons. The streamside trees and vegetation are well adapted to the environment and recover with amazing rapidity.

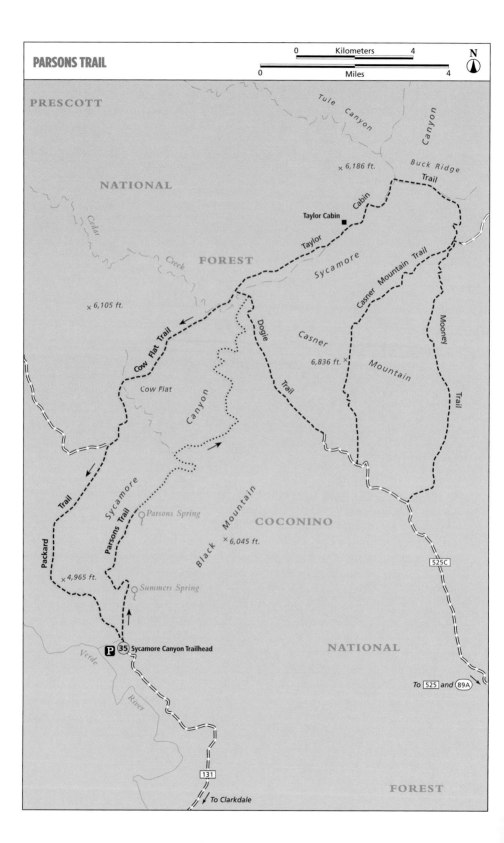

PARSONS TRAIL

0   Kilometers   4
0   Miles   4

N

PRESCOTT

Tule Canyon

Canyon

× 6,186 ft.

Buck Ridge
Trail

NATIONAL

Cedar

Creek

FOREST

Taylor Cabin ■

Cabin

Taylor

Sycamore

Casner Mountain Trail

× 6,105 ft.

Cow Flat Trail

Dogie

Casner

Mooney

Cow Flat

Trail

6,836 ft. ×

Mountain

Trail

Canyon

Trail

Sycamore

Parsons Trail

○ Parsons Spring

Black

COCONINO

Mountain

× 6,045 ft.

Packard

525C

× 4,965 ft.

○ Summers Spring

Trail

P 35 Sycamore Canyon Trailhead

NATIONAL

Verde

To 525 and 89A

River

131

To Clarkdale

FOREST

Above Parsons Spring, the source for Sycamore Creek, the creekbed dries up. Continue up Sycamore Creek by boulder-hopping along the broad, dry wash. You may see seasonal pools of water in the bends of the creek. Watch for petroglyphs along the rock walls of the canyon. Although strenuous, progress up the creekbed is relatively fast because the periodic floods keep the bed clear of brush. The gorge becomes shallower after about 6 miles. The Dogie Trail crosses Sycamore Creek 7.6 miles above Parsons Spring. Turn left (west) onto the Dogie Trail, which joins the Taylor Cabin and Cow Flat Trails above the west bank. Now turn left (south) onto the Cow Flat Trail. There are several good campsites for small groups on the bluffs overlooking the creek to the west. There is no water except for possible seasonal pools in Sycamore Creek.

After the confines of Sycamore Creek and the rugged boulder-hopping, it is a pleasure to walk the easy Cow Flat Trail southwest through the open piñon-juniper forest. Shortly the trail crosses Cedar Creek. (This creek is usually dry at the crossing, but water can sometimes be found about a mile upstream.) The trail climbs gradually for another mile and passes through a broad saddle to enter Sycamore Basin. The walking is very easy through this open basin, with fine views of the surrounding red-rock formations. Camping is unlimited—if you carry water for a dry camp. The trail crosses Cow Flat then skirts the head of a side canyon. It then climbs gradually to another pass. On the far side of the pass, the trail ends at a trailhead at the end of FR 181.

Now go south on the Packard Trail. Packard Mesa forms the west rim of lower Sycamore Canyon, and the trail generally stays near the crest of the mesa as it works its way south through open piñon pine and juniper stands. About 4 miles from FR 181, the trail turns east and descends into Sycamore Canyon. It crosses the creek and meets the Parsons Trail; turn right to return to the trailhead.

MILES AND DIRECTIONS

0.0   Start at the Sycamore Canyon Trailhead at the end of FR 131.

0.2   Reach Sycamore Creek and junction with the Packard Trail; stay right.
(FYI: The Packard Trail to the left, which crosses the creek, is the return trail.)

1.2   Pass Summers Spring.

3.6   Pass Parsons Spring.

11.2   Turn left onto the Dogie Trail.

11.3   Turn left onto the Cow Flat Trail.

11.7   Cross Cedar Creek.

12.7   Reach pass into Sycamore Basin.

15.8   Climb gradually to a second pass.

19.8   Reach rim of Sycamore Canyon.

21.2   Cross Sycamore Creek and turn right onto Parsons Trail.

21.4   Arrive back at the trailhead.

Sycamore Canyon

36 WEST FORK TRAIL

This is an easy and very popular hike along the spectacular West Fork of Oak Creek, the wilderness fork of Oak Creek Canyon. A fine forest of tall ponderosa pine and Douglas fir as well as a perennial stream grace the canyon floor, while red-rock formations and towering buttresses of white Coconino sandstone form the canyon walls.

Start: 11 miles north of Sedona
Distance: 6.0-mile out-and-back
Hiking time: About 3 hours
Difficulty: Easy
Trail surface: Dirt trails
Best seasons: Year-round
Water: West Fork of Oak Creek
Other trail users: None
Canine compatibility: Leashed dogs permitted

Fees and permits: None. The lower 6 miles of the West Fork is closed to camping.
Schedule: Trailhead parking is open daily 8 a.m. to dusk.
Maps: CalTopo.com MapBuilder Topo layer; Gaia GPS Trails Illustrated layer
Trail contacts: Coconino National Forest, 1824 S. Thompson St., Flagstaff, AZ 86001; (928) 527-3600; www.fs.usda.gov/coconino

FINDING THE TRAILHEAD:

From Sedona drive about 11 miles north on US 89A. Turn left into the West Fork Trailhead parking area. GPS: N34 59.431' / W111 44.518'

THE HIKE

The West Fork is an easy but extremely popular hike. It is not the place to go to escape crowds, especially on weekends. For solitude try the Thomas Point Trail on the opposite side of Oak Creek. Note that the Forest Service prohibits camping in the lower West Fork due to heavy use. Stay on the trail and do not pick flowers or otherwise disturb this fragile environment. Watch for poison ivy, which is common along the trail.

Follow the trail over the bridge across Oak Creek. The trail now goes south along the creek and then turns right (west) into the West Fork. Soon you'll leave the sounds of the busy highway behind and be able to hear the pleasant murmur of the creek and the whisper of the wind in the trees. Buttresses of Coconino sandstone tower on the left, while the canyon floor is filled with a tall ponderosa pine and Douglas fir forest. The trail crosses the creek several times and ends about 3 miles up the canyon. Walking is very easy to this point, which is the end of the hike.

West Fork Trail

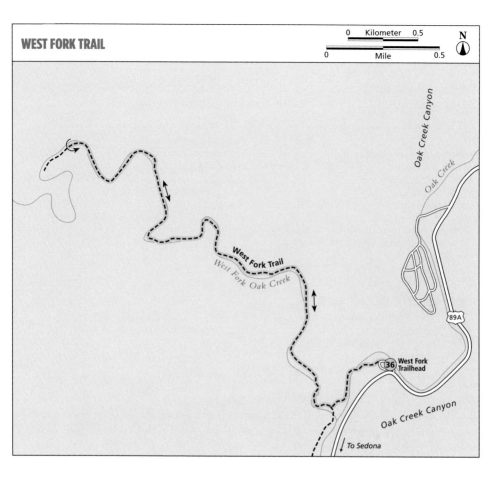

MILES AND DIRECTIONS

0.0 Start at the West Fork Trailhead.

0.4 Reach the mouth of the West Fork.

3.0 The trail ends. Retrace your steps.

6.0 Arrive back at the trailhead.

Options:

Experienced canyon hikers can continue up the West Fork to its head near FR 231. This hike requires wading in the creek and occasional swimming to cross deep pools. There is a serious danger of flash flooding. Do not continue unless you have a stable weather forecast and are prepared to handle the deep, often cold, pools.

Another possible hike for the adventurous, experienced canyon hiker is to climb to the south rim of the canyon and then hike to East Pocket Knob and use the AB Young Trail to descend back into Oak Creek Canyon. There is a route up the nameless canyon that is just west of West Buzzard Point.

37 GRANITE MOUNTAIN TRAIL

This popular hike climbs through rugged granite terrain to a viewpoint overlooking Granite Basin and the Sierra Prieta.

Start: 8.5 miles northwest of Prescott
Distance: 7.4-mile out-and-back
Hiking time: About 6 hours
Difficulty: Moderate
Trail surface: Dirt trails
Best seasons: Spring through fall
Water: None
Other trail users: Horses
Canine compatibility: Leashed dogs permitted

Fees and permits: None
Schedule: Open all year
Maps: CalTopo.com MapBuilder Topo layer; Gaia GPS Trails Illustrated layer
Trail contacts: Prescott National Forest, 344 S. Cortez St., Prescott, AZ 86303; (928) 443-8000; www.fs.usda.gov/prescott

FINDING THE TRAILHEAD

From Prescott drive northwest about 4.5 miles on Iron Springs Road. Turn right onto paved Granite Basin Road, and continue 4 miles to the Metate Trailhead. GPS: N34 36.925' / W112 33.069'

THE HIKE

The Granite Mountain Trail crosses a wash, then follows a drainage uphill through a forest of juniper, piñon pine, oak, and ponderosa pine. To the right there are occasional views of Granite Mountain, the destination for this hike. At Blair Pass you meet the junction with the Cedar Spring and Little Granite Mountain Trails. Turn right to continue on the Granite Mountain Trail. After following a broad ridge a short distance, the trail begins to ascend the rocky slopes in a series of switchbacks.

The terrain faces south here, and the increased heat and dryness cause the pines to give way to chaparral and juniper. Chaparral is not a single plant—it is an association of three shrubs that commonly grow together in the upper Sonoran life zone. The red-barked bush is manzanita; the brush with the oak-like prickly leaves is scrub oak; and the plant with longish leaves, curled under at the edges and fuzzy underneath, is mountain mahogany. Chaparral provides vital cover and habitat for wildlife.

The reward for the steady climb is expanding views. Little Granite Mountain forms a conspicuous landmark to the south; beyond are the pine-forested slopes of the Sierra Prieta. After reaching another pass, the trail turns east and climbs the beautiful west ridge of Granite Mountain, passing through stately groves of ponderosa pines and winding around granite slabs. Some of the slabs look almost glacial in origin. When the trail reaches the summit plateau, it turns south and ends at a viewpoint above Granite Mountain Wall. Granite Basin Lake, Prescott, and the northern Bradshaw Mountains are all visible. Although this is not the true summit of the mountain, the views are still excellent.

Granite Mountain Wilderness

WORLD-CLASS CLIMBING

As you start up the switchbacks above Blair Pass, you may see rock climbers taking an unmarked turnoff toward the prominent granite cliff above. Granite Mountain Wall offers world-class technical climbing on excellent granite.

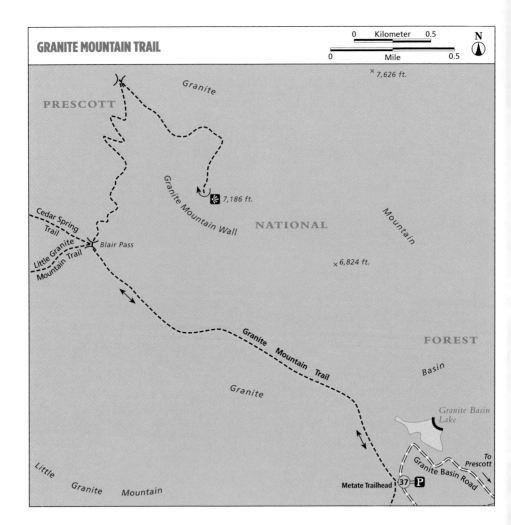

GRANITE MOUNTAIN TRAIL

PRESCOTT

Granite

× 7,626 ft.

7,186 ft.

Granite Mountain Wall

NATIONAL

Mountain

× 6,824 ft.

Cedar Spring Trail

Little Granite Mountain Trail

Blair Pass

Granite Mountain Trail

Granite

FOREST

Basin

Granite Basin Lake

Little Granite Mountain

Granite Basin Road

To Prescott

Metate Trailhead 37 P

MILES AND DIRECTIONS

0.0 Start at the Metate Trailhead on Granite Basin Road.

1.8 Reach Blair Pass and the junction with the Cedar Spring and Little Granite Mountain Trails. Turn right to continue on the Granite Mountain Trail.

2.9 Reach another pass.

3.7 Arrive at the viewpoint above the Granite Mountain Wall. Retrace your steps.

7.4 Arrive back at the trailhead.

Granite Mountain

38 CABIN LOOP

This loop hike on a series of historic trails connects several historic cabins north of the Mogollon Rim. The entire loop makes an enjoyable backpack trip, or you can do shorter segments as day hikes.

Start: 75.2 miles southeast of Flagstaff
Distance: 17.8-mile loop
Hiking time: About 2 days
Difficulty: Moderate
Trail surface: Dirt trails
Best seasons: Spring and fall
Water: Seasonally at Barbershop Canyon, Dane Canyon, Dane Spring, Coyote Spring, Barbershop Spring, Houston Draw, and Aspen Spring
Other trail users: Mountain bikes and horses

Canine compatibility: Leashed dogs permitted
Fees and permits: None
Schedule: Open all year
Maps: CalTopo.com MapBuilder Topo layer; Gaia GPS Trails Illustrated layer
Trail contacts: Coconino National Forest, 1824 S. Thompson St., Flagstaff, AZ 86001; (928) 527-3600; www.fs.usda.gov/coconino

FINDING THE TRAILHEAD

From Flagstaff drive about 55 miles southeast on Lake Mary Road (CR 3) to Clints Well. Turn left onto AZ 87, and go north 9 miles; turn right onto FR 95. Continue 11.1 miles on this maintained road, and then turn left onto FR 139A. Travel just over 0.1 mile, and park at the Pinchot Cabin Trailhead, where the Fred Haught Trail crosses the road. GPS: N34 30.56' / W111 11.79'

Clints Well can also be reached from Camp Verde by driving 30 miles east on the General Crook Trail (Forest Highway 9), then turning left onto AZ 87 and continuing 11 miles.

THE HIKE

This hike is part of the Cabin Loop, a system of trails that connect three historic cabins in the Mogollon Rim country. Sections of the trail are faint, but they are well marked with tree blazes.

Walk southeast along the Fred Haught Trail down into Houston Draw to Pinchot Cabin, where a junction marks the start of the Houston Brothers and U-Bar Trails. Turn left to start the U-Bar Trail, which follows an old road past the cabin and up the hill to the east. Note the standard Forest Service tree blazes, which consist of short and long vertical slashes. The entire trail is blazed with the same-style blazes. After less than 1 mile, turn right (south) onto another road (note the blaze and right arrow), and continue a short distance to a third road intersection. The trail crosses the road and continues east into the forest, ignoring both roads. The Cabin Loop trails are getting more and more use, but sections may still be faint. If the trail isn't clear, follow the blazes carefully. The trick is to walk from blaze to blaze, always keeping the last blaze in sight. If you lose the route, return to the last known blaze and locate the next one before continuing.

The route crosses Dick Hart Draw and meets another road. The U-Bar Trail now turns left (north) and follows the road past a large steel water tank. Watch carefully for the place where the trail turns sharply right (east) and leaves the road. Next the trail crosses a

General Springs Cabin on the Cabin Loop Trail System

maintained dirt road (FR 139), and a sign marks the U-Bar Trail. The trail veers some-what left as it crosses the road. The U-Bar Trail goes to the southeast out onto a point, then descends through a gate.

After the fence the trail becomes obvious as it descends into Barbershop Canyon. Serious trail construction was done on this section. Barbershop Canyon has a fine little perennial stream—a good goal for hikers wanting an easy day. For those on a backpack trip, there is very limited camping in the canyon bottom. It would be better to carry water up to the east rim, where there is unlimited camping.

The trail, still distinct, climbs the east wall of the canyon and crosses a faint road. Where the trail crosses a road at right angles, a sign marks the U-Bar Trail. On the east side of the main road, the U-Bar Trail follows an unmaintained road past a fine little meadow bordered by pines and aspens and containing McClintock Spring. Beyond the meadow the road joins another road; the U-Bar Trail continues across the road and descends into Dane Canyon. There are sections of historic trail construction along this section. Dane Canyon has a perennial stream and offers plentiful campsites in grassy meadows. A lush forest of Douglas fir and ponderosa pine covers the canyon walls, spiced by an occasional aspen, limber pine, or white fir.

After crossing the creek, the U-Bar Trail climbs east out of the canyon, then turns south along the east rim. This is one of the prettiest sections of the trail, staying below the heavily logged ridgetop. You'll soon reach Dane Spring, which is marked by the ruins of a log cabin. This is an excellent goal for a more ambitious day hike.

The U-Bar Trail continues south along the east side of a shallow drainage, then crosses the drainage and climbs to cross a road on a ridgetop. It descends into the next drainage to end at the junction with the Barbershop Trail. Turn right onto the Barbershop Trail, which passes Coyote Spring, follows the drainage west to Bill McClintock Draw, then climbs southwest to cross a low ridge. The next section of the Barbershop Trail crosses several drainages and follows several roads for short distances. Follow the blazes carefully so that you don't miss the places where the trail leaves the roads.

The Barbershop Trail crosses upper Dane Canyon at a sign. The trail climbs up a drainage to the west, crosses a maintained road, then drops into Barbershop Canyon, which usually has flowing water. The trail climbs steeply for a couple hundred yards then contours into a meadow at Barbershop Spring. After the spring the trail goes up the bed of a shallow drainage to the west and then climbs out on the right to cross FR 139. The Barbershop Trail ends just west of the road, at the signed junction with the Houston Brothers Trail.

U-Bar Trail, Cabin Loop Trail System

Old cabin at Dane Spring, Cabin Loop Trail System

Turn right and follow the Houston Brothers Trail north along Dick Hart Ridge. Very little of the original trail remains along this section; follow the tree blazes carefully. If you lose the trail, you can always walk east to FR 139, which is never more than 0.25 mile away. Eventually the trail crosses FR 139A and descends into Houston Draw, where it becomes a distinct footpath. The forest at the head of Houston Draw is a delightful mix of Douglas fir, white fir, and ponderosa pine. Soon the trail emerges into a series of fine alpine meadows, bordered with quaking aspen. You'll pass McFarland and then Aspen Springs. There is also an intermittent flow in the creek.

The Houston Brothers Trail ends at Pinchot Cabin, completing the loop. Turn left onto the Fred Haught Trail and walk to the end of the hike at the Pinchot Trailhead.

MILES AND DIRECTIONS

0.0 Start at the Pinchot Cabin Trailhead and hike southeast on the Fred Haught Trail.

0.4 Reach Pinchot Cabin in a meadow at the junction of the Fred Haught, Houston Brothers, and U-Bar Trails. Turn left onto the U-Bar Trail, which follows an old road northeast of the cabin.

1.2 Turn right onto a road.

1.4 Come to a T intersection; cross the road and follow the blazed trees east.

1.9 The trail turns left (north) along a road.

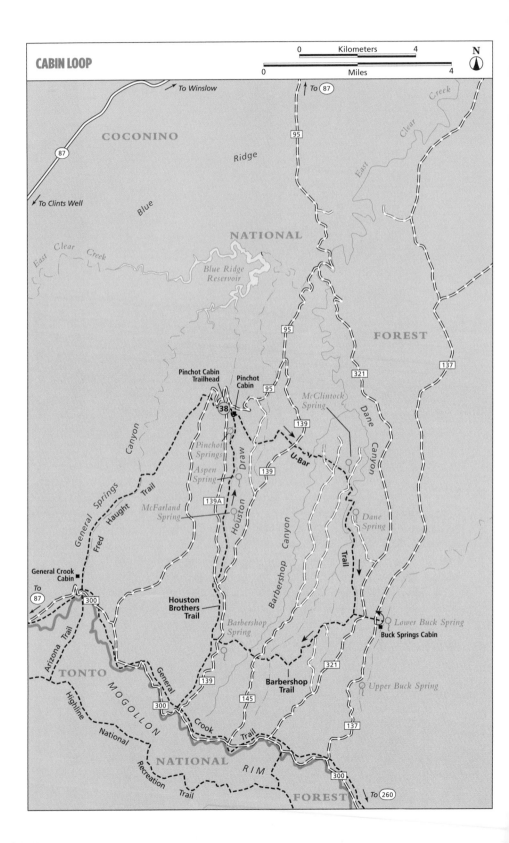

CABIN LOOP

0   Kilometers   4

0   Miles   4

N

To Winslow

To 87

COCONINO

95

Ridge

87

To Clints Well

Blue

East Clear Creek

NATIONAL

Blue Ridge
Reservoir

FOREST

95

321

137

Pinchot Cabin
Trailhead

Pinchot
Cabin

95

McClintock
Spring

38

139

Pinchot
Springs

Dane Canyon

U-Bar

Aspen
Spring

Houston Draw

139

McFarland
Spring

139A

Dane
Spring

General Springs Trail

Fred Haught

Barbershop Canyon

Trail

General Crook
Cabin

To 87

300

Houston
Brothers
Trail

Lower Buck Spring

Buck Springs Cabin

Barbershop
Spring

Arizona Trail

TONTO

MOGOLLON

General

139

Barbershop
Trail

321

Highline

300

145

Upper Buck Spring

National

Crook

Trail

Recreation

Trail

NATIONAL

RIM

137

300

FOREST

To 260

2.1 Pass a steel water tank; turn sharply right, leave the road, and follow the blazed trail east.

2.6 Cross FR 139, where a sign marks the U-Bar Trail; follow the blazes carefully.

3.2 Cross Barbershop Canyon. (FYI: Very limited camping is available in the canyon bottom.) (*Option:* Turn around here for an easy day hike.)

4.2 Pass McClintock Spring.

4.9 Cross the creek in Dane Canyon.

6.2 Reach Dane Spring. (*Option:* This is a good turnaround point for a longer day hike.)

8.2 Turn right onto the Barbershop Trail. (*Option:* Turn left and hike 0.5 mile to the Buck Springs Cabin Trailhead.)

8.4 Pass Coyote Spring, which may be dry.

8.6 Cross Bill McClintock Draw.

10.6 Cross Dane Canyon.

11.3 Cross Barbershop Canyon.

11.7 Reach Barbershop Spring.

12.0 Cross FR 139.

12.1 Barbershop Trail ends. Turn right onto the Houston Brothers Trail, which parallels FR 139 just to the west.

13.7 Cross FR 139A, and follow the trail north into the head of Houston Draw.

15.3 Pass McFarland Spring.

16.1 Pass Aspen Spring.

17.4 The Houston Brothers Trail ends at the Pinchot Cabin. Turn left onto the Fred Haught Trail.

17.8 Arrive back at the trailhead.

Options: From the junction of the Barbershop and Houston Brothers Trails, continue south another 1.4 miles on the Houston Brothers Trail to reach FR 300. Cross the road to the edge of the Mogollon Rim. The view of the rim country and the central mountains to the south is a treat, marred only slightly by the carnage wreaked on the forest by the Dude Fire in 1990. This side hike adds 2.8 miles round-trip and 150 feet of elevation gain to the hike.

39 HIGHLINE TRAIL

This long, scenic trail wanders along the base of the ramparts of the Mogollon Rim. There are six trailheads, so you can hike the entire trail or pick segments. A number of side trails branch from the Highline Trail, most climbing to the top of the Mogollon Rim.

Start: 12.9 miles north of Payson
Distance: 53.2 miles one way with a shuttle
Hiking time: 5–7 days
Difficulty: Strenuous
Trail surface: Dirt trails
Best seasons: Spring through late fall
Water: Weber Creek, East Verde River, Tonto Creek, Horton Spring, and Christopher Creek; seasonal springs and creeks possible after a wet winter

Other trail users: Mountain bikes and horses
Canine compatibility: Leashed dogs permitted
Fees and permits: None
Schedule: Open all year
Maps: CalTopo.com MapBuilder Topo layer; Gaia GPS Trails Illustrated layer
Trail contacts: Tonto National Forest, 2324 E. McDowell Rd., Phoenix, AZ 85006; (602) 225-5200; www.fs.usda.gov/tonto

FINDING THE TRAILHEADS

Pine Trailhead: From Payson drive 12.9 miles north on AZ 87. Turn right into the Pine Trailhead; this is the western trailhead. GPS: N34 22.444' / W111 26.602'
Two-Sixty Trailhead: From Payson drive 26.5 miles east on AZ 260 to the trailhead on the left. (Because of construction on AZ 260, the exact mileage may change.) GPS: N34 18.424' / W110 57.091'

THE HIKE

The Highline National Recreation Trail runs along the base of the Mogollon Rim, and it crosses numerous drainages. Because the trail was developed by ranchers on horseback in a piecemeal fashion, it tends to climb over ridges rather than contour around, so you can expect constant climbing and descending. Also, even though the trail crosses numerous creeks, as elsewhere in Arizona, the term *creek* usually refers to a seasonal stream—don't expect to find water at every creek crossing.

Vegetation along the trail ranges from tall stands of ponderosa pine to dense thickets of chaparral. Chaparral is common at the elevations and exposures of the Highline Trail and refers to a mixture of scrub oak, mountain mahogany, and manzanita. Several large fires have burned the south slopes of the Mogollon Rim in recent years; the Highline Trail passes through these burns.

From the Pine Trailhead the Highline Trail climbs east a short distance before leveling off and passing the Donahue Trail. The Highline Trail now contours east along the south slopes of Milk Ranch Point. Redrock Trail forks right, and the Highline Trail begins to turn northeast and then north. It passes Geronimo Trail just before reaching the Geronimo Trailhead and crossing Webber Creek Road.

Now the Highline Trail climbs northeast past Geronimo Spring to Bear Spring before leveling off and heading east along the base of the Mogollon Rim. It crosses numerous

Along the Highline Trail below the Mogollon Rim

seasonal creeks before crossing Mail Creek and a road. Here the trail skirts the Washington Park summer home area on the north by climbing over a ridge before descending to the East Verde River and Washington Park Trailhead on FR 32.

After leaving the East Verde River, the Highline Trail climbs east just a bit before leveling off and heading southeast along the base of the Mogollon Rim. The trail crosses several seasonal creeks before meeting the Myrtle Trail and turning south to descend along Ellison Creek. Near the old Pyle Ranch the Highline Trail again turns eastward and climbs gradually to the base of Myrtle Point. After crossing Big Canyon the trail reaches the Hatchery Trailhead.

After crossing Tonto Creek the Highline Trail continues east, crossing under a power line and reaching Horton Creek Trail and Horton Spring. This spring gushes from the base of the rim and creates Horton Creek, one of several beautiful creeks issuing from the rim. After Horton Spring the Highline Trail crosses the East Fork of Horton Creek and climbs through a fine stand of quaking aspen before turning south along Promontory Butte. As the trail begins to turn southeast around Promontory Butte, the Derrick Trail forks southwest. The Highline Trail continues around Promontory Butte and descends to the See Canyon Trailhead.

Crossing Christopher Creek, the Highline Trail continues east, climbing to regain the base of the Mogollon Rim. As the trail levels off, the Drew Trail forks left. The final section of the Highline Trail closely parallels the rim and crosses numerous unnamed drainages before ending at the Two-Sixty Trailhead.

MILES AND DIRECTIONS

0.0 Start on the Arizona Trail at the Pine Trailhead.

1.0 Turn right on the Highline Trail—you will follow this trail for the remainder of the hike.

8.3 Pass Geronimo Trail; stay right.

8.6 Reach Geronimo Trailhead.

9.2 Pass Geronimo Spring.

10.3 Pass Bear Spring.

16.6 Cross Mail Creek.

17.6 Pass the Washington Park Trailhead and cross East Fork Verde River.

26.8 Junction with Myrtle Trail; stay right on the Highline Trail.

34.8 Hatchery Trailhead.

38.6 Pass the Horton Creek Trail.

41.5 Junction with the Derrick Trail.

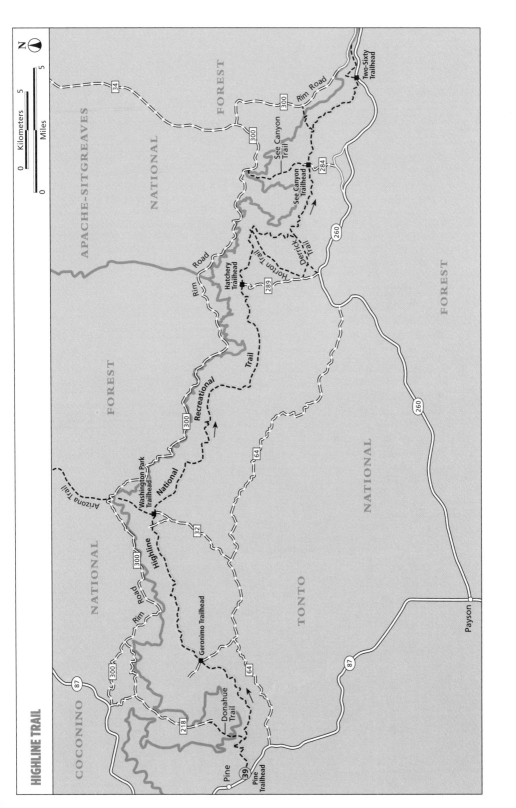

HIGHLINE TRAIL

46.5 See Canyon Trailhead.

49.1 Junction with the Drew Trail.

53.2 Arrive at Two-Sixty Trailhead and your shuttle vehicle.

Options:

Donahue Trail (at 0.5 mile) leaves the Highline Trail east of the Pine Trailhead and climbs 2.2 miles northwest onto the Mogollon Rim at Milk Ranch Point, ending at FR 218.

Redrock Trail (at 2.1 miles) leaves the Highline Trail west of the Geronimo Trailhead and descends 0.6 mile southeast to end at Control Road (FR 64).

Geronimo Trail (at 5.8 miles) forks north just west of the Geronimo Trailhead and runs 1.3 miles past Camp Geronimo to a trail junction in the Webber Creek basin. Three trails leave this junction: The West Webber Trail goes left and climbs 1.9 miles west to Milk Ranch Point and the Mogollon Rim, ending on FR 218. The Turkey Trail, the center choice, heads 1.8 miles past Turkey Spring; it also climbs to Milk Ranch Point and the Mogollon Rim, ending at FR 218. The East Webber Trail, the right fork, climbs 2.4 miles up Webber Creek before ending under the cliffs of the Mogollon Rim.

Arizona Trail (at 13.4 miles) leaves the Highline Trail at the Washington Park Trailhead and climbs 2 miles north to cross the Rim Road (FR 300) on the Mogollon Rim.

Myrtle Trail (at 26.8 miles) leaves the Highline Trail west of Myrtle Point and climbs 1 mile north to the Mogollon Rim and the Rim Road (FR 300).

Babe Haught Trail (at 34.8 miles) leaves the Highline Trail at the Hatchery Trailhead and climbs 1.3 miles north to the Mogollon Rim. The trail ends 1 mile north of the rim at the Rim Road (FR 300).

Horton Creek Trail (at 38.6 miles) meets the Highline Trail at Horton Spring and descends 3.2 miles southwest along beautiful Horton Creek to Upper Tonto Creek Campground on Tonto Creek Road (FR 289).

Derrick Trail (at 41.5 miles) leaves the Highline Trail along the west side of Promontory Butte and descends 2.2 miles west to Upper Tonto Creek Campground on Tonto Creek Road (FR 289). The Derrick Spur Trail forks off to the southwest from Derrick Trail and descends 0.7 mile to Lower Tonto Creek Campground on Tonto Creek Road (FR 289).

See Canyon Trail (at 46.5 miles) leaves the Highline Trail at the See Canyon Trailhead and follows Christopher Creek 3 miles north to the Mogollon Rim and the Rim Road (FR 300). A 0.5-mile spur trail (the See Spring Trail) leads to See Spring.

Drew Trail (at 49.1 miles) leaves the Highline Trail east of Christopher Creek and climbs 1 mile northeast to the Mogollon Rim and the Rim Road (FR 300).

40 MAZATZAL PEAK LOOP

This classic route travels around the range's highest peak and through a remarkable variety of terrain in the Mazatzal Mountains. These trails are better maintained and easier to find than most other trails in the Mazatzal Wilderness.

Start: 72 miles north of Mesa
Distance: 11.6-mile loop
Hiking time: About 8 hours
Difficulty: Strenuous
Trail surface: Dirt trails
Best seasons: Spring through fall
Water: Seasonal at Y Bar Tanks
Other trail users: Horses
Canine compatibility: Leashed dogs permitted

Fees and permits: None. Group size limited to 15; 14-day stay limit
Schedule: Open all year
Maps: CalTopo.com MapBuilder Topo layer; Gaia GPS Trails Illustrated layer
Trail contacts: Tonto National Forest, 2324 E. McDowell Rd., Phoenix, AZ 85006; (602) 225-5200; www.fs.usda .gov/tonto

FINDING THE TRAILHEAD

From Mesa drive about 67 miles north on AZ 87, then turn left onto the Barnhardt Road (this turnoff is just south of the Gisela turnoff). Continue 5 miles to the end of the maintained dirt road to the trailhead. GPS: N34 5.574' / W111 25.313'

THE HIKE

Start on the Barnhardt Trail; just a dozen yards from the trailhead, turn left onto the Y Bar Trail (sometimes called the Shake Tree Trail). The Barnhardt Trail will be your return. The Y Bar Trail climbs up a broad ridge in a series of rocky switchbacks, heading generally southwest through piñon pine and juniper forest. When the trail passes the wilderness boundary, it turns more to the south and climbs along the east slopes of Mazatzal Peak, crossing numerous small canyons. After about a mile of this, the trail crosses into Shake Tree Canyon and climbs along the west slopes. Below to the east, Shake Tree Canyon cuts through a spectacular area of cliffs and rock fins.

The trail continues up Shake Tree Canyon, entering a pine-forested northeast-facing slope, then works its way across the slopes west of the canyon's bed. The climb ends as the trail reaches the saddle between Mazatzal Peak and Cactus Ridge. It's possible to camp here, although the nearest water is at Y Bar Tanks. The Y Bar Trail descends southwest from the saddle, then levels out and contours across a small drainage. A small seep spring here, Y Bar Tanks, often has water. If it doesn't, follow the drainage downstream a hundred yards, where you may find large pools. After the seep the trail contours westward, then turns northwest and climbs to Windsor Saddle. There is limited camping in Windsor Saddle.

Turn right onto the Mazatzal Divide Trail, which heads north and contours the west slopes of Mazatzal Peak. You'll have fine views of the rocky summit, as well as the head of

Barnhardt Trail, Mazatzal Peak Loop

the South Fork of Deadman Creek to the west. The well-constructed trail (also the route of the Arizona Trail) descends gradually northwest as it works its way around ridges and ravines. You'll pass the junction with Brody Trail (Brody Seep is 0.7 mile northwest and there are several campsites nearby); stay right on the Divide Trail. You'll turn northward again and pass through several small stands of ponderosa pine as the trail contours to the saddle at the head of Barnhardt Canyon.

Turn right here, onto the Barnhardt Trail. This popular trail is well constructed and easy to find. It heads generally east, contouring the south slopes of the broad basin at the head of Barnhardt Canyon. The trail passes through several stands of ponderosa pine, but much of the basin is covered with dense chaparral brush. Stay right at the junction with the Sandy Saddle Trail (Casterson Seep, shown on the maps where the Sandy Saddle Trail crosses Barnhardt Creek, is not reliable). The Barnhardt Trail swings around a ridge, where you can leave the trail momentarily and walk a few yards north to a viewpoint overlooking the impressive gorge of Barnhardt Canyon. The trail swings south after this point and crosses a drainage where there may be seasonal pools a short distance upstream from the trail. In cold weather the waterfall above the upper pool is often graced with a beautiful tapestry of icicles.

Now the trail descends eastward along the south slopes of Barnhardt Canyon, skirting some impressive cliffs. Note the bent and twisted layers of metamorphic rock—mute testimony to the inconceivable forces that created these mountains. The trail turns north and descends a steep ridge in a series of switchbacks until it is close to the canyon bottom, then heads east again and stays just above the bed all the way to the Barnhardt Trailhead.

Spring flowers in the Mazatzal Mountains

THE WILLOW FIRE

Much of the Mazatzal high country burned in the Willow Fire during the summer of 2004. Ongoing drought combined with trees killed by bark beetles have created conditions for wildfires of unprecedented size in Arizona in recent years, including the Willow Fire, which burned more than 100,000 acres. Large stands of ponderosa pine were burned in the fire, as were large areas of chaparral brush and grasslands. While the brush and grass will quickly grow back, it will be difficult for the pine forests to reestablish themselves at these marginal elevations. However, fires have always been part of the Arizona forest ecology, and numerous other fires have burned in the Mazatzal Mountains in the past. Pockets of pine trees have survived all these fires and will undoubtedly survive future ones.

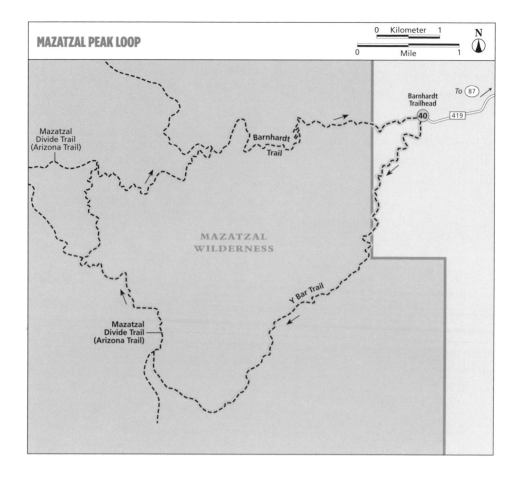

MILES AND DIRECTIONS

0.0 Start at the Barnhardt Trailhead on Barnhardt Road. In a few yards turn left onto the Y Bar Trail.

4.2 Reach saddle between Mazatzal Peak and Cactus Ridge.

4.8 Pass Y Bar Tanks. (FYI: This small spring often has water.)

5.7 Reach Windsor Saddle; turn right onto the Mazatzal Divide Trail.

6.9 Pass Brody Trail junction; stay right.

8.3 Turn right onto the Barnhardt Trail.

11.6 Arrive back at the trailhead.

41 MARGIES COVE TRAIL

This hike takes you across Sonoran Desert plains and into a scenic canyon in the North Maricopa Mountains, part of the Sonoran Desert National Monument.

Start: 61.2 miles west of Phoenix
Distance: 7.6-mile out-and-back
Hiking time: 4 hours
Difficulty: Moderate
Trail surface: Dirt trails
Best seasons: Fall through spring
Water: No water available
Other trail users: Horses
Canine compatibility: Leashed dogs permitted

Fees and permits: None
Schedule: Open all year
Maps: CalTopo.com MapBuilder Topo layer; Gaia GPS Trails Illustrated layer
Trail contacts: Bureau of Land Management, Lower Sonoran Field Office, 21605 N. Seventh Ave., Phoenix, AZ 85027-2929; (623) 580-5500; https://www.blm.gov /visit/sonoran-desert

FINDING THE TRAILHEAD

From Phoenix drive about 30 miles west on I-10, then exit south on AZ 85. Drive about 21 miles south and exit at Woods Road. Turn left, cross the overpass, and turn left again onto the frontage road. Drive north about 1 mile to reach the Margies Cove Road; turn right (east). After 4 miles, turn right (south) and continue 5.2 miles to the Margies Cove West Trailhead. These dirt roads are passable to cars if driven with care. GPS: N33 7.54' / W112 34.92'

THE HIKE

Starting from the Margies Cove West Trailhead, the trail follows a closed road and meanders up the broad, gently sloping valley. You'll pass an old windmill site in the first 0.5 mile. Gradually the mountains close in on either side. After about 3.1 miles the trail starts following a gravelly wash as the old road veers away. Watch for rock cairns and BLM trail markers along this section. The rugged peaks and canyon walls add to the wilderness atmosphere. Your hike ends where the Brittlebush Trail comes in from the right, about 3.8 miles from the trailhead.

Gila monster on the trail

THE NORTH MARICOPA MOUNTAINS

The North Maricopa Mountains are a jumble of long ridges and isolated peaks separated by extensive, saguaro-studded bajadas and wide desert washes. Cholla, ocotillo, prickly pear, paloverde, ironwood, and Mexican jumping bean complement the thick stands of saguaro to form classic Sonoran Desert vistas. Commonly seen wildlife include desert mule deer, javelinas, desert bighorn sheep, coyotes, desert tortoises, and numerous varieties of lizards and birds.

A segment of the 1850s Butterfield Stage Line runs along the southern boundary of the wilderness. This stage line was the first reliable, relatively fast method of transportation between the eastern United States and California. The stage carried people, mail, and freight more than 2,700 miles in less than 25 days. The stage boasted that it was late only three times in its 3-year history.

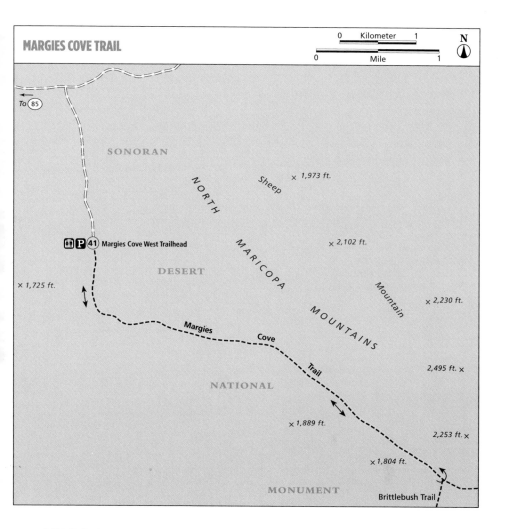

MILES AND DIRECTIONS

0.0 Start at the Margies Cove West Trailhead.

2.8 The trail leaves the old road and starts following a gravelly wash.

3.8 The Brittlebush Trail comes in from the right. This is the end of the hike and your turnaround point.

7.6 Arrive back at the trailhead.

42 PASS MOUNTAIN TRAIL

This loop day hike through the western Goldfield Mountains northeast of Mesa offers a fine sense of remoteness, considering its location on the very edge of the greater Phoenix area. The backside of the loop offers a sweeping view of the wild Superstition and southern Mazatzal Mountains.

Start: Just northeast of Mesa
Distance: 7.7-mile loop
Hiking time: About 4 hours
Difficulty: Moderate
Trail surface: Dirt trails
Best seasons: Fall through spring
Water: No water available
Other trail users: Mountain bikes and horses
Canine compatibility: Leashed dogs permitted

Fees and permits: Park entrance fee
Schedule: Open all year
Maps: CalTopo.com MapBuilder Topo layer; Gaia GPS Trails Illustrated layer
Trail contacts: Maricopa County Parks and Recreation, 234 N. Central Ave., Suite 6400, Phoenix, AZ 85004; (602) 506-2930; www.maricopa.gov /parks

FINDING THE TRAILHEAD

From Mesa go north on Ellsworth Road, which becomes Usery Pass Road. Turn right at the park entrance and go to the horse staging area, which is the trailhead. GPS: N33 27.99' / W111 36.43'

THE HIKE

Begin at the Pass Mountain Trailhead. After a couple hundred yards, turn left at a T intersection to start the loop portion of the hike. The trail wanders north along the east side of the park facilities. After passing a final ramada and parking area, you'll pass the Wind Cave Trail; stay left on the Pass Mountain Trail. The trail now works its way north along the west slopes of Pass Mountain. A fence marks the boundary of the Tonto National Forest. Now the trail climbs gradually around the north side of the mountain. As the trail crosses a ridge, the remainder of the Goldfield mountain range becomes visible to the northeast and, beyond, the distinctive summits of Four Peaks. Continuing to climb, the trail turns south into a canyon and climbs to a pass. This spot is the high point of the hike. With the bulk of Pass Mountain hiding the metropolitan area to the southwest, this saddle is a wild and rugged spot.

The descent is eroded and steep at first, but then a newer trail branches right and continues the descent at a more gradual rate. As you reach the mouth of the canyon and the southern foothills, the trail starts to swing west along the base of the mountain. Ignore an unsigned trail branching left and keep right. Stay right again at the junction with the Cat Peaks Trail. When you reach the T intersection near the horse staging area, turn left to return to the trailhead.

Sonoran desert foothills

Superstition Mountains

Teddybear cholla, Superstition Mountains

Superstition Mountains

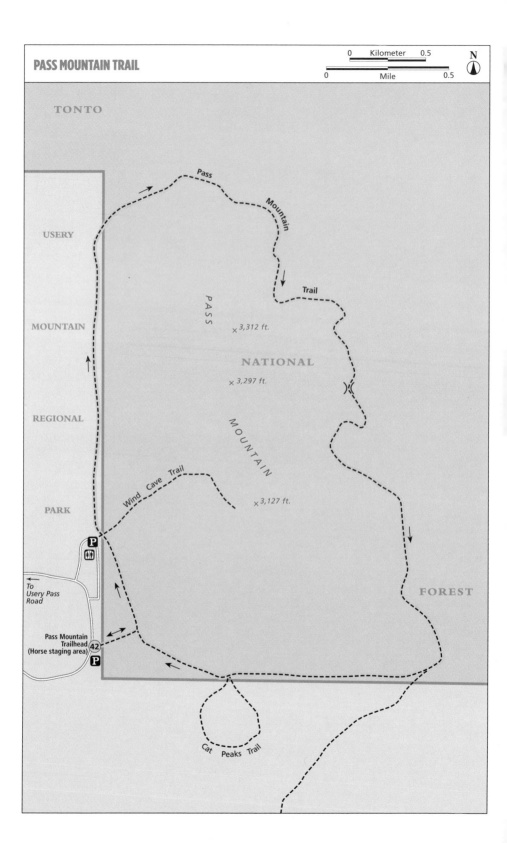

PASS MOUNTAIN TRAIL

0   Kilometer   0.5

0   Mile   0.5

N

TONTO

USERY

MOUNTAIN

REGIONAL

PARK

To
Usery Pass
Road

Pass Mountain
Trailhead
(Horse staging area)

42

PASS

×3,312 ft.

NATIONAL

×3,297 ft.

MOUNTAIN

×3,127 ft.

Wind Cave Trail

Pass Mountain Trail

FOREST

Cat Peaks Trail

Saguaro cactus, Superstition Mountains

MILES AND DIRECTIONS

0.0   Start at the horse staging area near the park entrance. Head east on the Pass Mountain Trail and then turn left at the T intersection.

0.7   Stay left at the junction with the Wind Cave Trail.

2.3   Reach the Tonto National Forest boundary.

4.4   Reach a pass, the high point of the hike.

4.6   The old trail forks left; stay right, on the new trail.

6.1   Stay right at an unsigned trail junction.

7.1   Stay right at the junction with the Cat Peaks Trail.

7.6   Turn left at the T intersection to return to the trailhead.

7.7   Arrive back at the horse staging area.

43 DUTCHMANS LOOP

This popular loop through the western Superstition Mountains, known by its many fans as "the Sups," takes in a lot of interesting country, following well-graded, easy trails throughout. The hike can be done as a long day hike but is an especially good overnight hike for those new to the sport of backpacking.

Start: 16.5 miles east of Apache Junction
Distance: 14.8-mile loop
Hiking time: About 9 hours or 2 days
Difficulty: Moderate
Trail surface: Dirt trails
Best seasons: Fall through spring
Water: Seasonal at Crystal, Bluff, La Barge, Charlebois, and White Rock Springs
Other trail users: Horses

Canine compatibility: Leashed dogs permitted
Fees and permits: None. Group size limited to 15; 14-day stay limit.
Schedule: Open all year
Maps: CalTopo.com MapBuilder Topo layer; Gaia GPS Trails Illustrated layer
Trail contacts: Tonto National Forest, 2324 E. McDowell Rd., Phoenix, AZ 85006; (602) 225-5200; www.fs.usda .gov/tonto

FINDING THE TRAILHEAD

From Apache Junction drive about 8.5 miles east on US 60. Turn left onto Peralta Road (FR 77), which becomes maintained dirt after passing a subdivision. Continue 8 miles to the end of the road at the Peralta Trailhead. GPS: N33 23.84' / W111 20.87'

THE HIKE

Hike east on the Dutchmans Trail over a low ridge. The trail passes the junction with the Coffee Flat Trail, then loops around the base of Miners Needle, climbing to Miners Summit via a couple of switchbacks. It then descends northwest to Crystal Spring at the base of Bluff Spring Mountain. Turning northeast, the good trail descends Bluff Spring Canyon, passing the spur trail to Bluff Spring, and then turns more to the north and works its way down to La Barge Canyon and the junction with the Red Tanks Trail. La Barge Spring is located just east of this junction, on the north side of the canyon. There are several campsites in the area.

Stay left on the Dutchmans Trail, and follow it down La Barge Canyon to the northwest. A spur trail leads to Music Spring. At the junction with the Peters Trail, you can reach Charlebois Spring by following the Peters Trail a short distance into the side canyon. There are several popular campsites near this spring. The main trail continues down La Barge Canyon to Marsh Valley and the junction with the Cavalry Trail. White Rock Spring usually has water, and there is limited camping nearby.

Again, stay left on the Dutchmans Trail and climb west to a low saddle. Here, at the junction with the Bull Pass Trail, the Dutchmans Trail turns south and drops into Needle Canyon. After following Needle Canyon for a while, turn right at the junction with the Terrapin Trail and follow the Dutchmans Trail up an unnamed drainage south of Black Top Mesa. The trail reaches Upper Black Top Mesa Pass, then descends northwest into

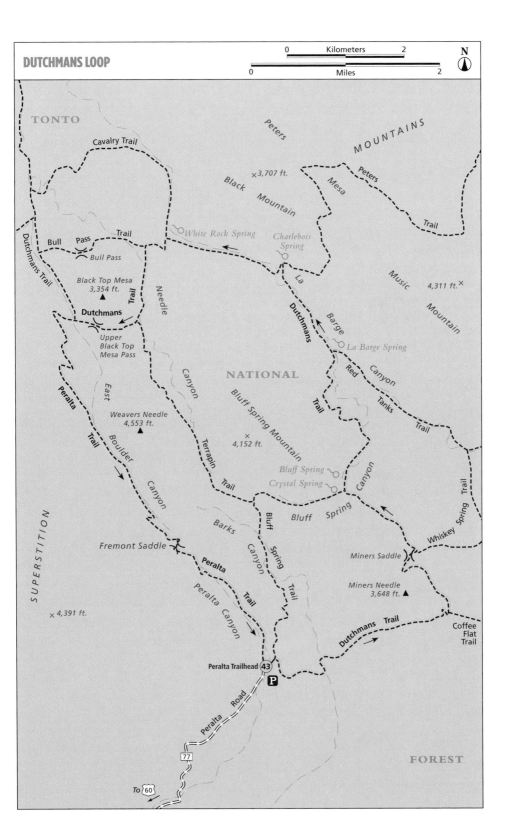

DUTCHMANS LOOP

Weavers Needle, Superstition Mountains

East Boulder Canyon to meet the Peralta Trail. There are campsites in this scenic basin, which is dominated by towering Weavers Needle to the south. Seasonal water can be found in the bed of the wash.

Turn left onto the Peralta Trail, which climbs west in well-graded switchbacks to the ridge south of Palomino Mountain, then heads south on a slope above a small canyon. A few switchbacks take the trail over a saddle next to a rock outcrop, and then the trail descends back into East Boulder Canyon below triple-summited Weavers Needle. It then works its way up the scenic head of East Boulder Canyon. Water can sometimes be found in the creekbed. The Peralta Trail climbs to Fremont Saddle in a couple of switchbacks and then descends scenic Peralta Canyon to the Peralta Trailhead.

MILES AND DIRECTIONS

0.0   Start at the Peralta Trailhead at the end of FR 77, hiking east on the Dutchmans Trail.

2.2   Pass junction with the Coffee Flat Trail.

2.6   Reach Miners Summit and junction with the Whiskey Spring Trail. Stay on the Dutchmans Trail.

3.8   Pass the Bluff Spring Trail; turn right to stay on the Dutchmans Trail.

5.0   Stay left at Red Tanks Trail junction and La Barge Spring. (FYI: There are several campsites in the area.)

6.1   Stay left again at Peters Trail and Charlebois Spring. (FYI: There are several campsites near the spring.)

7.4   Reach Marsh Valley, White Rock Spring, and the Cavalry Trail; stay left. (FYI: There is limited camping near White Rock Spring.)

7.8   At junction with Bull Pass Trail, stay left on the Dutchmans Trail.

8.6   At junction with Terrapin Trail, stay right on the Dutchmans Trail.

9.4   Turn left onto the Peralta Trail in East Boulder Canyon. (FYI: There are campsites in the basin.)

13.0   Reach Fremont Saddle, and begin to descend Peralta Canyon.

14.8   Arrive back at the Peralta Trailhead.

44 MOUNT BALDY

This day hike takes you to the highest point of the White Mountains and Arizona's second-highest mountain. On the way you'll follow a trout stream as it winds through alpine meadows, then climb through a beautiful forest of Douglas fir, Colorado blue spruce, and quaking aspen to reach the alpine tundra along the summit ridge.

Start: 43 miles east of Show Low
Distance: 12.0-mile out-and-back
Hiking time: About 7 hours
Difficulty: Strenuous
Trail surface: Dirt trails
Best seasons: Summer through fall
Water: West Fork of the Little Colorado River
Other trail users: Horses
Canine compatibility: Leashed dogs permitted

Fees and permits: None. Baldy Peak and all of the Fort Apache Indian Reservation are closed to all entry.
Schedule: Open all year
Maps: CalTopo.com MapBuilder Topo layer, Gaia GOS Gaia Topo layer
Trail contacts: Apache-Sitgreaves National Forest, PO Box 640, Springerville, AZ 85938; (928) 333-4301; www.fs.usda.gov/asnf

FINDING THE TRAILHEAD

From Show Low, drive about 39 miles east on AZ 260. Turn right on AZ 273 and drive 4 miles to the trailhead, on the right. GPS: N33 57.94' / W109 29.99'

THE HIKE

The popular West Baldy Trail begins along the bank of the West Fork of the Little Colorado River and climbs through lovely blue spruce forest and alpine meadows. During the short summer months, aster, fleabane, penstemon, cinquefoil, and iris bloom. There is evidence of past glacial activity—glacial erratics, large boulders deposited by flowing ice—along the valley floor.

West Fork contains brook, rainbow, and cutthroat trout, but the trail is only close to the stream near the trailhead. About 3 miles in, the trail crosses a tributary to West Fork. The trail then reaches the ridge leading to Mount Baldy and the junction with the East Baldy Trail, where you are treated to spectacular vistas of the White Mountain region. The boundary of the Fort Apache Indian Reservation runs along the west side of the summit ridge. (**Note:** The Apache Tribe has closed the reservation to all access, which includes Baldy Peak at the south end of the Mount Baldy ridge. Trespassers have had their packs confiscated and have been fined for trying to sneak to the top of Baldy Peak.)

According to the USGS Mount Baldy topo, the actual high point of the mountain is the Mount Baldy ridge, which has a final contour line at 11,420 feet. This makes the ridge 17 feet higher than Baldy Peak (11,403 feet). It's safe to leave the West Baldy Trail where it runs along the treeline and walk to the high point of the ridge. If you look closely, you'll see small metal survey caps just below the ridge crest to the west. These mark the actual boundary of the reservation. Feel free to point these out to any Apache ranger who questions your presence on the ridge crest.

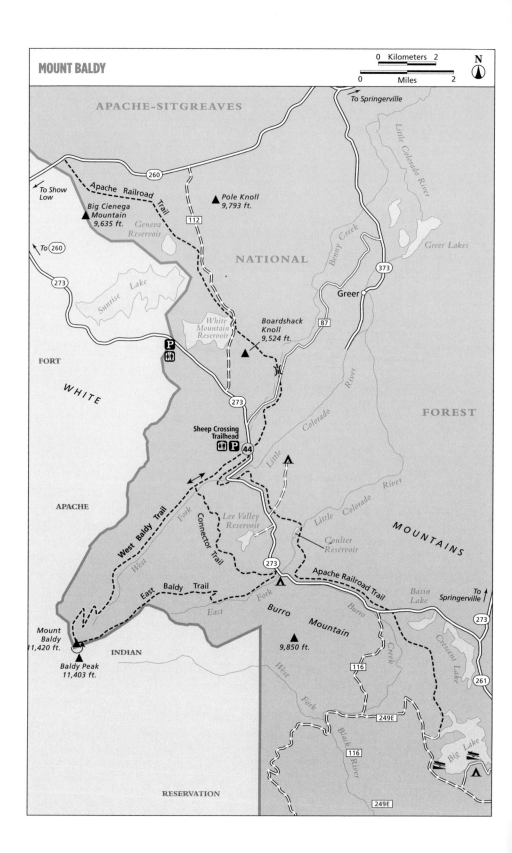

Although this is the turnaround point for the hike, the trail continues, descending into the East Fork of the Little Colorado River.

MILES AND DIRECTIONS

0.0   Start at the Sheep Crossing Trailhead.

3.0   Cross a tributary to the West Fork of the Little Colorado River.

4.4   Reach ridge leading to Mount Baldy.

5.3   Reach the reservation boundary. (Do not trespass on reservation land.)

5.4   Reach junction with East Baldy Trail.

5.6   Reach a saddle just north of Baldy Peak.

6.0   Arrive at the true, unnamed summit of Mount Baldy, your turnaround point. (Again, do not trespass on the reservation.)

12.0   Arrive back at the trailhead.

Summit ridge of Mount Baldy

West Fork Trail, Mount Baldy

45 WEST FORK SABINO CANYON

This hike takes you up two gorgeous canyons to fine seasonal pools in the Front Range of the Santa Catalina Mountains.

Start: Northeast side of Tucson
Distance: 8.8-mile out-and-back
Hiking time: About 6 hours
Difficulty: Moderate
Trail surface: Dirt trails
Best seasons: Fall through spring
Water: Seasonal in Sabino Canyon and West Fork Sabino Canyon
Other trail users: None
Canine compatibility: Leashed dogs permitted

Fees and permits: Entrance and tram fees
Schedule: Open all year
Maps: CalTopo.com MapBuilder Topo layer; Gaia GPS Gaia Topo layer
Trail contacts: Coronado National Forest, 300 W. Congress, Tucson, AZ 85701; (520) 388-8300; www.fs.usda.gov/coronado

FINDING THE TRAILHEAD

From I-10 in Tucson exit at Grant Road and go 8.5 miles east. Turn left onto Tanque Verde Road and continue 0.5 mile; turn left onto Sabino Canyon Road and drive 4.4 miles to the Sabino Canyon Visitor Center. GPS N32 18.597' / W110 49.384'. Take the Sabino Canyon Tram (fee) to the Sabino Canyon Trailhead. GPS: N32 20.611' / W110 46.829'

THE HIKE

The Sabino Canyon Trail switchbacks up the slope east of Sabino Creek, passes the Telephone Ridge Trail, and then climbs more gradually. After passing through a saddle at 0.9 mile, the trail contours along the east side of Sabino Canyon, well above the canyon bed. The trail crosses an unnamed drainage and then meets the West Fork, East Fork, and Mount Lemmon Trails at 2.2 miles; turn left onto the West Fork Trail. After crossing the East Fork of Sabino Canyon, the trail heads west along the north side of Sabino Canyon. At 3.6 miles the trail meets the West Fork of Sabino Canyon. Follow the trail across the West Fork and up the slope to the west. Watch for several spur trails to the right. These go to several large pools along the bed of the creek, our goal for the hike.

WEST FORK SABINO CANYON

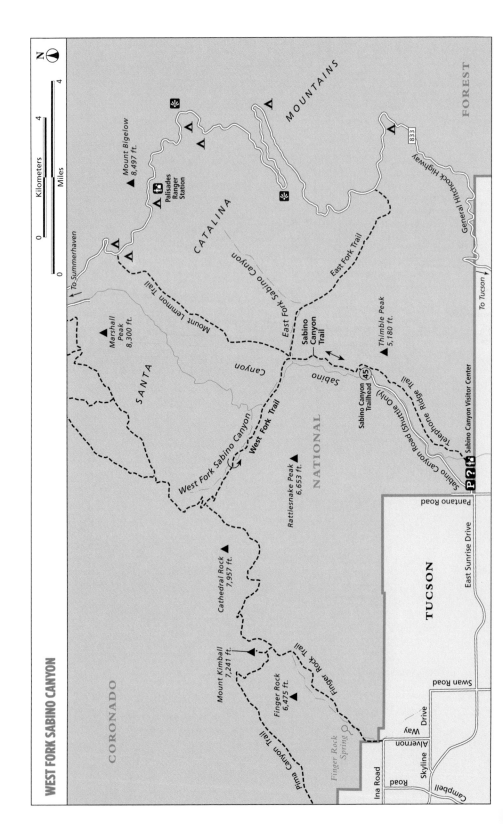

N

Kilometers
0   4

Miles
0   4

To Summerhaven

CORONADO

SANTA

Mount Kimball
7,241 ft.

Finger Rock
6,475 ft.

Cathedral Rock
7,957 ft.

Marshall
Peak
8,300 ft.

Mount Bigelow
8,497 ft.

Palisades
Ranger
Station

CATALINA

MOUNTAINS

FOREST

Pima Canyon Trail

Finger Rock Trail

Finger Rock
Spring

West Fork Sabino Canyon

West Fork Trail

Rattlesnake Peak
6,653 ft.

Mount Lemmon Trail

Sabino Canyon

East Fork Sabino Canyon

East Fork Trail

East Fork

Sabino
Canyon
Trail

NATIONAL

Sabino Canyon
Canyon

Thimble Peak
5,180 ft.

Sabino Canyon
Trailhead

45

Telephone Ridge Trail

General Hitchcock Highway

833

To Tucson

Sabino Canyon Road (Shuttle Only)

Sabino Canyon Visitor Center

P ?

Pantano Road

TUCSON

East Sunrise Drive

Swan Road

Skyline Drive

Alvernon Way

Campbell

Ina Road

Saguaro cactus in the Santa Catalina foothills

MILES AND DIRECTIONS

0.0 Start at the Sabino Canyon Trailhead and begin to climb on switchbacks.

0.2 Pass junction with the Telephone Ridge Trail; stay left.

0.9 Pass through a saddle.

2.2 At junction with multiple trails, turn left onto the West Fork Trail.

3.6 Reach the West Fork of Sabino Canyon. Follow the trail across the fork and up the slope.

4.4 Watch for spur trails to large pools along the creekbed. Retrace your steps.

8.8 Arrive back at the trailhead.

46 TANQUE VERDE RIDGE

This is a long day hike up a scenic desert ridge in the Rincon Mountains. It takes you from saguaro cactus "forest" to piñon pine–juniper woodland.

Start: East side of Tucson
Distance: 12.4-mile out-and-back
Hiking time: About 8 hours
Difficulty: Strenuous
Trail surface: Dirt trails
Best seasons: Fall through spring
Water: No water available
Other trail users: Horses
Canine compatibility: Dogs prohibited

Fees and permits: Permit and fee required for backcountry camping; camping allowed only in designated wilderness campsites
Schedule: Open all year
Maps: CalTopo.com MapBuilder Topo layer; Gaia GPS Trails Illustrated layer
Trail contacts: Saguaro National Park, 3693 S. Old Spanish Trail, Tucson, AZ 85730; (520) 733-5153; www.nps.gov /sagu

FINDING THE TRAILHEAD

From I-10 in Tucson exit at Speedway Boulevard and drive 12.4 miles east to Houghton Road. Turn right; go 2.7 miles and turn left onto Old Spanish Trail. Go another 2.7 miles, and turn left into Saguaro National Park. Turn right at the visitor center and go about 2 miles to the Tanque Verde Trailhead. GPS: N32 9.93' / W110 43.46'

THE HIKE

The Tanque Verde Ridge Trail first heads southeast across the desert foothills, climbing onto the west end of Tanque Verde Ridge. Here the trail swings northeast and starts a steady climb up this long ridge. The trail dips and winds around small hills and across small drainages but always tends to follow the main ridge. At first you will be in the saguaro cactus "forest." The national park was established to protect this unique and beautiful desert landscape, as well as its plants and animals.

As the trail climbs along the ridge, the cactus forest gradually gives way to high-desert grassland and piñon pine–juniper forest. Saguaros are not tolerant of frost, so they disappear from the cooler, north-facing slopes first. There are many points with good views of the Tucson area and its mountains along the lower portion of the ridge. As the miniature piñon–juniper forest becomes thicker, views become limited. Below an unnamed peak (6,300 feet), the trail turns southeast and contours to cross a drainage. The trail then turns east and follows another shallow drainage to Juniper Basin. This wilderness campground is a good turnaround point for a day hike and a good goal for an overnight backpack trip.

Saguaro cactus in the Rincon Mountains

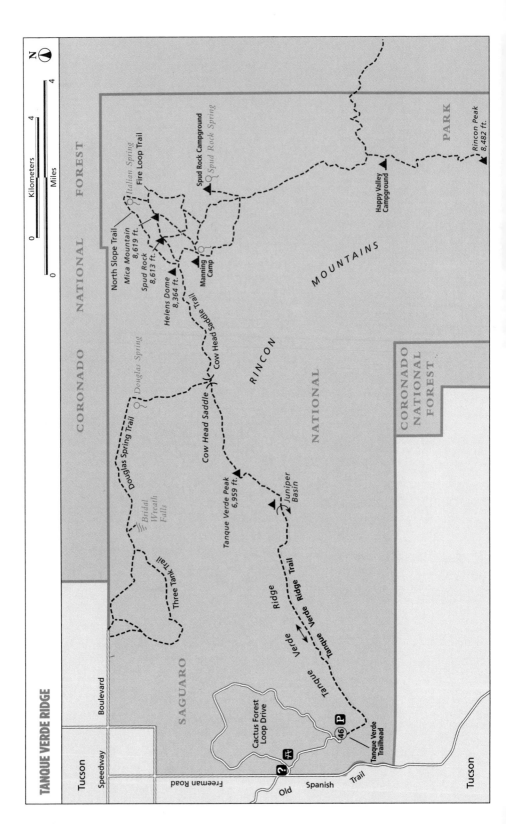

TANQUE VERDE RIDGE

N

Kilometers
0   4

Miles
0   4

Tucson
Speedway
Boulevard

CORONADO **NATIONAL** **FOREST**

Freeman Road

Old Spanish Trail

Tucson

SAGUARO

Cactus Forest Loop Drive

46 P

Tanque Verde Trailhead

Three Tank Trail

Douglas Spring Trail

Bridal Wreath Falls

○ *Douglas Spring*

Cow Head Saddle

Cow Head Saddle Trail

Tanque Verde Peak
6,959 ft.

Juniper Basin ▲

▲

Verde Ridge

Tanque Verde Ridge Trail

RINCON

NATIONAL

MOUNTAINS

North Slope Trail

○ *Italian Spring*

Fire Loop Trail

Mica Mountain
8,619 ft. ▲

Spud Rock
8,613 ft. ▲

Helens Dome
8,364 ft. ▲

Manning Camp ○

Spud Rock Campground ▲

○ *Spud Rock Spring*

Happy Valley Campground ▲

PARK

Rincon Peak
8,482 ft. ▲

CORONADO NATIONAL FOREST

Manning Camp, Rincon Mountains

MILES AND DIRECTIONS

0.0 Start at the Tanque Verde Trailhead and head southeast across the desert foothills.

0.8 Reach the west end of Tanque Verde Ridge.

3.4 Pass through a small saddle.

3.6 Pass through a second small saddle.

4.7 Cross a small drainage.

4.9 The trail turns southeast below an unnamed peak.

6.2 Reach Juniper Basin, your turnaround or overnight point.

12.4 Arrive back at the trailhead.

47 ARAVAIPA CANYON

This delightful hike along one of Arizona's best desert riparian areas follows a desert stream through a canyon cut across the northern end of the Galiuro Mountains.

Start: 23 miles south of Winkelman
Distance: 10.0-mile one way with a shuttle
Hiking time: About 7 hours
Difficulty: Moderate
Trail surface: Cross-country walking along and in Aravaipa Creek
Best seasons: Year-round
Water: Aravaipa Creek
Other trail users: None
Canine compatibility: Dogs prohibited

Fees and permits: Advance permit and fee required
Schedule: Open all year
Maps: CalTopo.com MapBuilder Topo layer; Gaia GPS Gaia Topo layer
Trail contacts: Bureau of Land Management, Safford Field Office, 711 14th Ave., Safford, AZ 85546-3337; (928) 348-4400; https://www.blm .gov/arizona

FINDING THE TRAILHEAD

From Winkelman take AZ 77 south for 11 miles to the Aravaipa Road. Follow the Aravaipa Road 12 miles east to the western trailhead. GPS: N32 54.19' / W110 33.99'

Access to the eastern trailhead is 10 miles northwest of Klondyke on the Aravaipa Canyon Road, which requires a high-clearance vehicle. Some lands around and within the wilderness are not federally administered. Please respect the property rights of the owners, and do not cross or use these lands without permission. GPS: N32 53.931' / W110 25.150'

THE HIKE

There is no established trail through Aravaipa Canyon. You simply follow the stream. Stream wading and numerous crossings (up to knee deep), as well as hiking through dense riparian brush, can slow your pace and extend your travel time. It takes a strong hiker about 10 hours to hike the length of the canyon. Topographic maps are handy for keeping track of your progress. The main attractions along the route, other than delightful Aravaipa Creek itself, are the numerous side canyons along the way, each of which invites exploration. Such side trips can add hours to the hike, so if you plan much side exploration, you may want to do this hike as an overnight backpack trip.

Aravaipa Creek

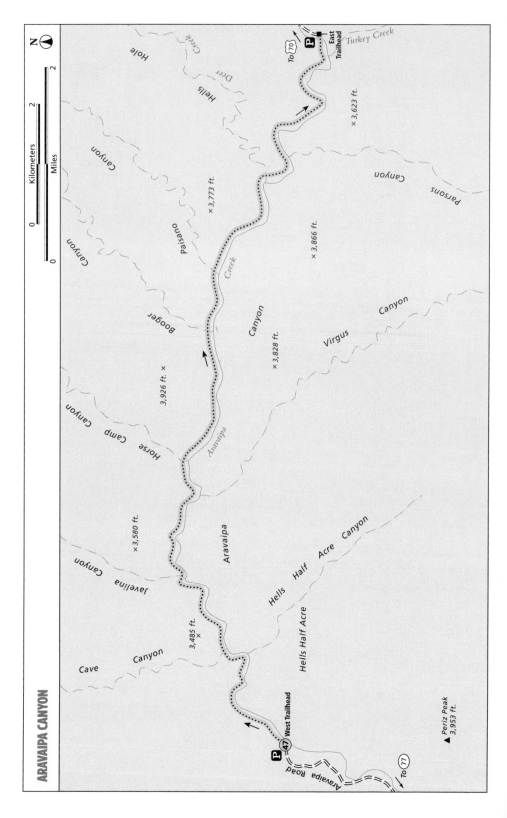

ARAVAIPA CANYON

ARAVAIPA CANYON

Aravaipa Canyon, which cuts through the northern part of the Galiuro Mountains, has long been recognized for its spectacular scenery and important wildlife habitat. A 19,410-acre designated wilderness area consists of Aravaipa Canyon plus surrounding tablelands and nine side canyons. Thousand-foot cliffs rise above a green ribbon of rich riparian habitat found along the 11-mile segment of Aravaipa Creek that flows through the wilderness. More than 200 species of birds live among the shady cottonwoods and willows growing along the perennial waters of Aravaipa Creek. During late spring and summer, birders can expect yellow-billed cuckoos, vermilion flycatchers, northern beardless-tyrannulets, yellow warblers, yellow-breasted chats, and summer tanagers. Two federally listed threatened fish occur in the creek—spikedace and loach minnow. There are an additional five species of native fish, which makes Aravaipa Creek one of the best native fisheries remaining in Arizona. The stream has been recommended as a National Wild and Scenic River.

MILES AND DIRECTIONS

0.0 Start at the western trailhead and begin following the stream. Be prepared for stream wading and numerous crossings.

1.3 Hells Half Acre Canyon enters from the right.

1.6 Cave Canyon enters from the left.

2.7 Javelina Canyon enters from the left.

3.7 Virgus Canyon enters from the right.

4.1 Horse Camp Canyon enters from the left.

5.7 Booger Canyon enters from the left.

6.3 Paisano Canyon enters from the left.

7.5 Deer Creek enters from the left.

8.0 Parsons Canyon enters from the right.

9.9 Turkey Creek enters from the right.

10.0 Arrive at the eastern trailhead and your shuttle.

48 **BULL PASTURE**

This is a day hike to a desert "meadow" perched on the west slopes of the rugged Ajo Mountains.

Start: 41 miles south of Ajo
Distance: 3.6-mile out-and-back
Hiking time: About 2 hours
Difficulty: Moderate
Trail surface: Dirt trails, optional cross-country
Best seasons: Fall through spring
Water: No water available
Other trail users: None

Canine compatibility: Dogs prohibited
Fees and permits: None
Schedule: Open all year
Maps: CalTopo.com MapBuilder Topo layer; Gaia GPS Gaia Topo layer
Trail contacts: Organ Pipe Cactus National Monument, 10 Organ Pipe Dr., Ajo, AZ 85321-9626; (520) 387-6849; www.nps.gov/orpi

FINDING THE TRAILHEAD

From Ajo drive 33 miles south on AZ 85 to the Organ Pipe Cactus National Monument headquarters. Turn left onto Ajo Mountain Loop Drive. Drive 8 miles to the signed Bull Pasture Trailhead at the Estes Canyon Picnic Area. GPS: N32 0.962' / W112 42.720'

THE HIKE

The popular trail leaves the picnic area and climbs to a ridge overlooking Bull Pasture, a scenic basin high on the flanks of the Ajo Range. As the name suggests, Bull Basin was a favorite cattle pasture prior to the creation of Organ Pipe Cactus National Monument in 1937.

In 1971 a hiker wandered into Bull Pasture and was never seen again despite repeated searches, which continued off and on for years after the official search ended.

Organ pipe cactus, Bull Pasture Trail

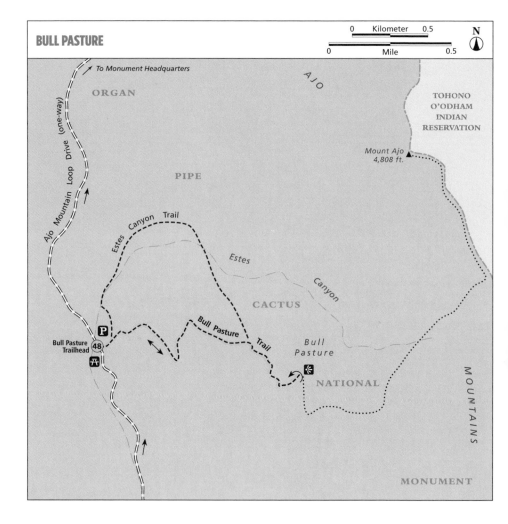

BULL PASTURE

0 Kilometer 0.5
0 Mile 0.5

N

To Monument Headquarters

ORGAN

Ajo Mountain Loop Drive (one-way)

AJO

TOHONO
O'ODHAM
INDIAN
RESERVATION

Mount Ajo
4,808 ft.

PIPE

Estes Canyon Trail

Estes

Canyon

CACTUS

Bull Pasture Trail

Bull
Pasture

P

Bull Pasture
Trailhead 48

NATIONAL

MOUNTAINS

MONUMENT

MILES AND DIRECTIONS

0.0 Start at the Bull Pasture Trailhead at the Estes Canyon Picnic Area.

1.8 Reach the overlook above Bull Pasture. Retrace your steps.

3.6 Arrive back at the trailhead.

Options:

From the trail's end at the overlook, a rough but rewarding cross-country hike leads to the summit of Mount Ajo—at 4,808 feet the highest point in the monument. The route goes from trail's end around the head of Bull Pasture basin, trending generally eastward toward the steep slopes on the far side. The route then goes up and to the right to gain the main north–south ridge. You will have to pick your way around some cliff bands. Once on the ridge, the route is a straightforward walk north about a mile to the summit.

From the top of Mount Ajo, you can see far into Mexico to the south, west across the monument, and north and east across the vast Tohono O'odham Reservation toward the Baboquivari Mountains. This option adds 3.6 miles to the hike.

49 MOUNT WRIGHTSON

This long day hike or overnight backpack follows a well-graded trail to the summit of Mount Wrightson, the highest peak in the Santa Rita Mountains. The trail starts alongside Madera Creek, a small perennial stream that is a destination for Mexican bird species rarely sighted in Arizona. The views along this hike encompass much of southern Arizona and extend well into northern Mexico.

Start: 37 miles south of Tucson
Distance: 13.7-mile loop with a cherry stem
Hiking time: About 9 hours or 2 days
Difficulty: Strenuous
Trail surface: Dirt trails
Best seasons: Spring through fall
Water: Seasonally in Madera Canyon; at Sprung, Baldy, and Bellows Springs
Other trail users: Horses

Canine compatibility: Leashed dogs permitted
Fees and permits: Trailhead parking fee
Schedule: Open all year
Maps: CalTopo.com MapBuilder Topo layer; Gaia GPS Gaia Topo layer
Trail contacts: Coronado National Forest, 300 W. Congress, Tucson, AZ 85701; (520) 388-8300; www.fs.usda.gov/coronado

FINDING THE TRAILHEAD

From Tucson go about 24 miles south on I-19. Exit at Continental, and drive east through Continental. Continue 13 miles on paved Madera Canyon Road to its end at the Roundup Trailhead. GPS: N31 42.81' / W110 52.41'

THE HIKE

This hike uses the newer, well-graded Super Trail to take you most of the way to the summit of Mount Wrightson, the highest point in the Santa Rita Mountains. The steeper but shorter Old Baldy Trail is used for the final ascent of the peak and for part of the return hike.

The Super Trail almost immediately crosses Madera Creek, then switchbacks up the east side of the canyon through chaparral brush and oak. This trail is well named because the ascent, though steady, is always moderate. After climbing along the east side of the creek for a bit, the trail gradually returns to the creek side. Beautiful Arizona sycamores grace the creek, which is nearly always flowing. More switchbacks take the trail out on the east side of the canyon once again. The trail works its way south toward the head of the canyon through silverleaf, Emory, and Arizona white oaks; Arizona madrone; and alligator junipers. You'll get occasional views of Mount Wrightson high to the east, but usually the summit is hidden behind closer ridges. After the trail passes Sprung Spring, it climbs into Josephine Saddle at 3.5 miles. Here a sign memorializes three Boy Scouts who died while camping here during a severe late-fall snowstorm.

Several trails depart Josephine Saddle, but your route remains on the Super Trail, which switchbacks northeast out of the saddle. At 3.7 miles you'll pass the Old Baldy Trail in a minor saddle, which will be your return. The Super Trail now heads southeast across

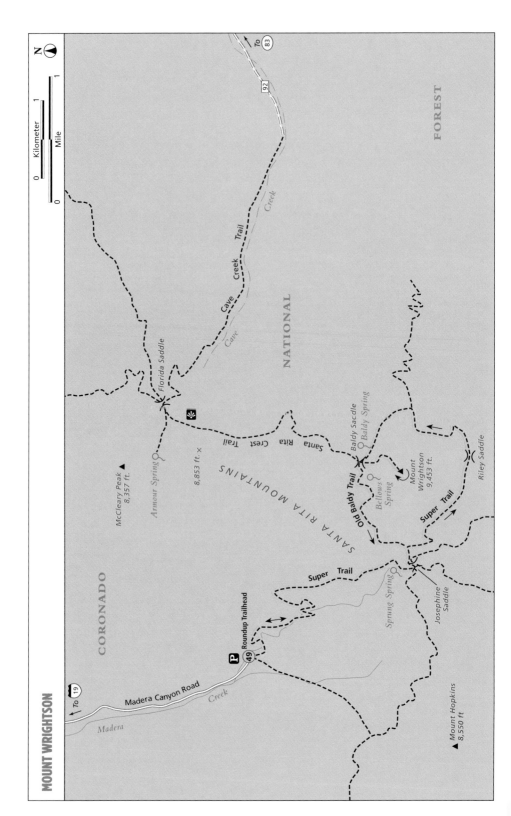

MOUNT WRIGHTSON

N

0 1 Kilometer
0 1 Mile

To 19

Madera Canyon Road

Madera Creek

P 49 Roundup Trailhead

CORONADO

McCleary Peak
8,357 ft.

Armour Spring

8,853 ft. ×

SANTA RITA MOUNTAINS

Florida Saddle

Cave Creek Trail

Cave Creek

Santa Rita Crest Trail

NATIONAL

FOREST

Baldy Saddle
Baldy Spring

Old Baldy Trail

Bellows Spring

Mount Wrightson
9,453 ft.

Super Trail

Riley Saddle

Super Trail

Sprung Spring

Josephine Saddle

Mount Hopkins
8,550 ft.

To 83

92

the slopes of Mount Wrightson, passing through Riley Saddle at 5.2 miles. Continuing to circle the mountain, the trail climbs northeast and then northwest, passing Baldy Spring. The Super Trail ends at Baldy Saddle at 6.8 miles; turn left onto the Old Baldy Trail. At first the Old Baldy Trail heads across the northeast slopes of Mount Wrightson, but it soon begins to switchback steeply, climbing around to the southeast face. The open, rocky terrain gives you great views. Early in the season, snow and ice can be a hazard on this section. A final climb takes you to the rocky summit dome, 7.6 miles from the start at the Roundup Trailhead.

Return to Baldy Saddle and the junction with the Super Trail, and then stay left to remain on the Old Baldy Trail. This trail switchbacks steeply down the rugged terrain below the saddle, then swings south past Bellows Spring and descends through stands of Mexican white pine and Douglas fir to meet the Super Trail just above Josephine Saddle. Turn right, and follow the Super Trail through Josephine Saddle and back to the Roundup Trailhead.

MILES AND DIRECTIONS

- **0.0** Start at the Roundup Trailhead and almost immediately cross Madera Creek on the Super Trail.
- **3.5** Reach Josephine Saddle.
- **3.7** Pass the Old Baldy Trail. (FYI: This will be the return trail.)
- **5.2** Pass through Riley Saddle.
- **6.8** Reach Baldy Saddle, and turn left onto the Old Baldy Trail.
- **7.6** Reach the summit of Mount Wrightson.
- **8.4** Return to Baldy Saddle; turn left to remain on the Old Baldy Trail.
- **10.0** Turn right onto the Super Trail.
- **10.2** Pass through Josephine Saddle.
- **13.7** Arrive back at the trailhead.

Madera Creek, Santa Rita Mountains

50 HEART OF ROCKS

This aptly named hike takes you away from the crowds and into a remote area featuring some of the best of the stone hoodoos in Chiricahua National Monument.

Start: 39.1 miles southeast of Willcox
Distance: 6.7-mile cherry stem
Hiking time: About 5 hours
Difficulty: Moderate
Trail surface: Dirt trails
Best seasons: Year-round
Water: No water available
Other trail users: None
Canine compatibility: Dogs prohibited

Fees and permits: Entrance fee
Schedule: Open all year
Maps: CalTopo.com MapBuilder Topo layer; Gaia GPS Gaia Topo layer
Trail contacts: Chiricahua National Monument, 12856 E. Rhyolite Creek Rd., Willcox, AZ 85643; (520) 824-3560; www.nps.gov/chir

FINDING THE TRAILHEAD

From Willcox on I-10, drive 34 miles southeast on AZ 186. Turn left onto AZ 181. Continue 5.1 miles to the Chiricahua National Monument Visitor Center and the trailhead. GPS: N32 0.34' / W109 21.39'

THE HIKE

The trail starts at the national monument visitor center parking lot and heads east along the south side of Rhyolite Canyon, climbing gradually. At 1.5 miles turn right onto the Sarah Deming Trail, which ascends a little faster as it turns southeast up Sarah Deming Canyon. Near the head of the canyon, the trail turns abruptly north and climbs out of the canyon into a land of strange-shaped rock formations. You'll meet the Heart of Rocks Trail at 2.9 miles; turn left to hike this scenic loop. The trail returns to the same

LITTLE-UNDERSTOOD GEOLOGY

The story behind this fantastic collection of rocks is not completely understood, but geologists believe that about 27 million years ago violent volcanic eruptions spewed red-hot pumice and ash over a 1,200-square-mile area. The hot particles became "welded" together to form an 800-foot-thick layer of tuff with a composition of rhyolite. As cooling took place, the tuff contracted and vertical cracks (joints) formed. The extent and thickness of this deposit indicates eruptions substantially greater than the Mount St. Helens eruption in 1980.

From 25 to 5 million years ago, the Earth's crust stretched and broke into large fault-bounded blocks. One uplifted block created the Chiricahua Mountains, and the masters of erosion—water, wind, and ice—began to sculpt the rock into odd formations. The horizontal bedding planes and joints provided weak places for erosion to act upon. Fanciful names such as Organ Pipe, Sea Captain, China Boy, Punch and Judy, and Duck on a Rock describe some of the strange rock shapes. Although many pinnacles and rocks appear to be precariously balanced, they were sufficiently stable to withstand the magnitude-7.2 earthquake that shook southeastern Arizona in 1887.

Hoodoos, Chiricahua National Monument

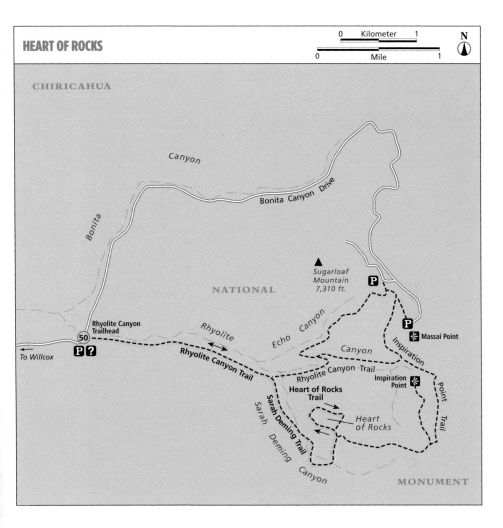

junction at 3.8 miles. Stay left, and return to the visitor center via the Sarah Deming and Rhyolite Canyon Trails.

The Heart of Rocks Loop features rock caricatures of people and animals and the most massive balanced rock in the monument. There are sweeping views of Sulphur Springs Valley, Cochise Head, and the Chiricahua Mountains.

MILES AND DIRECTIONS

0.0 Start at the Rhyolite Canyon Trailhead and head east.

1.5 Turn right onto the Sarah Deming Trail.

2.9 Reach junction with the Heart of Rocks Trail; turn left onto the loop.

3.8 Complete the loop and turn left onto the Sarah Deming Trail.

5.2 Turn left onto the Rhyolite Canyon Trail.

6.7 Arrive back at the trailhead.

WESTERN NEW MEXICO

51 BISTI BADLANDS

This cross-country day hike takes you into the weirdly eroded badlands of the Bisti/De-Na-Zin Wilderness. There are no trails but the walking is easy so you are free to explore.

Start: 38.8 miles south of Farmington
Distance: Variable, up to 6-mile loop
Hiking time: About 2 hours
Difficulty: Easy
Trail surface: Cross-country
Best seasons: Spring and fall
Water: None
Other trail users: None
Canine compatibility: Leashed dogs permitted

Fees and permits: None
Schedule: Open all year
Maps: CalTopo.com MapBuilder Topo layer
Trail contacts: Bureau of Land Management, Farmington Field Office, 6251 College Blvd., Suite A, Farmington, NM 87402; (505) 564-7600; https://www.blm.gov/visit/bisti-de-na-zin-wilderness

FINDING THE TRAILHEAD

To reach the Bisti Trailhead from Farmington, drive 36 miles south on NM 371, and turn east on gravel Road 1290. Continue 1.9 miles to a T-intersection and turn left. Drive 0.9 mile to the Bisti Trailhead, which is just south of a broad wash on the east side of the road. There is another, smaller parking area 0.25 mile farther north. GPS: N36 15.544' / W108 15.544'

THE HIKE

It is a good idea to mark the trailhead location on a GPS unit so that you can find your way back in this maze-like landscape.

From the trailhead, work your way generally north and east up the gently sloping plain toward the hoodoos. Watch for petrified wood in the clay layers, and for seams of dark coal deposits. When you are finished exploring, walk generally downhill to return to the trailhead. If you get disoriented, remember that walking downhill in a westerly direction will take to you the gravel road that runs along the west boundary of the wilderness.

Hoodoos are weird-looking towers and pinnacles that are created when hard cap rocks protect softer layers below from erosion. The Bisti contains a mix of sedimentary rocks, primarily soft shale, with occasional layers of hard sandstone. In arid climates, shale erodes into badlands, which consist of small, steep hills with an abrupt transition to flat ground. The soil formed is highly alkaline, and plant life has a difficult time getting a foothold.

Bisti badlands

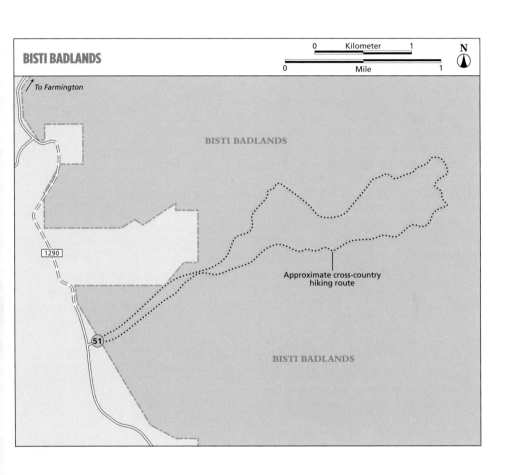

BISTI BADLANDS

0   Kilometer   1

0   Mile   1

N

To Farmington

BISTI BADLANDS

1290

Approximate cross-country
hiking route

BISTI BADLANDS

51

52 **PENASCO BLANCO**

This day hike takes you to the ruins of a great house in Chaco Culture National Historic Park.

Start: 66.5 miles south of Bloomfield
Distance: 7.2-mile out-and-back
Hiking time: About 4 hours
Difficulty: Moderate
Trail surface: Closed dirt road, dirt trails
Best seasons: Spring and fall
Water: None
Other trail users: None
Canine compatibility: Dogs permitted on leash; must be 6 feet or less

Fees and permits: Entrance fee
Schedule: Open all year; roads are impassable when wet, which happens after winter storms and during late summer thunderstorms
Maps: CalTopo.com MapBuilder Topo layer
Trail contacts: Chaco Culture National Historic Park, PO Box 220, Nageezi, NM 87037; (505) 786-7014; https://www.nps.gov/chcu

FINDING THE TRAILHEAD

From Bloomfield, drive south for 39.0 miles on US 550, then turn right on CR 7900. Continue 5.1 miles, then turn right on CR 7950 and drive 22.4 miles into the park and past the visitor center to the end of the road at the Pueblo del Arroyo parking area. N36 3.744' / W107 57.916'

THE HIKE

From the parking lot, walk northwest on the old road, which follows the broad, sandy floor of Chaco Canyon. You'll soon pass Kin Kletso, an impressive ruin on the right side of the trail, and then Casa Chiquita ruin. Watch for petroglyphs on the north wall of the canyon, about 0.5 mile beyond Casa Chiquita. Where the trail crosses Chaco Wash, take a short spur trail to pictographs painted on the walls and roof of an overhang. Researchers think that one of the paintings may represent the supernova of 1054 AD.

Rock art falls broadly into two categories—pictographs, and petroglyphs. The difference is simple—pictographs are painted onto the rock, and petroglyphs are pecked into the rock. Both are extremely fragile and can be ruined by the oil from your skin. Please respect this 1,000-year-old art and look, take photos, but do not touch.

Chaco Canyon was the center of the Ancestral Pueblo people between 800 and 1150 AD, whose culture encompassed a large portion of the Four Corners region in northwest New Mexico, northeast Arizona, southwest Colorado, and southeast Utah. Trade routes, including constructed roads, connected many of the major centers to Chaco Canyon. Structures built at Chaco Canyon were the largest in North America until the advent of European colonization.

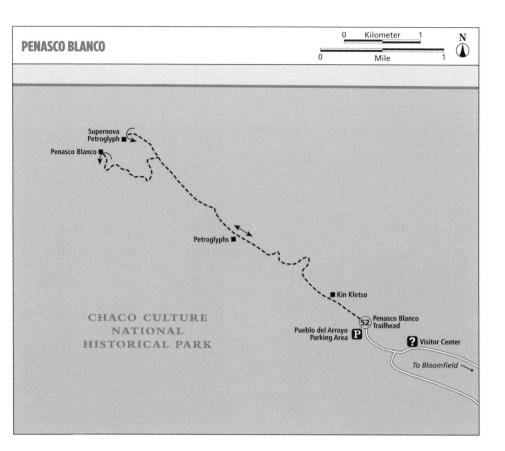

MILES AND DIRECTIONS

0.0 Trailhead; walk northwest on a closed dirt road, downstream along Chaco Wash.

0.3 Kin Kletso ruin on the right.

0.9 Casa Chiquita ruin on the right.

1.4 Petroglyphs.

2.4 Go right on a short spur trail to supernova petroglyph.

2.8 Supernova petroglyph; retrace your steps to the main trail.

3.2 Turn right on the main trail.

4.0 Penasco Blanco; retrace your steps to the trailhead, except for the supernova spur trail.

7.2 Trailhead.

53 SAN PEDRO PARKS

This is a 2- to 3-day backpack trip into the San Pedro Parks Wilderness, a unique 10,000-foot land of open meadows and alpine forest, in stark contrast to most of New Mexico's mountains, which are steep and rugged.

Start: 12.7 miles east of Cuba
Distance: 17.5-mile loop with a cherry stem
Hiking time: 2–3 days
Difficulty: Strenuous
Trail surface: Dirt and rocks
Best seasons: Summer through fall
Water: Plentiful along the many creeks
Other trail users: Horses

Canine compatibility: Leashed dogs permitted
Fees and permits: None
Schedule: Open all year
Maps: CalTopo.com MapBuilder Topo layer
Trail contacts: Santa Fe National Forest, 11 Forest Ln., Santa Fe, NM 87508; (505) 438-5300; https://www.fs.usda.gov/santafe/

FINDING THE TRAILHEAD

From Cuba, drive 10 miles east on NM 126, then turn left on FR 70. Continue 2.7 miles to the trailhead. GPS: N36 1.655' / W106 50.784'

THE HIKE

This loop hike is just a sample of the gorgeous and relatively easy backpacking to be had in the San Pedro Parks.

From the trailhead, head north on the Vacas Trail #51 through the beautiful alpine forest and follow it around the east side of San Gregorio Reservoir. After the trail climbs over a saddle, it reaches Clear Creek and the junction with Damien Trail #436. Turn left to remain on the Vacas Trail and follow it north up Clear Creek. The trail meets Upper Clear Creek Trail #417, which will be your return from the loop portion of the hike; stay right here and follow the Vacas Trail as it climbs up a drainage then levels out, heading northeast. The trail drops down to the Rio de las Vacas and the Palomas Trail #50 comes in from the right; stay left on the Vacas Trail and follow it upriver.

Very shortly, the Anastacio Trail #435 comes in from the left; stay right here and follow the Vacas Trail up the Rio de las Vacas. Where Trail #32 comes in from the right, bear left and follow the Vacas Trail northwest through a series of meadows. You'll cross the Rio Puerco in a broad meadow, and on the far side, reach a junction. Turn left here on Trail 46 and follow it downriver into a shallow gorge that gradually becomes deeper as you head southwest. The trail finally leaves the river and climbs to a saddle to the west.

At this crossroads, go straight ahead on the Lucero Trail #34 and follow it south back to the banks of the Rio Puerco. Continue downstream 2.3 miles, then follow the trail up a small side canyon to the east. After the trail crosses a broad ridge, it drops southeast into Clear Creek and meets Trail 417. Turn right here and follow Trail 417 for 0.5 mile south along the creek, where you'll meet Vacas Trail #51 coming in from the left, closing the loop.

Stay right on Vacas Trail and return to the trailhead the way you came.

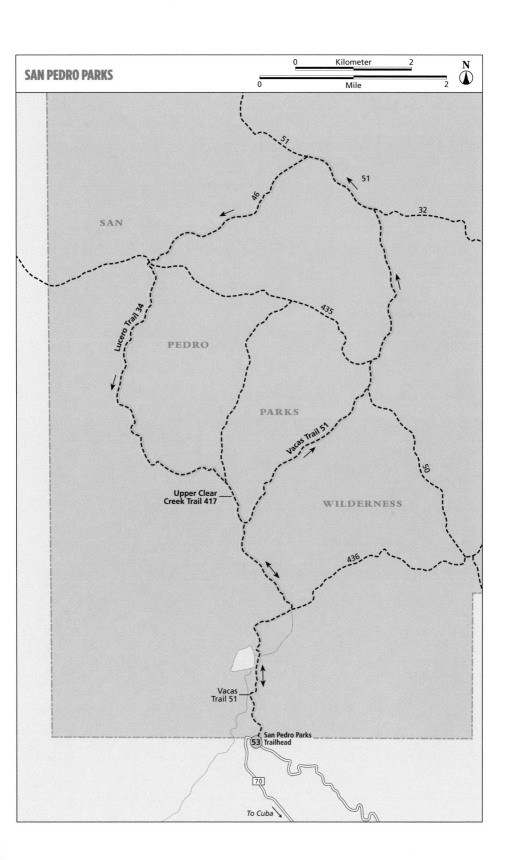

MILES AND DIRECTIONS

0.0 Head north on the Vacas Trail 51.

0.9 Pass San Gregorio Reservoir on the east.

1.9 Junction with Damien Trail 436; go left to remain on Vacas Trail 51.

3.0 Junction with Upper Clear Creek Trail 417; this will be our return from the loop portion of the hike. For now, turn right to stay on the Vacas Trail 51.

5.1 Junction; stay left on Vacas Trail 51.

5.4 Junction with Trail 435; turn right to stay on the Vacas Trail 51.

7.3 Trail 32 comes in from the right; bear left to stay on Vacas Trail 51.

8.3 Junction; turn left on Trail 46.

10.5 Junction; Trail 46 goes right and Trail 435 goes left. Go straight ahead on the Lucero Trail 34.

14.0 Junction; stay right on Trail 417.

14.5 Trail 51 joins from the left, closing the loop portion of the hike. Turn right on Trail 51 and retrace your steps to the trailhead.

17.5 Trailhead.

54 **ALCOVE HOUSE**

Bandelier National Monument is the location for this day hike to pre-Columbian ruins in a sheltering alcove high above Frijoles Canyon.

Start: 43.8 miles west of Santa Fe
Distance: 2.7-mile loop with an out-and-back section
Hiking time: About 2 hours
Difficulty: Easy
Trail surface: Paved and dirt trails, ladders at Alcove House
Best seasons: Spring through fall
Water: None
Other trail users: None
Canine compatibility: Dogs not permitted
Fees and permits: Entry fee. Permit required for overnight backpacking.

From June through mid-Oct, access to the Frijoles Canyon Visitor Center and trailheads is by free shuttle bus only, starting from the White Rock Visitor Center. Check the park website for updates.
Schedule: Open all year
Maps: CalTopo.com MapBuilder Topo layer; Gaia GPS Trails Illustrated layer
Trail contacts: Bandelier National Monument, 15 Entrance Rd., Los Alamos, NM 87544; (505) 672-3861 x0; https://www.nps.gov/band

FINDING THE TRAILHEAD

From Santa Fe, drive 16 miles north on US 84, then turn left on NM 502. Drive 10 miles west, then turn left onto NM 4. Drive 6.2 miles to the White Rock Visitor Center, which is your trailhead if the shuttle is required. Otherwise, continue 8.3 miles, then turn left on the Bandelier National Monument entrance road, and continue 3.3 miles to the Frijoles Visitor Center and trailhead. GPS: N35 46.719' / W106 16.225'

THE HIKE

Start by walking northwest up the canyon on the main paved trail, staying on the north side of the creek. Almost immediately, a trail forks left and crosses the creek. This will be the return from the loop portion of the hike. Stay right and then turn right again at a second fork and walk through Tyuonyi Ruin.

Just past Tyuoniyi, stay right at another junction and hike past Talus House. Then, stay left at the junction with the Frey Trail, and then almost immediately go right on the trail upstream to Long House.

After passing Long House, the trail crosses the creek to meet the Frijoles Trail. This is the start of the out-and-back portion of the walk. Turn right and follow the trail upstream through stands of ponderosa pine and riparian trees. When you reach the spur trail to Alcove House, turn right and follow it up to the ruin. Ladders give access to the partly restored and stabilized ruin, but access may be limited for restoration work.

To return to the trailhead, retrace your steps to the junction with the Pueblo Loop Trail at the stream crossing, but stay right and don't cross the creek. Just before the visitor center, cross the creek at a junction.

Frijoles Canyon, the setting for this hike, was home to a community of Ancestral Pueblo people (formerly known as Anasazi) from about 1100 to 1550 AD. While many Ancestral Pueblo villages were abandoned by 1250 AD, the inhabitants of this area stayed

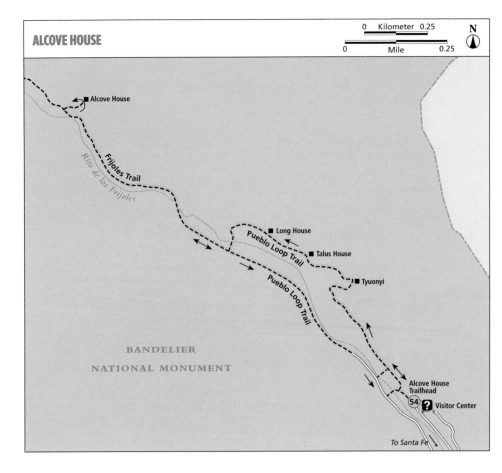

on for three more centuries. It appears that exhaustion of local resources as well as a severe drought forced the people to move to better sites along the Rio Grande.

MILES AND DIRECTIONS

0.0   From the Frijoles Visitor Center, walk northwest on the paved trail.

0.1   Stay right at a junction (the left fork will be the return trail).

0.2   Stay right at a junction and walk past Tyuonyi Ruin.

0.4   Just past Tyuonyi, turn right on a short loop past Talus House.

0.5   Stay left at the junction with the Frey Trail, then almost immediately, turn right on the trail to Long House.

0.8   After crossing the stream, turn right on Frijoles Trail. This is the start of the out-and-back portion of the hike.

1.4   Turn right on the short spur trail up to Alcove House.

1.5   Alcove House; retrace your steps to the junction at the stream crossing.

2.1   Junction; stay right.

2.6   Junction, turn left, cross the stream, then turn right.

2.7   Visitor center and trailhead.

55 RIO GRANDE GORGE

This hike takes you into the unique rocky gorge created by the Rio Grande, in Rio Grande del Norte National Monument.

Start: 38.1 miles north of Taos
Distance: 5.6-mile out-and-back
Hiking time: About 4 hours
Difficulty: Moderate
Trail surface: Dirt and rocks
Best seasons: All year
Water: Campground at trailhead, and Big and Little Arsenic Springs
Other trail users: Horses
Canine compatibility: Dogs are not permitted.

Fees and permits: Entrance fee
Schedule: Open all year
Maps: CalTopo.com MapBuilder Topo layer; Gaia GPS Trails Illustrated layer
Trail contacts: Bureau of Land Management, Taos Field Office, Wild Rivers Visitor Center, Cerro, NM 87519; (575) 758-8851; https://www.blm.gov/visit/rgdnnm

FINDING THE TRAILHEAD

From Taos, drive 4.1 miles north on US 64, then continue straight onto NM 522. Drive 22.7 miles, then turn left on NM 378. Continue 11.1 miles, then bear right to stay on the right branch of NM 378. Drive 0.2 mile to Big Arsenic Springs Campground and the trailhead. GPS: N36 40.490' / W105 40.906'

THE HIKE

This hike into a desert volcanic canyon makes quite a change from the usual high mountain trails. And unlike the mountains, this hike can be done year-round, although it can be hot in summer.

From the campground, follow the Big Arsenic Trail down switchbacks into the gorge. When the trail forks, go right to make a short side trip to Big Arsenic Springs and some petroglyphs. Beyond the springs, watch for a faint trail going left. At the petroglyphs, retrace your steps to the junction.

Back on the main trail, stay right and hike downriver. The trail soon descends to the riverbank. Follow the trail downstream to the confluence of the Rio Grande and Red Rivers, where it ends. Retrace your steps to the trailhead, except for the side trail to the petroglyphs.

MILES AND DIRECTIONS

0.0 Start on the trail behind the small campground.

0.6 Junction; turn right and go to Big Arsenic Springs.

0.8 Petroglyphs; retrace your steps back to the junction.

1.0 Turn right (downriver).

1.4 The trail reaches the bottom of the gorge.

3.4 Confluence of the Rio Grande and Red Rivers; return the way you came, except skip the side trip to the petroglyphs.

5.6 Trailhead.

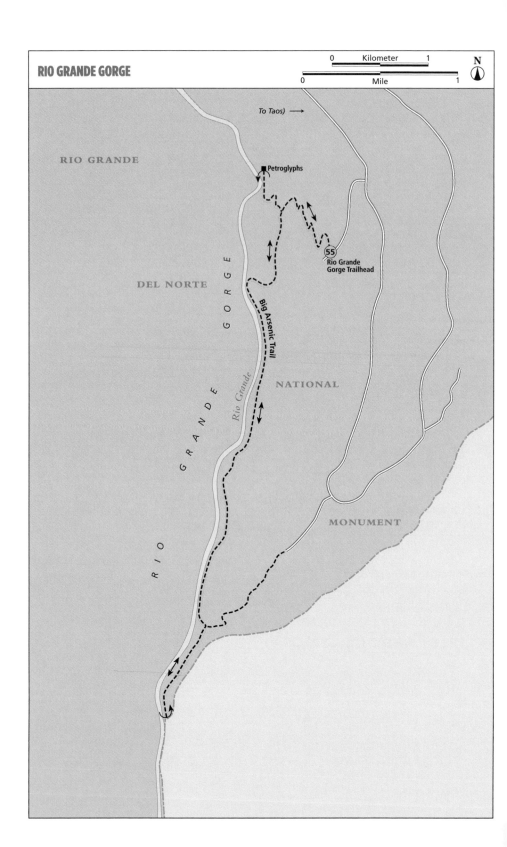

RIO GRANDE GORGE

0   Kilometer   1

0   Mile   1

N

To Taos) →

RIO GRANDE

■ Petroglyphs

DEL NORTE

RIO GRANDE GORGE

Big Arsenic Trail

55
Rio Grande
Gorge Trailhead

NATIONAL

Rio Grande

MONUMENT

RIO

56 WHEELER PEAK

This is a long day hike or overnight backpack trip to the highest peak in New Mexico.

Start: 18.6 miles northeast of Taos
Distance: 14.6-mile out-and-back
Hiking time: About 9 hours or 2 days
Difficulty: Strenuous
Trail surface: Dirt and rocks
Best seasons: Summer through fall
Water: Taos Ski Valley at trailhead, Middle Fork Red River
Other trail users: Horses

Canine compatibility: Leashed dogs permitted
Fees and permits: None
Schedule: Open all year
Maps: CalTopo.com MapBuilder Topo layer; Gaia GPS Trails Illustrated layer
Trail contacts: Carson National Forest, 208 Cruz Alta Rd., Taos, NM 87571; (575) 758-6200; https://www.fs.usda.gov/carson

FINDING THE TRAILHEAD

 From Taos, drive 4 miles north on US 64, then turn right on NM 150. Continue 14.6 miles to the large parking lot and trailhead at Twinning Campground, just below Taos Ski Valley. GPS: N36 35.819' / W105 27.021'

THE HIKE

Summer brings monsoon thunderstorms, so it is a very good idea to do this hike early in the morning so that you can be off exposed ridges by early afternoon.

Follow the Wheeler Peak Trail, #90 from the signed trailhead, and head northeast up the valley bottom. Numerous dirt roads and use trails branch off this section; remember to always stay on Trail 90, which is the most heavily used trail. A few sections follow dirt roads through private land—again, you will stay on Trail 90 to the top of Wheeler Peak.

After 2.0 miles you'll reach Bull of the Woods Pasture. Turn right to remain on Trail 90 and follow it south as it climbs out of the canyon, then climbs around the west side of Bull of the Woods Mountain. On the south side of the mountain, the old road forks right and Trail 90, now a foot trail, goes left. Continue on Trail 90.

The trail climbs steadily south along the ridge, passing just east of Frazer Mountain, before descending to cross the Middle Fork Red River. This is the last place to get water before the summit. The climb resumes as the trail switchbacks south and rejoins the crest. Finally, the trail climbs over Mount Walter before reaching Wheeler Peak. After enjoying the incredible view, return the way you came.

The high ridges and peaks surrounding Mount Wheeler are the most extensive areas of alpine tundra in New Mexico. Cirques on the northeast sides of the mountains contain small alpine lakes and show that these mountains were carved by glaciers. The last glaciers melted about 10,000 years ago, and only a few perennial snowfields remain.

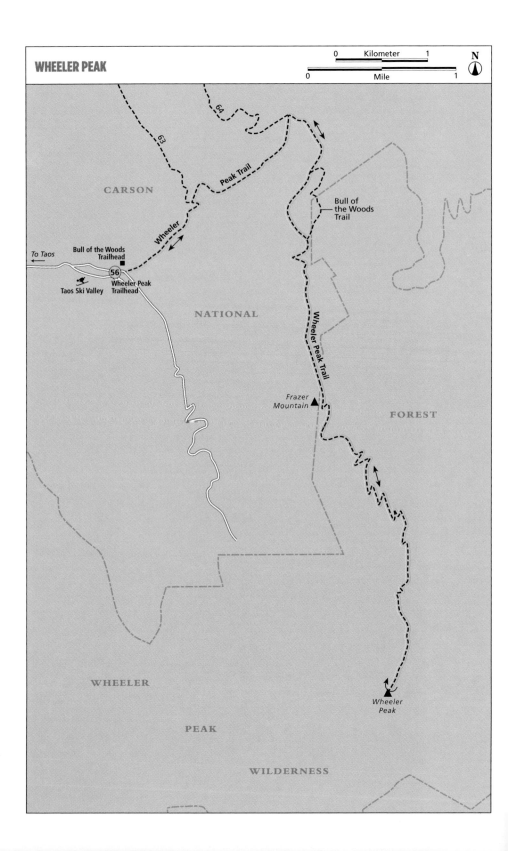

WHEELER PEAK

0   Kilometer   1

0   Mile   1

N

CARSON

64

63

Wheeler

Peak Trail

Bull of
the Woods
Trail

To Taos

Bull of the Woods
Trailhead

56

Taos Ski Valley

Wheeler Peak
Trailhead

NATIONAL

Wheeler Peak Trail

Frazer
Mountain

FOREST

WHEELER

PEAK

Wheeler
Peak

WILDERNESS

MILES AND DIRECTIONS

0.0 Start on the Wheeler Peak Trail, #90. You will stay on Trail 90 to Wheeler Peak.

0.8 Junction with Trail 63; stay right on Trail 90.

2.0 Junction with Trail 64; stay right on Trail 90.

2.4 Junction with Bull of the Woods Trail; stay right on Trail 90.

3.0 End of old road and start of foot trail.

4.8 Cross Middle Fork Red River.

7.3 Wheeler Peak; return the way you came.

14.6 Trailhead.

57 SANTA FE BALDY

This popular hike takes you to the summit of a 12,632-foot peak in the Santa Fe National Forest.

Start: 15.4 miles northeast of Santa Fe
Distance: 13.4-mile out-and-back
Hiking time: About 8 hours or 2 days
Difficulty: Strenuous
Trail surface: Dirt and rocks
Best seasons: Later summer through fall
Water: Rio Nambe, East Fork Rio Nambe
Other trail users: Horses

Canine compatibility: Leashed dogs permitted
Fees and permits: None
Schedule: Open all year
Maps: CalTopo.com MapBuilder Topo layer; Gaia GPS Trails Illustrated layer
Trail contacts: Santa Fe National Forest, 11 Forest Ln., Santa Fe, NM 87508; (505) 438-5300; https://www.fs.usda.gov/santafe/

FINDING THE TRAILHEAD

From Santa Fe, drive east on NM 475 for 15.4 miles to the parking area just before the ski area. GPS: N35 47.731' / W105 48.261'

THE HIKE

Start off on the well-traveled Windsor Trail, #254, which climbs to a saddle east of Aspen Peak and crosses the Pecos Wilderness boundary. Now, follow the trail as it descends slightly to the junction with Trail 403. Stay right on Trail 254 as it contours through beautiful alpine forest before descending to cross the Rio Nambe.

A side trail here goes right to Nambe Lake, but you'll continue on Trail 254 as it climbs gradually across a north-facing slope. Trail 403 branches left, but you'll stay on Trail 254. Just before Trail 254 reaches the East Fork Rio Nambe, Trail 160 goes left; stay right on Trail 254.

Once across the river, the trail ascends in a series of switchbacks. After the trail levels out a bit, turn left on to Trail 251 to Lake Katherine (Trail 254 goes right.) Broad switchbacks lead to the ridge crest. Here, leave the trail and follow an informal trail northwest and north to the summit. After enjoying the incredible view, return the way you came.

In eastern Arizona and western New Mexico, high summits that reach above timberline are often called "baldy," which refers to the fact that their summits are devoid of trees.

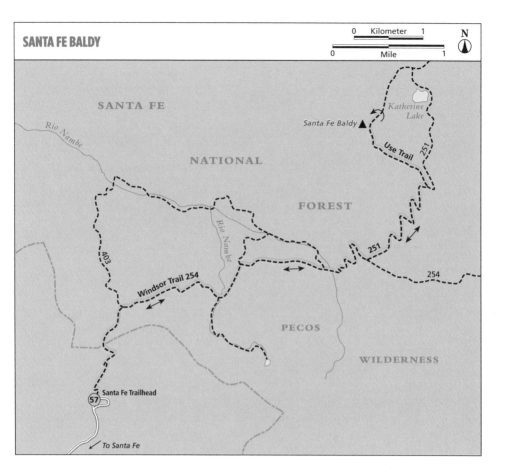

MILES AND DIRECTIONS

0.0 Start on the Windsor Trail 254.

1.2 Trail 403 goes left; stay right on Trail 254.

2.3 Cross Rio Nambe, remaining on Trail 254.

2.6 Junction; stay right on Trail 254.

3.4 Junction; stay right on Trail 254.

3.5 Cross the east fork of Rio Nambe.

4.2 Trail 254 goes right; turn left on Trail 251.

5.7 Main crest; leave the trail and climb the ridge to the northwest and north.

6.7 Santa Fe Baldy; return the way you came.

13.4 Trailhead.

58 MOUNT TAYLOR

A beautiful day hike to the top of Mount Taylor, the most prominent summit in northwestern New Mexico.

Start: 18.7 miles northwest of Grants
Distance: 6.0-mile out-and-back
Hiking time: About 4 hours
Difficulty: Strenuous
Trail surface: Dirt and rocks
Best seasons: Summer and fall
Water: None
Other trail users: Horses
Canine compatibility: Leashed dogs permitted

Fees and permits: None
Schedule: Open all year
Maps: CalTopo.com MapBuilder Topo layer
Trail contacts: Cibola National Forest, 2113 Osuna Rd. NE, Albuquerque, NM 87113; (505) 346-3900; https://www.fs.usda.gov/cibola

FINDING THE TRAILHEAD

From Grants, drive 13.5 miles northeast on NM 547, then turn right onto FR 193. Continue 5.2 miles on this gravel road to the trailhead, marked by "Trail 77" signs. GPS: N35 13.214' / W107 38.217'

THE HIKE

Follow the Gooseberry Spring Trail #77 as it steadily climbs northeast up a ridge, which is dominated by ponderosa pine and quaking aspen forest. The trail briefly turns southeast and crosses a drainage, where there is a seasonal spring. Now, the trail climbs steadily along the slopes south of the drainage. An old road branches left and goes a short distance to seasonal Gooseberry Spring. Stay right on Trail 77.

Above the spring junction, the trail soon emerges into open meadows that feature great views, including the summit of Mount Taylor high above you to the northeast. The trail turns more to the north for the final climb to the summit.

From this highest peak in the area, the views are stunning, including the 14,000-foot peaks of southwest Colorado on a clear day. Mount Taylor is an old volcano, one of many on this plateau. Basalt flows and cinder cones cover the area, including the 2,000-year-old lava flows at El Malpais National Monument to the south.

MOUNT TAYLOR

MILES AND DIRECTIONS

0.0 Hike northwest on Trail 77.

1.1 Old road to Gooseberry Spring; stay right on Trail 77.

3.0 Mount Taylor; return the way you came.

6.0 Trailhead.

59 ZUNI-ACOMA TRAIL

This is a long day hike or overnight backpack trip across the lava flows of El Malpais National Monument. It can optionally be done one way with a car shuttle.

Start: 16 miles south of Grants
Distance: 15.8-mile out-and-back (7.9 miles with a car shuttle)
Hiking time: About 8 hours or 2 days (4–5 hours with a car shuttle)
Difficulty: Strenuous
Trail surface: Rocky lava flow, dirt
Best seasons: Spring and fall
Water: None
Other trail users: None

Canine compatibility: Leashed dogs permitted, but be aware that the lava is very hard on paws
Fees and permits: None
Schedule: Open all year
Maps: CalTopo.com MapBuilder Topo layer
Trail contacts: El Malpais National Monument, 1900 E. Santa Fe Ave., Grants, NM 87020; (505) 876-2783; https://www.nps.gov/elma

FINDING THE TRAILHEAD

To reach the west trailhead from Grants, drive 16 miles south on NM 53 to the trailhead. GPS: N34 57.414' / W107 56.610'

To reach the east trailhead from Grants, drive 5.4 miles southeast on NM 66. After the highway crosses I-14, it becomes NM 117. Continue south 14.9 miles to the east trailhead. GPS: N34 53.943' / W107 51.524'

THE HIKE

This historic route has been used by the people of the Zuni and Acoma pueblos for at least 1,000 years to cross the plateau between their villages. This section crosses five different lava flows of different ages. As much of the hiking is on bare lava rock, wear sturdy boots. In places the trail crosses area where soil has had time to form, it is a distinct footpath, but in areas of bare rock, it is marked by cairns—small piles of rock. Hiking a cairned route requires different navigation skills than trail hiking. Always have the next cairn in sight before leaving the last cairn. Respect this historic route by not disturbing existing cairns and refraining from building new ones.

Hike generally southeast along the route. Twisted piñon pines, junipers, and ponderosa pines underscore the difficulty of existence on this raw landscape. At first, the hike crosses the El Calderon Lava Flow, at 60,000 years the oldest lava flow along the trail. Soon, you're walking across the Twin Craters Lava Flow, which is about 18,000 years old. At a little over 2 miles you cross onto the Bandera Flow, which is about 11,000 years old. Most of the second half of the trail is on the McCarty Flow, which is only 2,000 years old. Just before the east trailhead, you cross the Hoya de Cibola Flow, which is older—about 11,000 years. In terms of the vastness of geologic time, these are all very young landscapes.

Aspens, El Malpais National Monument

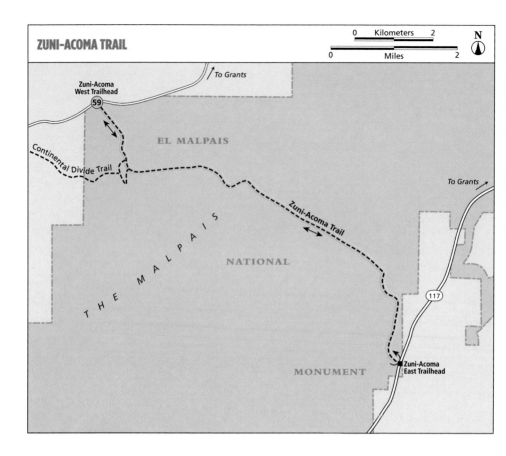

MILES AND DIRECTIONS

0.0 West trailhead on NM 53.

1.2 Continental Divide Trail joins from the right.

7.9 East trailhead on NM 117; return the way you came unless you are doing a car shuttle.

15.8 West trailhead.

60 SOUTH SANDIA CREST

This scenic loop starts from Sandia Crest and loops below the crest for some dramatic views, then returns through the cool, shady, alpine aspen and fir forest on the crest. This is another great hike for fall color.

Start: 35.6 miles east of Albuquerque
Distance: 3.1-mile loop
Hiking time: About 2 hours
Difficulty: Easy
Trail surface: Dirt and rocks
Best seasons: Summer through fall
Water: None
Other trail users: Horses
Canine compatibility: Leashed dogs permitted

Fees and permits: Trailhead parking fee
Schedule: Open all year
Maps: CalTopo.com MapBuilder Topo layer; Gaia GPS Trails Illustrated layer
Trail contacts: Cibola National Forest, 2113 Osuna Rd. NE, Albuquerque, NM 87113; (505) 346-3900; https://www.fs.usda.gov/cibola

FINDING THE TRAILHEAD

From the junction of I-40 and I-25 in Albuquerque, drive east 14.5 miles on I-40 to exit 175. Turn left on NM 333, drive 0.8 mile, and then turn left on NM 14. Drive 6.9 miles, and then turn left on NM 536. Continue 13.4 miles to the end of the road, and park in the main parking lot. GPS: N35 12.635' / W106 26.969'

THE HIKE

Start on the Crest Spur Trail, which drops off the ridgeline to the south. The trail then descends gradually to end where it meets the La Luz Trail in a saddle. Turn left and follow the La Luz Trail as it contours south and east to meet the Crest Trail just north of the upper tram terminal. Turn left on the Crest Trail and follow it back to the northwest along the crest through Kiwanis Meadow. After passing Sandia Crest with its crown of radio towers, the Crest Trail returns to the Sandia Crest Trailhead.

The Sandia Peak Tramway, whose upper terminal is at the south end of this loop hike, is the longest aerial tram in the world, spanning 2.7 miles and rising 4,000 feet. It serves as both a scenic tram and a fast way to reach the top of the Sandia Peak Ski Area, taking just 15 minutes for the trip. It was constructed by a Swiss engineering company, took 2 years to build, and was completed in 1966. Construction was complicated by the difficult, rocky terrain, and the cable alone took 5 months to lay. Even the Swiss experts admitted that the Sandia Peak Tram was the hardest of the more than fifty aerial trams they'd previously constructed.

Sandia Crest Trail

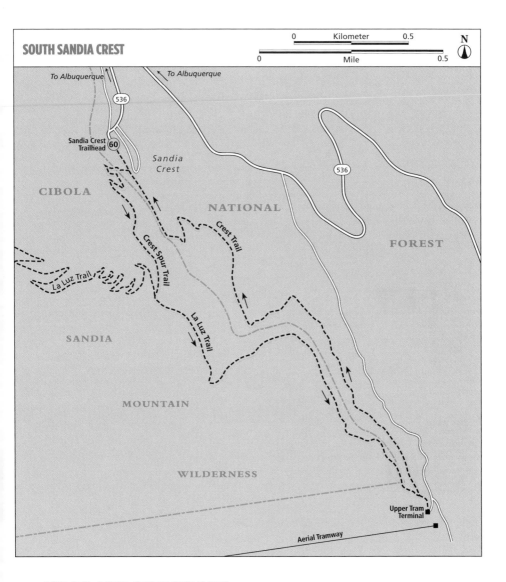

0   Kilometer   0.5

0   Mile   0.5

N

To Albuquerque

To Albuquerque

536

Sandia Crest
Trailhead   60

*Sandia
Crest*

536

CIBOLA

NATIONAL

Crest Trail

FOREST

Crest Spur Trail

La Luz Trail

La Luz Trail

SANDIA

MOUNTAIN

WILDERNESS

Upper Tram
Terminal

Aerial Tramway

MILES AND DIRECTIONS

0.0   Leave the Sandia Crest Trailhead and start on the Crest Spur Trail.

0.6   The Crest Spur Trail ends at the La Luz Trail; turn left on the La Luz Trail.

1.8   Meet the Crest Trail at the upper tram terminal; turn left on the Crest Trail.

3.1   Return to the Sandia Crest Trailhead.

61 THE CATWALK

This short but spectacular day hike follows the Catwalk National Recreation Trail up Whitewater Creek in the Gila National Forest. It takes its name from a section of trail that is suspended from the canyon walls.

Start: 65 miles northwest of Silver City
Distance: 2.4-mile out-and-back
Hiking time: 1 hour
Difficulty: Easy, moderate, strenuous
Trail surface: Paved and dirt trails and steel bridge
Best seasons: All year
Water: None
Other trail users: None

Canine compatibility: Leashed dogs permitted
Fees and permits: Parking fee
Schedule: Open all year
Maps: CalTopo.com MapBuilder Topo layer; Gaia GPS Trails Illustrated layer
Trail contacts: Gila National Forest, 3005 E. Camino del Bosque, Silver City, NM 88061; (575) 388-8201; https://www.fs.usda.gov/gila

FINDING THE TRAILHEAD

From Silver City, drive 60 miles north on US 180, then turn right on NM 174. Continue 1.0 mile, then turn right onto Catwalk Road. Continue 4 miles to the end of the road at the picnic area and trailhead. GPS: N33 22.334' / W108 50.565'

THE HIKE

The Catwalk and trail were originally built in the late 1800s to maintain waterworks that supplied a mill at the town site of Graham near the trailhead. Most of the town site and water line have been washed away in floods. Major floods after the 300,000-acre Whitewater Baldy Fire of 2012 wiped out much of the trail but the lower 1.2 miles have been rebuilt.

Start by hiking upstream on the newer paved trail on the right side of the creek. You'll soon reach the Catwalk. After the bridge ends, continue across a fiberglass bridge and through an arch. When the trail becomes unnavigable, retrace your steps to the trailhead.

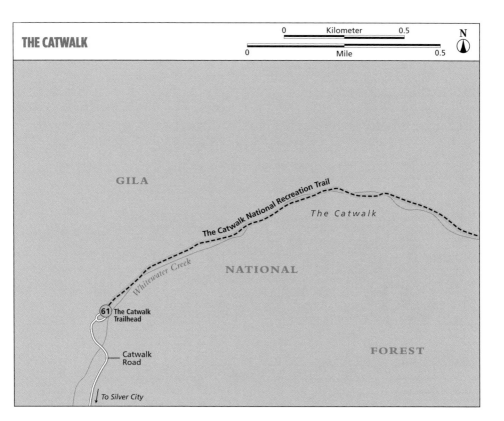

THE CATWALK

0   Kilometer   0.5

0   Mile   0.5

N

GILA

The Catwalk National Recreation Trail

The Catwalk

Whitewater Creek

NATIONAL

61 The Catwalk Trailhead

Catwalk Road

FOREST

To Silver City

MILES AND DIRECTIONS

0.0   Hike upstream on the newer paved trail on the right side of the creek.

0.3   Start of Catwalk.

0.5   End of Catwalk.

1.2   End of maintained trail; return the way you came.

2.4   Trailhead.

62 MOGOLLON BALDY

A 2- or 3-day backpack trip, this hike takes you along the crest of the Mogollon Mountains in the Gila Wilderness area, the first wilderness area established in the United States. Parts of the forest were burned in the 300,000-acre Whitewater Baldy Fire of 2012.

Start: 21 miles east of Glenwood
Distance: 22.8-mile out-and-back
Hiking time: 2-3 days
Difficulty: Strenuous
Trail surface: Dirt and rocks
Best seasons: Summer and fall
Water: Bead, Hummingbird, Little Hobo, West Fork Saddle, and Black Tail Springs. Don't trust any single spring; always carry enough water to get you to the next spring, or back to the last one, if a spring is dry.

Other trail users: Horses
Canine compatibility: Leashed dogs permitted
Fees and permits: None
Schedule: Open all year
Maps: CalTopo.com MapBuilder Topo layer; Gaia GPS Trails Illustrated Topo layer
Trail contacts: Gila National Forest, 3005 E. Camino del Bosque, Silver City, NM 88061; (575) 388-8201; https://www.fs.usda.gov/gila

FINDING THE TRAILHEAD

From Glenwood, drive 3.7 miles north on US 180, then turn right on NM 159. Continue 17.3 miles to the Sandy Point Trailhead, on the left. NM 159 becomes gravel after it passes through the town of Mogollon. GPS: N33 22.349' / W108 41.156'

THE HIKE

Much of the beautiful pine-fir-aspen forest that formerly covered the high country of the Mogollon Mountains has been burned in a series of wildfires, the worst being the fire in 2012. The upside of this devastation is that you can see the forces of natural forest regeneration at work. At these altitudes, the first trees to return are quaking aspen, which sprout from their interconnected root systems. Soon the pines and firs will follow. The other plus side of the fires is that much of this hike now has 100-mile views from the trail along the crest. Before the fire the only views were from the peaks, Whitewater and Mogollon Baldy.

Across the road from the parking area, follow the Crest Trail, #182, as it climbs steadily across the north and east sides of Willow Mountain. Just past the wilderness boundary lies Bead Spring, in a drainage of the left side of the trail. The trail gains the crest in a saddle southeast of Willow Mountain, and then stays on or near the crest all the way to Mogollon Baldy.

Just north of Whitewater Baldy, the trail drops into Hummingbird Saddle. Hummingbird Spring lies one switchback down Trail 207, to the right. Follow the Crest Trail around the east side of Whitewater Baldy to the junction with the Iron Creek Trail; stay right on the Crest Trail.

Just northeast of Center Baldy, the Holt-Apache Trail 181 forks right; stay left on the Crest Trail and follow it east along south-facing slopes. At the junction with the

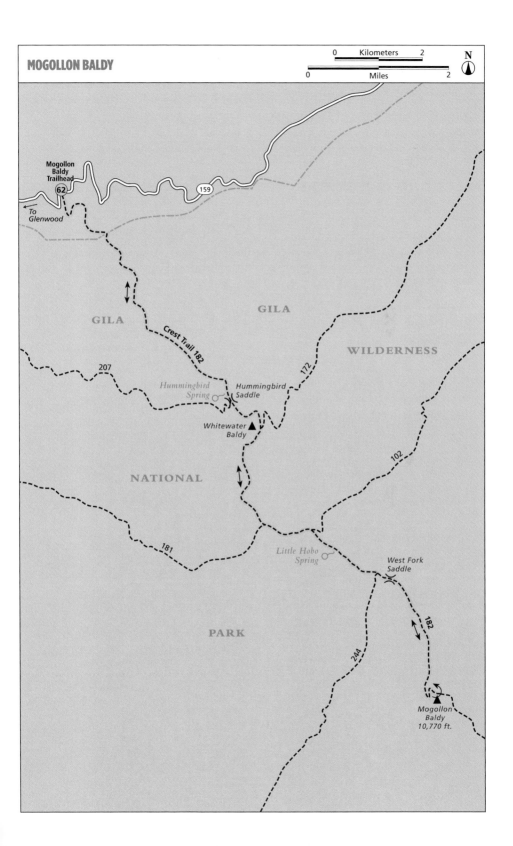

0   Kilometers   2

0   Miles   2

N

Mogollon
Baldy
Trailhead
62
159

To
Glenwood

GILA

GILA

WILDERNESS

Crest Trail 182

207

172

Hummingbird
Spring

Hummingbird
Saddle

Whitewater
Baldy

NATIONAL

102

181

Little Hobo
Spring

West Fork
Saddle

PARK

182

244

Mogollon
Baldy
10,770 ft.

Turkeyfeather Mountain Trail, stay right on the Crest Trail. You'll soon come to Little Hobo Spring. Just before reaching West Fork Saddle, you'll pass Trail 224 on the right, and then West Fork Spring. Continuing on the Crest Trail, you'll stay mostly on the crest past a spur trail to Black Tail Spring, and then climb a short distance up the ridge to the summit of Mogollon Baldy. This 10,770-foot peak commands a stunning view of the Mogollon Mountains, western New Mexico, and eastern Arizona. A fire lookout tower is staffed during periods of high fire danger—please ask permission before climbing the stairs.

MILES AND DIRECTIONS

0.0   Start on the Crest Trail, #182, across the road from the parking area.

1.4   Junction with the short spur trail to Bead Spring, on the left. Continue on Trail 182.

4.6   Hummingbird Saddle and junction with Trail 207 on the right. Hummingbird Spring is a short distance down this trail. Continue on Trail 182.

5.4   Junction with Iron Creek Lake Trail 172; stay right on Trail 182.

7.1   Junction with Holt-Apache Trail 181; stay left on Trail 182.

7.8   Junction with Turkeyfeather Mountain Trail 102; stay right on Trail 182.

8.2   Little Hobo Spring.

9.0   Trail 244 forks right; stay left on Trail 182.

9.1   West Fork Saddle Spring.

9.2   West Fork Saddle.

10.7   Spur trail to Black Tail Spring on left; stay right on Trail 182.

11.4   Mogollon Baldy; return the way you came.

22.8   Trailhead.

63 SIERRA BLANCA

This popular day hike takes you to the summit of the highest mountain in southern New Mexico, 11,877-foot Sierra Blanca Peak.

Start: 23.8 miles west of Ruidoso
Distance: 9.6-mile out-and-back
Hiking time: About 6 hours
Difficulty: Strenuous
Trail surface: Dirt and rocks
Best seasons: Summer through fall
Water: Ice Spring
Other trail users: Horses
Canine compatibility: Leashed dogs permitted
Fees and permits: Permit required for the portion of the hike on the Mescalero Reservation

Schedule: Open all year
Maps: CalTopo.com MapBuilder Topo layer; Gaia GPS Trails Illustrated Topo layer
Trail contacts: Lincoln National Forest, 3463 Las Palomas, Alamogordo, NM 88310; (575) 434-7200; https://www.fs.usda.gov /lincoln. Mescalero Apache Tribe, PO Box 227, 108 Central Ave., Mescalero, NM 88340; (575) 464-4494; https:// mescaleroapachetribe.com/

FINDING THE TRAILHEAD

From Ruidoso, drive 11.9 miles north on NM 48, then turn left on CR 532. Continue 11.9 miles to the Sierra Blanca Trailhead, on the right. GPS: N33 23.971' / W105 47.367'

THE HIKE

During the summer, it's a good idea to get an early start on this hike. Summer thunderstorms are common and can build up very quickly. You do not want to be on the high ridges above timberline when lightning is striking. Dress in layers for warmth—sudden storms can drop the temperature by 50 degrees F, or more.

Begin by following Trail #15 to the junction with the Crest Trail 25. Turn left here and follow the trail through a burned area to the junction with the Lookout Mountain Trail 78. Ice Spring is located in the drainage below the trail. Turn left on the Lookout Mountain Trail and follow it south along the crest. After you pass the upper terminal of the ski area gondola, you'll reach the summit of Lookout Mountain.

Here the hike leaves the national forest and enters the Mescalero Apache Reservation. Make sure you have a permit from the tribal offices before continuing. If the reservation is closed to access, Lookout Mountain still makes a fine destination for the hike.

To reach Sierra Blanca, continue south on a use trail. You are hiking above timberline where the alpine vegetation is very fragile; stay on the trail as much as possible. As you can well imagine, the view from the lofty summit is fine in all directions.

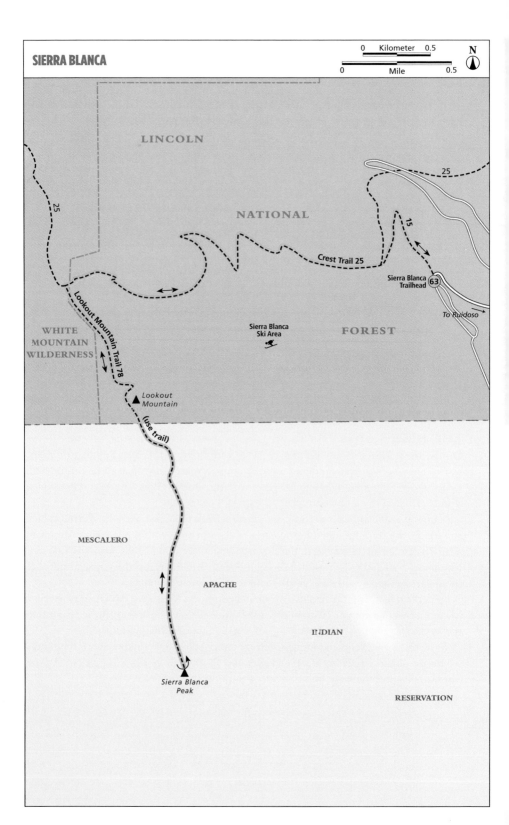

SIERRA BLANCA

0   Kilometer   0.5

0   Mile   0.5

N

LINCOLN

NATIONAL

25

25

15

Crest Trail 25

Sierra Blanca
Trailhead   63

To Ruidoso

WHITE
MOUNTAIN
WILDERNESS

Lookout Mountain Trail 78

Sierra Blanca
Ski Area

FOREST

Lookout
Mountain

(use trail)

MESCALERO

APACHE

INDIAN

Sierra Blanca
Peak

RESERVATION

Sunset in the Sierra Blanca

MILES AND DIRECTIONS

0.0 Start on Trail 15.

0.6 Junction; turn left on the Crest Trail #25.

2.5 Ice Spring.

2.8 The Crest Trail 25 goes right; turn left onto the Lookout Mountain Trail 78.

3.6 Lookout Mountain. Continue south on a use trail.

4.8 Sierra Blanca Peak; return the way you came.

9.6 Trailhead.

64 ARGENTINA CANYON

A beautiful loop day hike along mountain streams and through alpine forest in the White Mountain Wilderness.

Start: 18.8 miles west of Capitan
Distance: 6.0-mile loop
Hiking time: About 4 hours
Difficulty: Moderate
Trail surface: Dirt and rocks
Best seasons: Later spring through fall
Water: Argentina Spring, Spring Cabin Spring
Other trail users: Horses

Canine compatibility: Leashed dogs permitted
Fees and permits: None
Schedule: Open all year
Maps: CalTopo.com MapBuilder Topo layer; Gaia GPS Trails Illustrated Topo layer
Trail contacts: Lincoln National Forest, 3463 Las Palomas, Alamogordo, NM 88310; (575) 434-7200; https://www.fs.usda.gov/lincoln

FINDING THE TRAILHEAD

 From Capitan, drive 9.2 miles south on NM 48, then turn right on NM 37. Continue 1.3 miles, then bear left onto FR 107, the Bonito Lake Road. Drive 8.3 miles to the end of the road and the parking loop. GPS: N33 27.812' / W105 48.276'

THE HIKE

This hike loops up one beautiful canyon and down another in the Sierra Blanca. Water is plentiful along this loop, one of many possible loops in these mountains. And luckily, forest fires have largely spared the area of this hike, so far.

Start up Argentina Canyon Trail #39 and follow it west up Argentina Canyon alongside the rushing mountain stream. You'll pass through a beautiful mixed forest of pine, fir, and aspen. At the junction with Trail 38, stay right on the Argentina Canyon Trail 39. After a final climb up the head of the canyon, you reach Argentina Spring and the junction with Clear Water Trail 42. Turn left to stay on Trail 39, which ends at the Crest Trail 25 on the other side of a meadow.

Turn left on the Crest Trail 25 and follow it south across the bare crest and Argentina Mountain. The views from here extend for dozens of miles across southern New Mexico. After descending slightly from the peak, you'll reach a major trail junction. Turn sharply left here onto Trail 37 and follow it east down the drainage of Little Bonito Creek. You'll pass the junction with Trail 38; stay right on Trail 37.

The main arm of Bonito Creek comes in from the right, and with it Big Bonito Trail #36. Stay left and follow Big Bonito Trail east along Bonito Creek back to the trailhead.

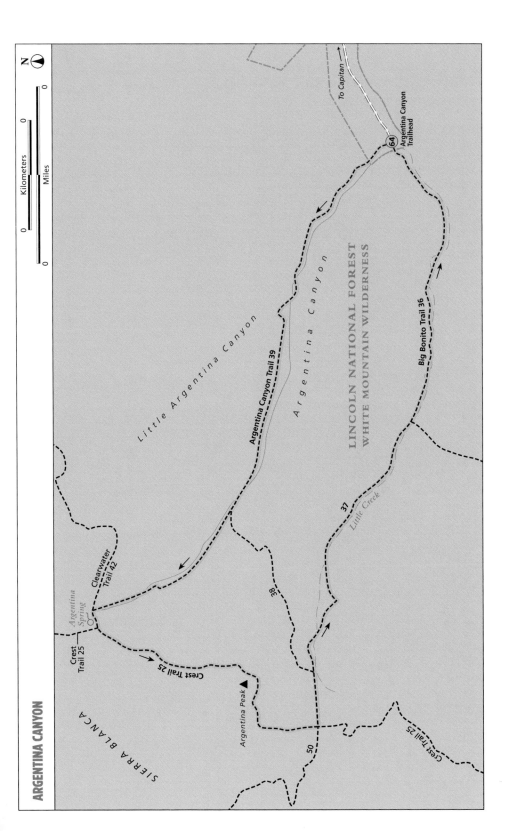

ARGENTINA CANYON

N

Kilometers

Miles

SIERRA BLANCA

Crest Trail 25

Argentina Spring

Clearwater Trail 42

Crest Trail 25

Argentina Peak

Little Argentina Canyon

Argentina Canyon Trail 39

Argentina Canyon

50

38

37

Little Creek

LINCOLN NATIONAL FOREST
WHITE MOUNTAIN WILDERNESS

Big Bonito Trail 36

Crest Trail 25

64

Argentina Canyon Trailhead

To Capitan

MILES AND DIRECTIONS

0.0   Start on the Argentina Canyon Trail #39.

1.6   Junction with Trail 38; stay right on Argentina Canyon Trail 39.

2.3   Junction with Clear Water Trail 42, and Argentina Spring. Turn left to stay on Argentina Canyon Trail.

2.4   Junction with the Crest Trail 25; turn left on the Crest Trail.

3.5   Crossroads with Trails 50, 29, and 37; turn left on Trail 37.

3.7   Trail 38 joins from left; stay right on Trail 37.

4.8   Junction with Big Bonito Trail 36; turn left.

6.0   Trailhead.

65 CAPITAN PEAK

This loop backpack trip takes you over the summit of 10,083-foot Capitan Peak and through one of the least-visited wilderness areas in New Mexico.

Start: 55.4 miles west of Roswell
Distance: 14.5-mile loop
Hiking time: 2 or 3 days
Difficulty: Strenuous
Trail surface: Dirt and rocks
Best seasons: Fall through spring
Water: Seasonal in Pine Lodge, Copeland, and Seven Cabins Canyons
Other trail users: Horses
Canine compatibility: Leashed dogs permitted

Fees and permits: None
Schedule: Open all year
Maps: CalTopo.com MapBuilder Topo layer; Gaia GPS Trails Illustrated Topo layer
Trail contacts: Lincoln National Forest, 3463 Las Palomas, Alamogordo, NM 88310; (575) 434-7200; https://www.fs.usda.gov/lincoln

FINDING THE TRAILHEAD

From Roswell, drive 4 miles north on US 285, then turn left onto NM 246. Continue 47.7 miles, then turn left on to FR 130. Drive 3.7 miles to the trailhead for the North Base Trail #65. GPS: N33 37.577' / W105 14.579'

THE HIKE

Portions of this loop, like many other forested areas of the Southwest, have been burned in recent wildfires. Trail 65 at the start and Trail 64 at the end have suffered the most. It is a good idea to check with the Forest Service office for current trail conditions while planning your trip. Carry topographic maps, a compass, and a GPS unit on this hike; trails may be faint or confused by old logging roads, especially along Trail 65. Where the forest hasn't burned, you'll be treated to beautiful stands of pine, fir, and aspen, in stark contrast to the Chihuahuan desert far below.

The North Base Trail 65 immediately crosses Pine Lodge Creek, then works its way west across the north slopes. Faint unofficial trails and old logging roads confuse this part of the trail. Climbing gradually with short descents, the trail crosses Red Lick Canyon then contours west to Copeland Canyon. Here it passes the Copeland Canyon Trail 63, which goes left, and FR 163, which goes right. Stay on the North Base Trail 65 and continue west. The trail finally drops into Seven Cabins Canyon, where there is seasonal water. This is your last chance to top off your water supply for the dry trip along the crest.

Turn left here and hike south up the canyon on Seven Cabins Trail 66. For about half a mile the trail climbs along the bed, but it soon switchbacks up the slope to the southwest to gain the ridge crest. A steady climb along the ridge west of Seven Cabins Canyon leads to the main east–west crest of the Capitan Mountains and a trail junction. Turn left on the Summit Trail 58.

Now the trail stays on the crest, crossing over a couple of minor summits before crossing the west side of Capitan Peak just below the summit. It's an easy walk through an open meadow to reach the 10,083-foot summit.

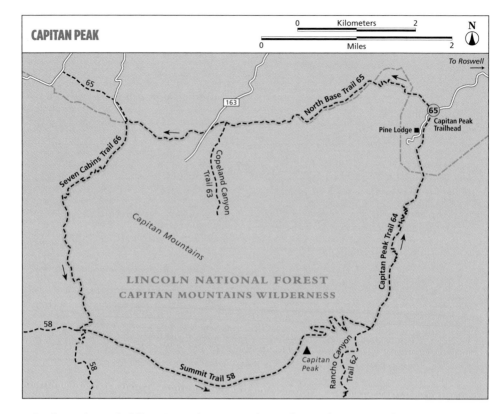

CAPITAN PEAK

Kilometers 0 ... 2

Miles 0 ... 2

N

To Roswell

65

163

North Base Trail 65

Pine Lodge ■

65

Capitan Peak Trailhead

Seven Cabins Trail 66

Copeland Canyon Trail 63

Capitan Mountains

LINCOLN NATIONAL FOREST
CAPITAN MOUNTAINS WILDERNESS

Capitan Peak Trail 64

58

58

Summit Trail 58

Capitan Peak

Rancho Canyon

Trail 62

Back on the trail, follow it northeast as it descends steeply via several switchbacks before meeting the Pancho Canyon and Capitan Peak Trails. Turn left on the Capitan Peak Trail 64.

This trail descends steeply down a ridge, often in short switchbacks, then crosses the wilderness boundary just before passing Pine Lodge. You'll reach the trailhead just after passing the lodge.

MILES AND DIRECTIONS

0.0 Start on the North Base Trail #65 and hike northwest.

0.3 Wilderness boundary.

2.7 Cross the Copeland Canyon Trail 63; continue west on North Base Trail 65.

2.9 FR 163 goes right—continue straight ahead (west) on the North Base Trail 65.

3.9 North Base Trail continues west; turn left (south) on Seven Cabins Trail 66.

7.1 Junction with Summit Trail 58 and Pierce Canyon Trail 61; turn left (east) on the Summit Trail 58.

9.7 High point of loop just below Capitan Peak.

11.4 Junction with the Capitan Peak Trail 64 and Pancho Canyon Trail 62; turn left (north) on the Capitan Peak Trail 64.

13.7 Wilderness boundary.

13.8 Pass Pine Lodge.

14.5 Trailhead.

66 WHITE SANDS

A very short but unique loop nature trail through the world's largest gypsum sand dune field.

Start: 18.4 miles west of Alamogordo
Distance: 1.0-mile loop with a cherry stem
Hiking time: About 1 hour
Difficulty: Easy
Trail surface: Sand
Best seasons: Fall through spring
Water: None
Other trail users: None

Canine compatibility: Dogs not permitted
Fees and permits: Entrance fee
Schedule: Open all year
Maps: CalTopo.com MapBuilder Topo layer; Gaia GPS Trails Illustrated layer
Trail contacts: White Sands National Park, PO Box 1086, Holloman AFB, NM 88330; (575) 479-6124; https://www.nps.gov/whsa

FINDING THE TRAILHEAD

From Alamogordo, drive 2.0 miles south on US 54, then turn right on US 70. Continue 13.6 miles to the visitor center, then turn right on Dunes Drive. Drive 2.8 miles to the marked Dune Life Nature Trail parking area. GPS: N32 47.642' / W108 12.752'

THE HIKE

Hike south on the trail toward the dunes. The trail is marked with blue trail markers—make sure you have the next one in sight before continuing. If the wind rises, visibility can become very poor in just minutes and it is easy to get lost. If this happens, turn around and retrace your steps to the trailhead.

There are fourteen trailside signs along the way, describing this unique area where the Chilhuahuan desert scrub meets the dunes. Although the area is home to many animals, including kit foxes, badgers, birds, coyotes, rodents, and reptiles, you're not likely to see any because most desert animals are nocturnal. But you'll see their tracks; each day, breezes erase the tracks from the dunes, and in the morning the animal activity has left a record.

At the start of the loop, turn left, and when the loop ends, turn left to return to the trailhead.

You can easily explore much farther into the dunes. In this case, you should carry a map, compass, and GPS unit.

Yucca on dune, White Sands National Monument

MILES AND DIRECTIONS

0.0   Walk south on the trail.

0.1   Start of loop; turn left.

0.9   End of loop; turn left to return to the trailhead.

1.0   Trailhead.

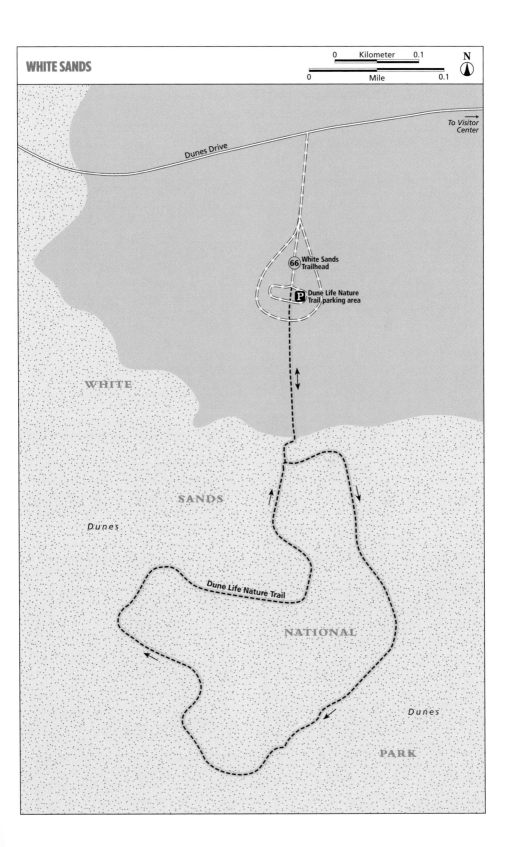

WHITE SANDS

0   Kilometer   0.1

0   Mile   0.1

N

To Visitor Center

Dunes Drive

66 White Sands Trailhead

P Dune Life Nature Trail parking area

WHITE

SANDS

Dunes

Dune Life Nature Trail

NATIONAL

Dunes

PARK

67 BLUFF SPRINGS

This day hike takes you along the historic Cloudcroft logging railroad grade, part of a system of railroad lines built into the Sacramento Mountains at the end of the 19th century.

Start: 14 miles south of Cloudcroft
Distance: 6.4-mile out-and-back
Hiking time: About 3 hours
Difficulty: Easy
Trail surface: Dirt and rocks
Best seasons: Late spring through late fall
Water: Bluff Springs at trailhead
Other trail users: Horses
Canine compatibility: Leashed dogs permitted

Fees and permits: None
Schedule: Open all year
Maps: CalTopo.com MapBuilder Topo layer; Gaia GPS Gaia Trails Illustrated layer
Trail contacts: Lincoln National Forest, 3463 Las Palomas, Alamogordo, NM 88310; (575) 434-7200; https://www.fs.usda.gov/lincoln

FINDING THE TRAILHEAD

From Cloudcroft, drive 1.8 miles south on NM 130, then turn right on Sunspot Highway, NM 6563. Continue 8.5 miles then turn left on to Upper Rio Penasco Road, FR 164. Drive 3.7 miles to the trailhead at Bluff Springs. GPS: N32 49.873' / W105 44.220'

THE HIKE

Cross the Rio Penasco on a footbridge, then join the old railroad grade (Willie White Spur Trail #112) at the base of the falls and follow it east as it climbs slowly out of the canyon. As Trail 112 crosses a ridge, the Willie White Trail 113 joins from the left. Stay right on Trail 113, which continues along the old railroad grade into Willie White Canyon. After the trail reaches the bottom of the canyon, it turns sharply left and climbs out of the canyon.

Shortly, Trail 113 makes a sharp bend to the right; go straight onto Trail 9277 (Trail 5008 on some maps), which is a continuation of the old railroad grade. The old railroad grade ends in a broad saddle—continue up a faint old road along the broad ridge to a round hill, marked "9135" on the topo maps. Return the way you came.

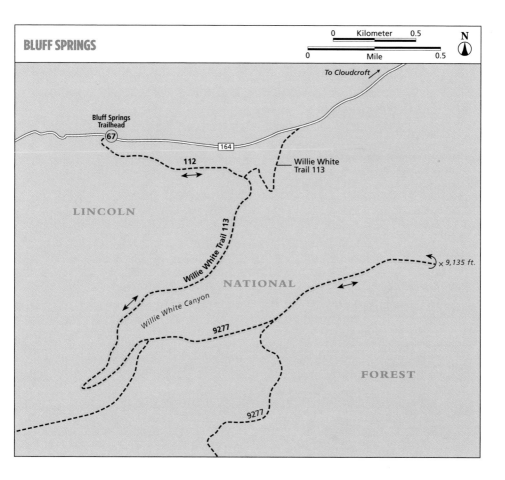

MILES AND DIRECTIONS

0.0   Cross the river and start on Trail 112.

0.6   Trail 112 ends where the Willie White Trail 113 joins from the left; stay right on Trail 113.

1.7   Trail 113 turns sharply left and leaves the canyon bottom.

2.0   Trail 113 turns sharply right; turn slightly left onto Trail 9277 (Trail 5008 on some maps).

2.5   Reach a saddle where Trail 9277 turns right; leave the official trail and follow a use trail west up the ridge.

3.2   Peak 9135 and the end of the hike; return the way you came.

6.4   Arrive back at the trailhead.

68 ICE CANYON

This is an easy day hike to a historic site on the west side of the dramatic Organ Mountains.

Start: 9.9 miles east of Las Cruces
Distance: 2.4-mile out-and-back with a small loop
Hiking time: About 2 hours
Difficulty: Easy
Trail surface: Dirt and rocks
Best seasons: Fall through spring
Water: Visitor center
Other trail users: None
Canine compatibility: Dogs not permitted
Fees and permits: Entrance fee

Schedule: 8 a.m. to 5 p.m. except winter holidays
Maps: CalTopo.com MapBuilder Topo layer
Trail contacts: Organ Mountains-Desert Peaks National Monument, Bureau of Land Management, 1800 Marquess St., Las Cruces, NM 88005-3370; (575) 525-4300; https://www.blm.gov/programs/national-conservation-lands/new-mexico/organ-mountains-desert-peaks-national-monument

FINDING THE TRAILHEAD

From I-25 in south Las Cruces, drive 9.9 miles east on Dripping Springs Road and park at the Dripping Springs Trailhead. GPS: N32 19.773' / W106 35.442'

THE HIKE

This trail leads to Dripping Springs, the site of a former mountain resort and, later, a sanatorium, dating from the 1870s. After checking in and paying the entrance fee at the visitor center, head southeast on the broad trail. Just as the canyon walls start to close in, you'll pass the ruins of an old stage stop.

When the trail splits into a small loop, stay right. You'll soon pass the ruins of Boyd's Sanatorium, which was established in 1917 when the resort went bankrupt. Just past the sanatorium ruins, you'll see the waters of Dripping Springs. Next, you'll pass the ruins of Colonel Eugene van Patten's Mountain Resort. Please don't molest or climb on any of the ruins, as they are protected under the American Antiquities Act.

At the end of the loop, stay right to return to the trailhead.

Organ Mountains

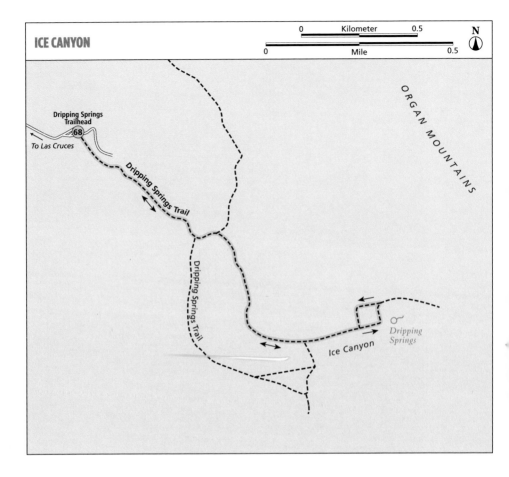

MILES AND DIRECTIONS

0.0 Trailhead.

1.1 Start of short loop section; stay right.

1.3 End of loop; stay right and retrace your steps.

2.4 Trailhead.

69 NORTH SLAUGHTER CANYON

This hike takes you into a rugged canyon in Carlsbad Caverns National Park.

Start: 16.5 miles southwest of Whites City
Distance: 5.6-mile out-and back
Hiking time: About 4 hours
Difficulty: Moderate
Trail surface: Dirt, gravel, and cobbles along dry wash
Best seasons: Fall through spring
Water: None
Other trail users: Horses

Canine compatibility: Dogs not permitted
Fees and permits: Free permit required for overnight camping
Schedule: Open all year
Maps: CalTopo.com MapBuilder Topo layer; Gaia GPS Trails Illustrated layer
Trail contacts: Carlsbad Caverns National Park; 3225 National Parks Hwy., Carlsbad, NM 88220; (575) 785-2232; https://www.nps.gov/cave/

FINDING THE TRAILHEAD

From Whites City, drive 5.4 miles southwest on US 62, then turn right onto NM 418. Continue 11.1 miles to the end of the road and the North Slaughter Canyon Trailhead. GPS: N32 6.631' / W104 33.754'

THE HIKE

From the trailhead, follow the trail north up North Slaughter Canyon, which starts out as an old road. When West Slaughter Canyon comes in from the left, the old road ends. Follow the faint trail, marked by rock cairns, north up North Slaughter Canyon. As the canyon gets narrower, Middle Slaughter Canyon comes in from the left; stay right and continue up North Slaughter Canyon. After swinging around a couple of small bends, the trail leaves the canyon bed on the left and climbs to the ridge between Middle and North Slaughter Canyons. Where the trail leaves the bed is the turnaround for the hike.

MILES AND DIRECTIONS

0.0 Start up North Slaughter Canyon following a former road.

1.0 West Slaughter Canyon comes in from the left; stay right and follow the faint trail, or the wash, up North Slaughter Canyon.

1.8 Middle Slaughter Canyon forks left; stay right in North Slaughter Canyon.

2.8 End of hike. Return the way you came. GPS: N32 8.340' / W104 34.385'

5.6 Arrive back at the trailhead.

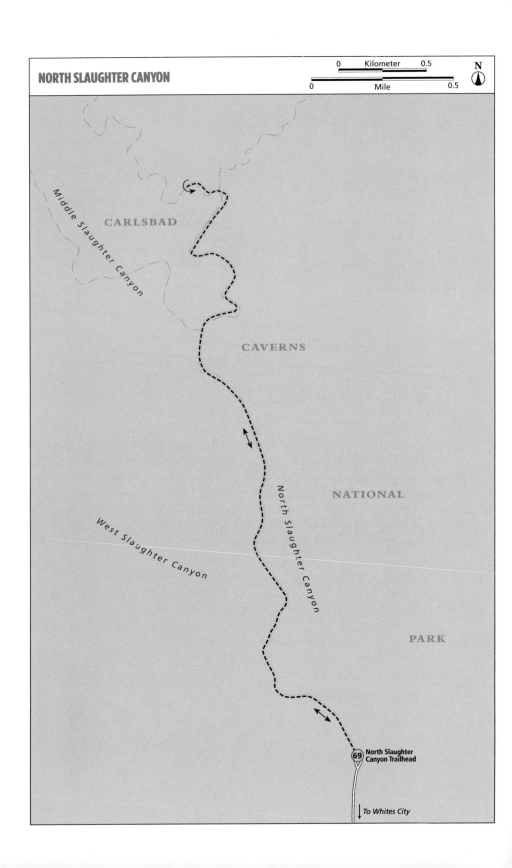

NORTH SLAUGHTER CANYON

0   Kilometer   0.5

0   Mile   0.5

N

Middle Slaughter Canyon

CARLSBAD

CAVERNS

NATIONAL

West Slaughter Canyon

North Slaughter Canyon

PARK

69 North Slaughter
    Canyon Trailhead

To Whites City

70 SITTING BULL CREEK

This day hike takes you to an impressive waterfall and one of the rare flowing streams in the Guadalupe Mountains.

Start: 41.5 miles west of Carlsbad
Distance: 2.0-mile out-and-back with a very short optional side hike to the top of the falls
Hiking time: About 1 hour
Difficulty: Easy
Trail surface: Dirt and paved trails
Best seasons: All year
Water: Trailhead, Sitting Bull Creek
Other trail users: None

Canine compatibility: Leashed dogs permitted
Fees and permits: None
Schedule: Open all year
Maps: CalTopo.com MapBuilder Topo layer; Gaia GPS Trails Illustrated Topo layer
Trail contacts: Lincoln National Forest, 3463 Las Palomas, Alamogordo, NM 88310; (575) 434-7200; https://www.fs.usda.gov/lincoln

FINDING THE TRAILHEAD

From Carlsbad, drive 11 miles north on US 283, then turn left onto NM 137. Continue 22.9 miles, then turn right onto FR 409, Sitting Bull Falls Road. Drive 7.6 miles to the trailhead at the end of the road. GPS: N32 14.719' / W104 41.810'

THE HIKE

Start the hike on Trail 68, which climbs up a bit to the west and then heads south toward the top of Sitting Bull Falls. A very short side hike on Trail 68A will take you to the top of the falls. This area is heavily used—protect it by staying on trails or bare rock.

Continue up Sitting Bull Creek on Trail 68, passing several deep pools along the way. The hike ends at Sitting Bull Spring. Return the way you came.

MILES AND DIRECTIONS

0.0 Start on Trail 68 from the north side of the parking lot.

0.4 Trail 68A goes left a short distance to the top of Sitting Bull Falls—this is optional.

1.0 Sitting Bull Spring; return the way you came.

2.0 Trailhead.

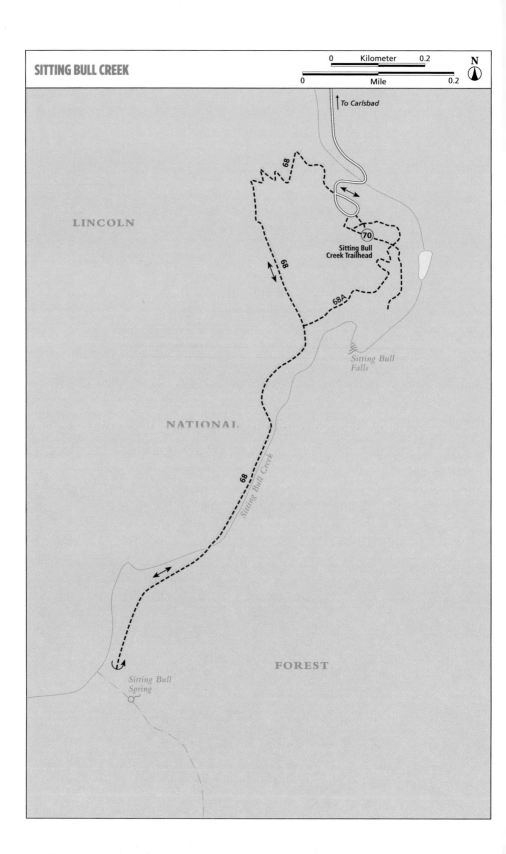

SITTING BULL CREEK

0   Kilometer   0.2

0   Mile   0.2

N

To Carlsbad

68

70

Sitting Bull
Creek Trailhead

68

LINCOLN

68A

Sitting Bull
Falls

NATIONAL

68

Sitting Bull Creek

FOREST

Sitting Bull
Spring

SOUTHWESTERN COLORADO

71 BIG DOMINGUEZ CANYON

This long day hike takes you up a red sandstone canyon cut into the Uncompahgre Plateau, leading past ancient rock art panels.

Start: 22.7 miles northwest of Delta
Distance: 12.6-mile out-and-back
Hiking time: About 8 hours
Difficulty: Strenuous
Trail surface: Dirt and rocks
Best seasons: Spring and fall
Water: Seasonal in Big Dominguez Canyon
Other trail users: Horses
Canine compatibility: Leashed dogs permitted

Fees and permits: None. No camping in lower Big Dominguez Canyon.
Schedule: Open all year
Maps: CalTopo.com MapBuilder Topo layer; Gaia GPS Trails Illustrated layer
Trail contacts: Dominguez-Escalante National Conservation Area, 2815 H Rd., Grand Junction, CO 81505; (970) 244-3000; https://www.blm.gov/programs/national-conservation-lands/colorado/dominguez-escalante-nca

FINDING THE TRAILHEAD

From Delta, drive 19.5 miles west on US 50, then turn left on Bridgeport Road. Continue 3.2 miles to the Dominguez Canyon Trailhead, on the right, next to the railroad tracks and the Gunnison River. GPS: N38 50.962' / W108 22.344'

THE HIKE

Watch for rock art panels along this hike, evidence that humans have been using Big Dominguez Canyon for at least 10,000 years. These petroglyphs are extremely fragile and are easily damaged by oil from your skin, so please do not touch.

The canyons are also home to desert bighorn sheep, which were reintroduced in the 1980s. Keep a lookout for these graceful animals along high ledges and the canyon rims. If you hike with a dog, be sure to keep it under control on a leash so that it doesn't stress the bighorn sheep and other wild animals.

The hike follows the Big Dominguez Canyon to the junction with the Cactus Park Trail, but you can hike as much or as little of the canyon as you want.

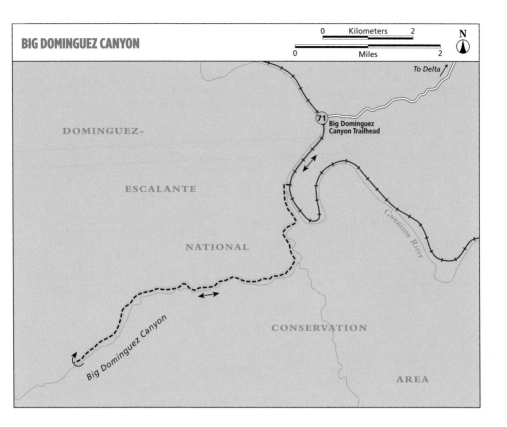

BIG DOMINGUEZ CANYON

0 Kilometers 2

0 Miles 2

N

To Delta

71 Big Dominguez
Canyon Trailhead

DOMINGUEZ–

ESCALANTE

NATIONAL

CONSERVATION

AREA

Gunnison River

Big Dominguez Canyon

MILES AND DIRECTIONS

0.0 Start along the railroad tracks. The first 0.3 mile follows the tracks—if a train is present, wait until it's gone before proceeding.

0.9 Private bridge across the river—do not use.

1.0 Cross the river on the public bridge.

1.7 Wilderness boundary in the mouth of Big Dominguez Canyon.

2.3 Confluence of Big and Little Dominguez Canyons; stay right on the trail to Big Dominguez Canyon.

3.1 Spur trail on the left, leading to a seasonal waterfall.

4.0 End of day-use area.

6.1 Old mine.

6.3 End of hike at Cactus Park Trail junction; return the way you came.

12.6 Arrive back at the trailhead.

This day hike runs along the north rim of the Black Canyon of the Gunnison and takes you to two spectacular viewpoints.

Start: 13.1 miles southwest of Crawford
Distance: 6.7-mile out-and-back with two small loops
Hiking time: 4 hours
Difficulty: Moderate
Trail surface: Dirt and rocks
Best seasons: Late spring through fall
Water: None
Other trail users: None
Canine compatibility: Dogs not permitted

Fees and permits: Entrance fee. Free backcountry permits are required for overnight trips or hiking in the inner canyon.
Schedule: Apr through Nov, depending on snowfall
Maps: CalTopo.com MapBuilder Topo layer; Gaia GPS Trails Illustrated layer
Trail contacts: Black Canyon of the Gunnison National Park, 800 Hwy. 347, Montrose, CO 81230; (970) 641-2337; https://www.nps.gov/blca/

FINDING THE TRAILHEAD

From Crawford, drive 3.8 miles west and south on Fruitland Mesa Road, then turn left on CR 7745. Continue 1.2 miles then turn right on Black Canyon Road. Drive 8.1 miles to the trailhead and the North Rim Ranger Station, on the right. GPS: N38 35.203' / W107 42.312'

THE HIKE

Follow the trail northwest through open sage meadows and piñon-juniper woodland. After about 0.5 mile, the trail skirts the north rim of Black Canyon, offering occasional excellent views. When the trail meets the spur trail to Exclamation Point, turn left and follow the trail out to the point and around the short loop. The point is well named and offers some of the best views of Black Canyon from either rim.

After the loop, retrace your steps to the main trail and turn left. After skirting a side canyon, the trail leaves the immediate rim and climbs northwest to the top of Green Mountain. A small loop trail offers 360-degree panoramic vistas of western Colorado, including the San Juan Mountains, the West Elks, Grand Mesa, the Uncompahgre Plateau, and an aerial perspective of the Black Canyon.

Unlike canyons made of softer rock, the hard metamorphic rocks of Black Canyon have created a deep and very narrow canyon. Without major tributaries to help widen the canyon, the Gunnison River has carved a slot more than 2,000 feet deep, as narrow as 40 feet at the river, and 1,100 feet wide at Chasm View. The Painted Wall, Colorado's tallest cliff, is more than 2,000 feet from base to rim.

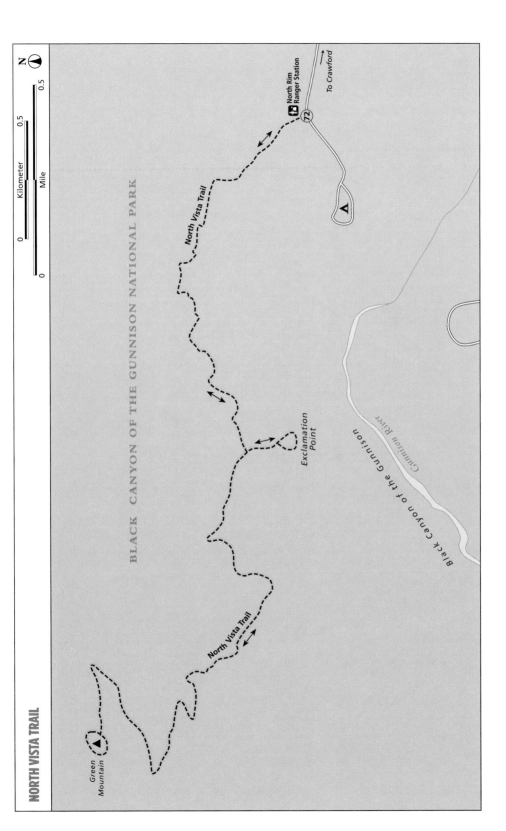

NORTH VISTA TRAIL

BLACK CANYON OF THE GUNNISON NATIONAL PARK

North Vista Trail

North Vista Trail

Green Mountain

Exclamation Point

North Rim Ranger Station

72

To Crawford

Black Canyon of the Gunnison

Gunnison River

N

Kilometer
0   0.5   0.5

Mile
0   0.5

MILES AND DIRECTIONS

0.0 Leave the trailhead and hike northwest on the North Vista Trail.

1.2 Turn left on the side trail to Exclamation Point. Follow the trail out to the viewpoint, around the short loop, and back out to the main trail.

1.6 Turn left on the North Vista Trail.

3.4 Start the short loop on the summit of Green Mountain by turning left.

3.6 Complete the loop and return the way you came.

6.7 Trailhead.

73 CASCADE AND PORTLAND LOOP

This loop day hike follows the Upper Cascade Falls and Portland trails to waterfalls and historic mining sites.

Start: East side of Ouray
Distance: 6.4-mile loop including a 3.1-mile out-and-back section
Hiking time: About 4 hours
Difficulty: Strenuous
Trail surface: Dirt and rocks
Best seasons: Late spring through early fall
Water: Portland and Cascade Creeks
Other trail users: Horses

Canine compatibility: Leashed dogs permitted
Fees and permits: None
Schedule: Open all year
Maps: CalTopo.com MapBuilder Topo layer; Gaia GPS Trails Illustrated layer
Trail contacts: Uncompahgre National Forest, 2250 S. Main St., Delta, CO 81416; (970) 874-6600; https://www.fs.usda.gov/gmug

FINDING THE TRAILHEAD

From Ouray, drive 0.9 mile south on US 550, then turn left on the Amphitheater Campground Road, FR 855. Drive 1.2 miles to the trailhead at the end of the campground. GPS: N38 1.326' / W107 39.631'

THE HIKE

Follow the trail southwest and then southeast from the trailhead to a junction. The loop portion of the hike starts here—turn left on the Upper Cascade Falls Trail and follow it as it switchbacks northeast up a ridge. It meets the Lower Cascade Falls Trail; stay right on the Upper Cascade Falls Trail. After a short climb to the east, turn left on the Upper Cascade Falls Trail. This is the start of the out-and-back section; the loop hike will resume from this junction.

The Upper Cascades Falls Trail switchbacks steeply up the slope to the north, then levels out and traverses the hillside to Cascade Creek and Upper Cascade Falls. Cross the creek, using care for the falls just below, and follow the trail west to the remains of the Chief Ouray Mine. From here, retrace your steps to the Portland Trail Junction.

Turn left to resume the loop portion on the Portland Trail. The trail descends east to cross a tributary of Portland Creek, then turns southwest along the ridge above Portland Creek itself. Broad switchbacks descend west through the spruce-fir-aspen forest to a trail junction, where you'll turn right on the Upper Cascade Falls Trail. A final junction closes the loop; turn left to hike the short distance to the trailhead.

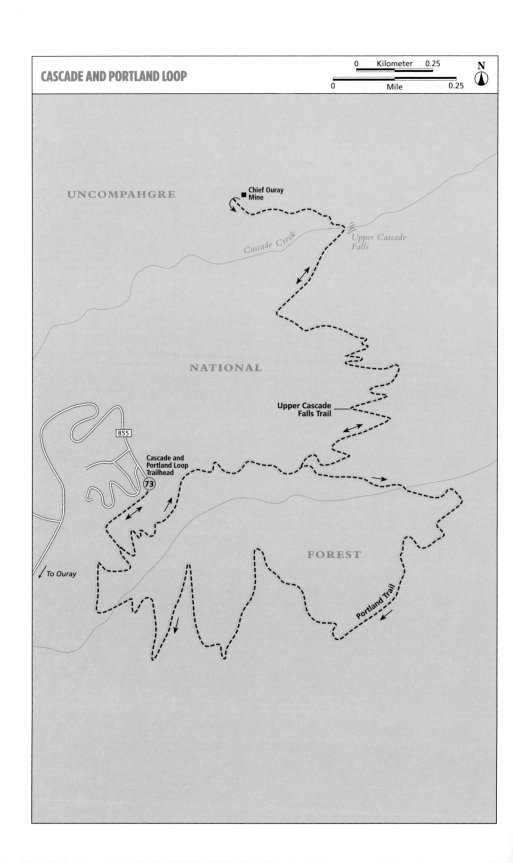

0   Kilometer   0.25

0   Mile   0.25

N

UNCOMPAHGRE

■ Chief Ouray
Mine

Cascade Creek

Upper Cascade
Falls

NATIONAL

Upper Cascade
Falls Trail

855

Cascade and
Portland Loop
Trailhead

73

FOREST

To Ouray

Portland Trail

MILES AND DIRECTIONS

0.0 Head southwest on the trail from the parking area.

0.2 Turn left on the Upper Cascade Falls Trail. You'll return to this junction after hiking the loop.

0.5 Junction with the Lower Cascade Falls Trail; stay right on the Portland Trail.

0.8 Turn left on the Upper Cascade Falls Trail; the Portland Trail goes right—this will be our loop trail after the out-and-back to Chief Ouray Mine.

2.1 Upper Cascade Falls.

2.3 Chief Ouray Mine; retrace your steps to the Portland Trail.

3.9 Turn left on the Portland Trail to continue the loop.

5.9 Junction—turn right on the Portland Trail.

6.2 Junction with the Upper Cascade Falls Trail; turn left to return to the trailhead.

6.4 Trailhead.

Just the approach to this hike along US 550, the "million dollar high-way," is stunning. The trail itself climbs through beautiful aspen forest to a 12,600-foot pass with amazing views of the southwestern Colorado mountains.

Start: 8 miles south of Ouray
Distance: 5.2-mile out-and-back
Hiking time: About 4 hours
Difficulty: Strenuous
Trail surface: Dirt and rocks
Best seasons: Summer through fall
Water: None
Other trail users: Horses
Canine compatibility: Leashed dogs permitted

Fees and permits: None
Schedule: Open all year
Maps: CalTopo.com MapBuilder Topo layer; Gaia GPS Trails Illustrated layer
Trail contacts: Uncompahgre National Forest, 2250 S. Main St., Delta, CO 81416; (970) 874-6600; https://www. fs.usda.gov/gmug

FINDING THE TRAILHEAD

 From Ouray, drive south 7.7 miles on US 550. Just 0.2 mile after passing CR 20D on the left, turn right onto a small dirt road, and then immediately left on another dirt road that ends at the small trailhead. GPS: N37 56.004' / W107 40.991'

THE HIKE

US 550 is an engineering marvel that traverses the rugged San Juan Mountains. Heavy snowfall and steep slopes combine to create a severe avalanche hazard in the winter, as shown by the snowshed structures protecting the most exposed parts of the highway, and by the numerous avalanche zone warning signs. A number of people have lost their lives in avalanches along the highway, including a Disney cameraman who was shooting avalanche control work. A lack of guardrails makes the highway seem even more vertiginous, but snowplow operators have nowhere to put the snow along many stretches of the road, so they have to push it over the edge.

The section between Ouray and the trailhead is highly mineralized and was once one of the most productive mining regions in Colorado. Remains of the mines are visible from the highway and the trail.

The first section of the trail follows an old road, but soon becomes a footpath as it steadily switchbacks up the mountainside through stands of quaking aspen. As you climb, you'll start to pick up views of the striking summits of Red Mountain #1, #2, and #3.

At the north end of the last switchback, a faint trail goes right; stay left on the Richmond Trail. The climb relents a bit as the trail comes out on a ridge with views of Richmond Mountain to the north, and Richmond Pass, your destination, to the northwest. A final climb takes you to the pass. After taking in the expansive views, return the way you came.

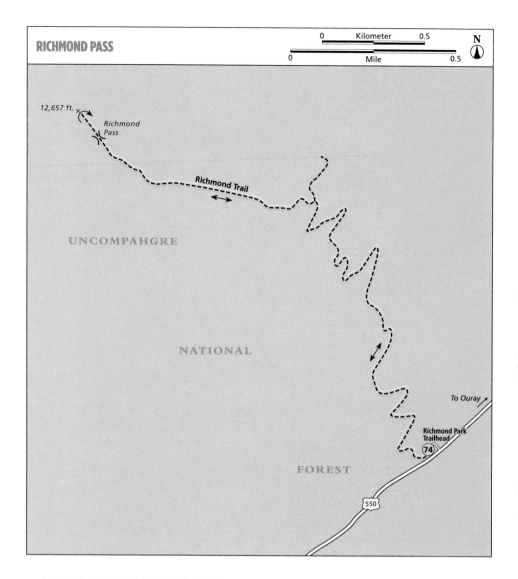

RICHMOND PASS

12,657 ft.

Richmond
Pass

Richmond Trail

UNCOMPAHGRE

NATIONAL

To Ouray

Richmond Park
Trailhead

74

FOREST

550

0   Kilometer   0.5

0   Mile   0.5

N

MILES AND DIRECTIONS

0.0 Start up the Richmond Trail.

1.7 Junction; stay left on the Richmond Trail.

2.6 Richmond Pass; return the way you came.

5.2 Trailhead.

75 BILK BASIN

This overnight backpack trip takes you into a scenic and less-visited western outlier of the San Juan Mountains. There are options for extended exploration.

Start: 15.7 miles south of Telluride
Distance: 18.8-mile out-and-back
Hiking time: 2 or 3 days
Difficulty: Strenuous
Trail surface: Dirt and rocks
Best seasons: Summer through fall
Water: Bilk Creek
Other trail users: Horses
Canine compatibility: Leashed dogs permitted

Fees and permits: None
Schedule: Open all year
Maps: CalTopo.com MapBuilder Topo layer; Gaia GPS Trails Illustrated layer
Trail contacts: Uncompahgre National Forest, 2250 S. Main St., Delta, CO 81416; (970) 874-6600; https://www.fs.usda.gov/gmug

FINDING THE TRAILHEAD

From Telluride, drive 15.7 miles south on US 550 to Lizard Head Pass. The Lizard Head Trailhead is on the right. GPS: N37 48.787' / W107 54.392'

THE HIKE

From the trailhead, follow the Lizard Head Trail northeast up the slopes above Lizard Head Pass. As the trail climbs across meadows and through stands of quaking aspen, you'll get great views of the pass and Trout Lake. A few switchbacks lead to a pass, where the trail turns southwest and climbs the long ridge over Black Face Mountain. You're above timberline now, and the views of the western San Juan Mountains are stunning in all directions. Black Face Mountain is just a high point on the ridge, but it makes a good turnaround point for a day hike.

The Lizard Head Trail drops west into the broad saddle at the head of Wilson Creek, then works its way up to the base of Lizard Head and the junction with the Cross Mountain Trail. Stay right here and follow the Lizard Head Trail across the south slopes of Lizard Head to the saddle between Lizard Head and Cross Mountain.

Follow the trail north as it descends into Bilk Basin and crosses the main arm of Bilk Creek, then contours along the west side of the basin. When the trail reaches the fork of Bilk Creek lying between Wilson and Gladstone Peaks, the Lizard Head Trail turns right and descends the canyon. Turn left here on an informal trail that heads west. After a few switchbacks, the trail heads west and comes out into a glacial cirque with a small, unnamed lake. This wild and isolated spot is the destination for this hike. There are excellent campsites in the area around the lake.

Extended trips are possible from this point. The informal trail continues over the pass to the west, and connects to trails into Navajo Basin and Silver Pick Basin.

Camp along the Lizard Head Trail

MILES AND DIRECTIONS

0.0   Leave the trailhead on the Lizard Head Trail.

2.1   Saddle.

3.4   Black Face Mountain; this is a good goal for a day hike.

4.5   Saddle.

6.0   Junction with the Cross Mountain Trail; stay right on Lizard Head Trail.

6.4   Pass.

8.2   Fork of Bilk Creek and trail junction; turn left on the informal trail and hike west into Bilk Basin.

9.4   Bilk Basin; return the way you came.

18.8 Trailhead.

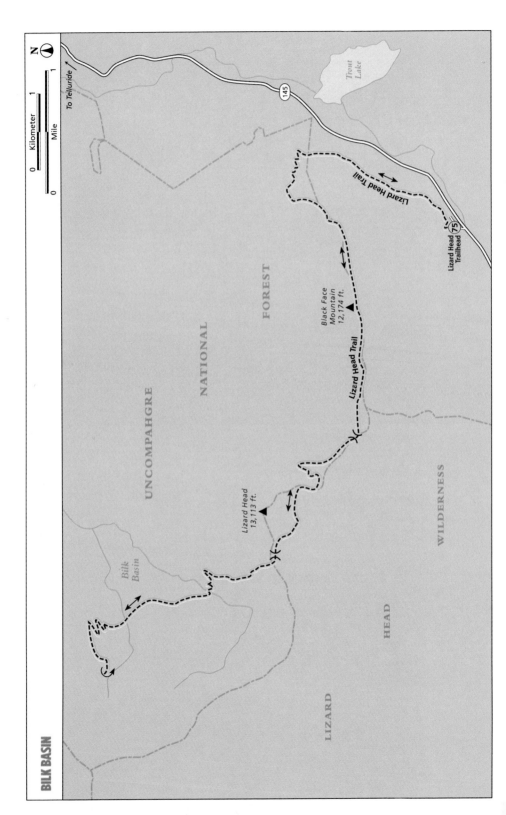

BILK BASIN

Bilk
Basin

Lizard Head
13,113 ft.

Lizard Head Trail

Black Face
Mountain
12,174 ft.

UNCOMPAHGRE

NATIONAL

FOREST

LIZARD

HEAD

WILDERNESS

Lizard Head Trail

Lizard Head
Trailhead

75

145

Trout
Lake

To Telluride

N

0   Kilometer   1

0   Mile   1

76 LAKE HOPE

This moderate day hike takes you to a beautiful artificial lake set in a high alpine cirque in the San Miguel Mountains.

Start: 17.3 miles south of Telluride
Distance: 4.4-mile out-and-back
Hiking time: About 4 hours
Difficulty: Moderate
Trail surface: Dirt and rocks
Best seasons: Summer through fall
Water: Creeks, Lake Hope
Other trail users: Horses
Canine compatibility: Leashed dogs permitted

Fees and permits: None
Schedule: Forest roads are closed by snow in winter and spring.
Maps: CalTopo.com MapBuilder Topo layer; Gaia GPS Trails Illustrated layer
Trail contacts: Uncompahgre National Forest, 2250 S. Main St., Delta, CO 81416; (970) 874-6600; https://www.fs.usda.gov/gmug

FINDING THE TRAILHEAD

From Telluride, drive 3 miles west on CO 145, then turn right to remain on CO 145. Continue 10.1 miles, then turn left on Trout Lake Road, FR 63. Drive 1.7 miles, then turn left on to Lake Hope Road, FR 627 (this road is closed in winter). Continue 2.5 miles to the trailhead, on the right. GPS: N37 48.296' / W107 51.107'

THE HIKE

Start out on the Lake Hope Trail, which heads east, crosses a creek in Poverty Gulch, then turns south, climbing steadily. The view soon opens out as you start to cross rock slides and avalanche paths on the west slopes of Vermilion Peak. After crossing an unnamed creek and then Lake Fork Creek, the trail starts to switchback up a steeper ridge. After emerging into alpine meadows above timberline, the trail climbs to a low pass, where Lake Hope comes into view.

Despite being a reservoir created by a small earth fill dam, Lake Hope's stunning setting makes it a worthy destination. This is also a great hike for summer wildflowers.

Blue columbine, Lake Hope Trail

MILES AND DIRECTIONS

0.0   Hike south on the Lake Hope Trail.

0.3   Cross Poverty Gulch, and follow the trail as it turns south.

0.9   Cross an unnamed creek.

1.1   Cross Lake Fork Creek.

2.2   Lake Hope; return the way you came.

4.4   Trailhead.

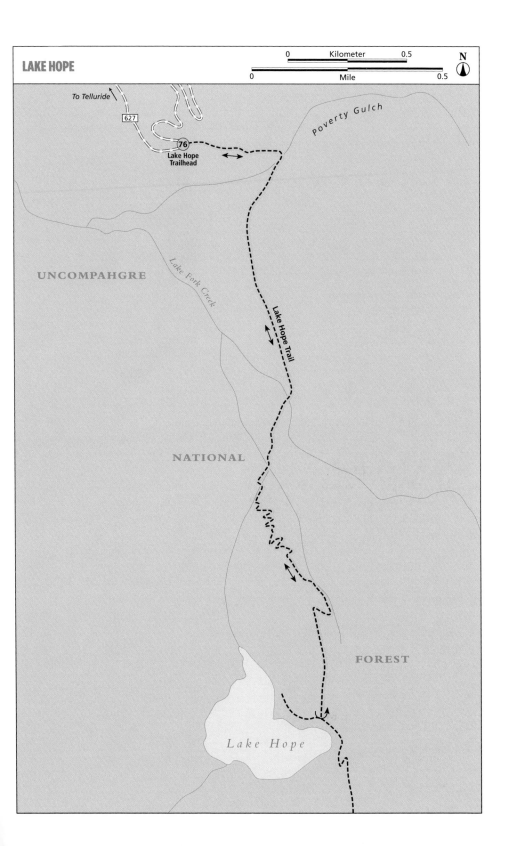

77 ICE LAKE TRAIL

Although extremely popular, the expansive alpine tundra, meadows, and lakes make this a hike that's worth the effort. It's best to arrive at the trailhead by 7 a.m., as all the parking is often taken later in the day.

Start: 6.9 miles east of Silverton
Distance: 8.0-mile out-and-back, with optional side trips
Hiking time: About 5 hours
Difficulty: Strenuous
Trail surface: Dirt and rocks
Best seasons: Summer and fall
Water: Streams near Ice Lake Basin, Ice Lake, Fuller Lake
Other trail users: Horses

Canine compatibility: Leashed dogs permitted
Fees and permits: None
Schedule: Open all year
Maps: CalTopo.com MapBuilder Topo layer; Gaia GPS Trails Illustrated layer
Trail contacts: San Juan National Forest, 15 Burnett Ct., Durango, CO 81301; (970) 247-4874; https://www .fs.usda.gov/sanjuan

FINDING THE TRAILHEAD

From Silverton, drive 3 miles north on US 550, then turn left on FR 585 and drive 3.9 miles to the trailhead, on the right. N37 48.389' / W107 46.417'

THE HIKE

From the trailhead, follow the Ice Lake Trail as it climbs generally westward along the heavily forested slopes above South Mineral Creek. Occasional switchbacks bring the well-used trail to timberline and Lower Ice Lake Basin, where there is a bit of a break from the climb. A final climb up the grassy slopes to the west brings you to the rim of Ice Lake Basin, a series of broad glacial cirques lying between Fuller and US Grant Peaks.

Just before reaching Ice Lake, the Island Lake Trail comes in on the right. This trail offers a 1.0-mile out-and-back side hike north to Island Lake, a small, nearly square lake with a small island in the middle.

Back on the main trail, follow it south up a broad bench past a small unnamed lake to Fuller Lake, the largest lake in the basin. From here, return the way you came.

Though the Ice Lake Trail and Ice Lake can be very crowded, Ice Lake Basin is a large, open expanse of alpine meadows that invites easy cross-country exploration.

MILES AND DIRECTIONS

0.0 Follow the Ice Lake Trail west as it climbs the forested slopes above the South Fork Mineral Creek.

2.2 Lower Ice Lake Basin.

3.1 Junction with optional Island Lake Trail in Ice Lake Basin; turn left on Ice Lake Trail.

3.3 Ice Lake.

3.5 Unnamed lake.

4.0 Fuller Lake; return the way you came.

8.0 Trailhead.

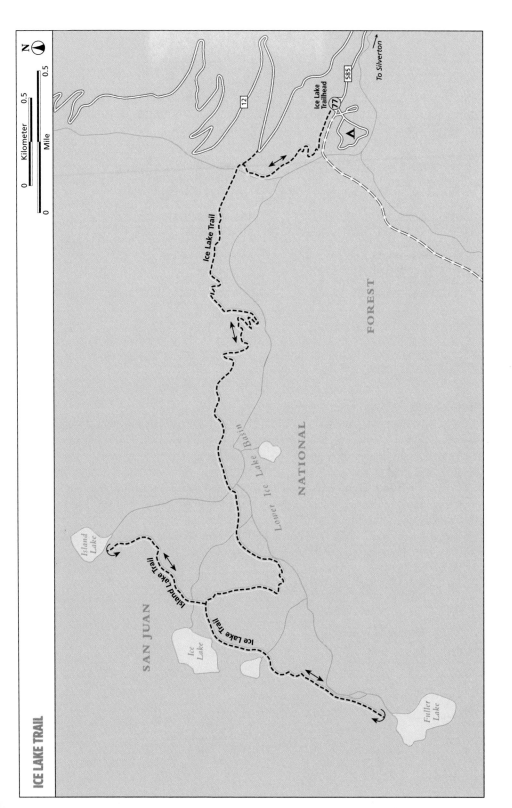

ICE LAKE TRAIL

N

0   Kilometer   0.5
0   Mile   0.5

To Silverton

585

Ice Lake Trailhead

77

12

Ice Lake Trail

FOREST

NATIONAL

Lower Ice Lake Basin

SAN JUAN

Island Lake

Island Lake Trail

Ice Lake

Ice Lake Trail

Fuller Lake

78 PASS CREEK TRAIL

This day hike takes you across alpine meadows to a high pass north of Engineer Mountain for fine views of the Weminuche Wilderness to the east. This is an excellent hike for viewing mountain wildflowers.

Start: 14.2 miles south of Silverton
Distance: 6.6-mile out-and-back
Hiking time: About 5 hours
Difficulty: Strenuous
Trail surface: Dirt and rocks
Best seasons: Summer through fall
Water: None
Other trail users: Horses
Canine compatibility: Leashed dogs permitted

Fees and permits: None
Schedule: Open all year
Maps: CalTopo.com MapBuilder Topo layer; Gaia GPS Trails Illustrated layer
Trail contacts: Uncompahgre National Forest, 2250 S. Main St., Delta, CO 81416; (970) 874-6600; https://www.fs.usda.gov/gmug

FINDING THE TRAILHEAD

From Silverton, drive 14.2 miles south on US 550. At Coal Bank Pass, turn right into the Engineer Mountain Trailhead (Pass Creek Trailhead on some maps). GPS: N37 41.949' / W107 46 7.38'

THE HIKE

Initially, the trail climbs north and northeast up the slope above Coal Bank Pass, but then soon reaches less-steep terrain. Turning west, the trail soon passes a small pond in a meadow then climbs west through alpine forest and meadow. You'll have great views of Engineer Mountain as you approach it.

Just before the base of the mountain, the trail climbs above timberline, then reaches a trail junction. Turn right on the Engineer Mountain Trail and head north. The trail drops slightly into a broad pass, which is the end of the hike.

There are many trails in the area that make longer loops and backpack trips possible, though you'll need a car shuttle for most of them.

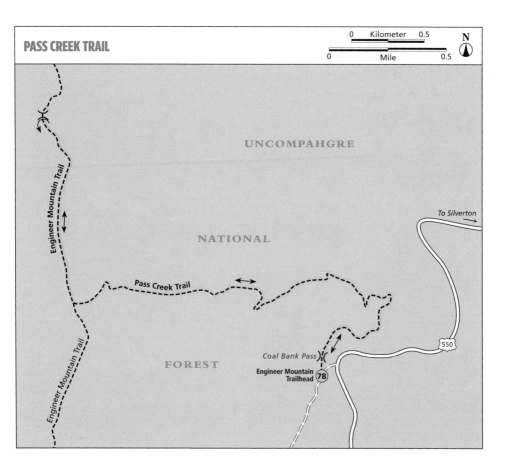

PASS CREEK TRAIL

0 Kilometer 0.5
0 Mile 0.5

N

UNCOMPAHGRE

To Silverton

NATIONAL

Engineer Mountain Trail

Pass Creek Trail

FOREST

Engineer Mountain Trail

Coal Bank Pass

Engineer Mountain
Trailhead 78

550

MILES AND DIRECTIONS

0.0   Start on the Pass Creek Trail.

1.1   Small pond on the left.

2.3   Engineer Mountain Trail; turn right.

3.3   Unnamed pass; return the way you came.

6.6   Arrive back at the trailhead.

79 ELDORADO LAKE

An overnight or longer backpack trip, this hike takes you across the Animas River gorge, up a scenic glacial canyon, and into the high peaks of the San Juan Mountains.

Start: 5 miles south of Silverton
Distance: 26.2-mile out-and-back
Hiking time: About 3 days
Difficulty: Strenuous
Trail surface: Dirt and rocks
Best seasons: Summer and fall
Water: Animas River, Elk Creek, Eldorado Lake
Other trail users: Horses

Canine compatibility: Leashed dogs permitted
Fees and permits: None
Schedule: Open all year
Maps: CalTopo.com MapBuilder Topo layer; Gaia GPS Trails Illustrated layer
Trail contacts: San Juan National Forest, 15 Burnett Ct., Durango, CO 81301; (970) 247-4874; https://www .fs.usda.gov/sanjuan

FINDING THE TRAILHEAD:

From Silverton, drive 5 miles south on US 550, then turn left onto the Molas Lake Road and park at the trailhead on the lakeshore. GPS: N27 44.904' / W107 41.034'

THE HIKE

From the trailhead on the north side of Molas Lake, follow the Molas Trail south along the west shore of the lake. After crossing the outlet stream from the lake, the trail descends and turns east along a bench above Molas Creek. Switchbacks then lead down to the confluence of Molas Creek and the Animas River. Cross the river on a footbridge, and follow the trail (now the Elk Creek Trail) south along the river. There are campsites along the river, and there won't be any more good campsites for several miles. After the trail crosses the tracks and enters the wilderness area, it begins to climb above the river. The trail turns east and crosses a forested ridge before descending to Elk Creek. Now the trail follows the creek eastward—in about a mile the canyon bottom opens a bit.

Now the trail climbs away from the creek onto a bench and eventually passes a small, unnamed lake with excellent campsites and views. The trail descends to creekside again and continues east through open meadows. Where a major tributary enters from the north, the main creek and the trail turn southeast. The trail turns east again and climbs along the north slopes in a few switchbacks. Finally, at the headwaters, the trail climbs above timberline and switchbacks up to the Continental Divide. The official trail (part of the Colorado Trail), turns left, but instead turn right here on an informal trail. Follow the ridge south for about 0.3 mile, then turn right on another informal trail and hike west down easy, open slopes to Eldorado Lake.

There are unlimited campsites near the lake that can serve as a base for further exploration of the San Juan Mountains.

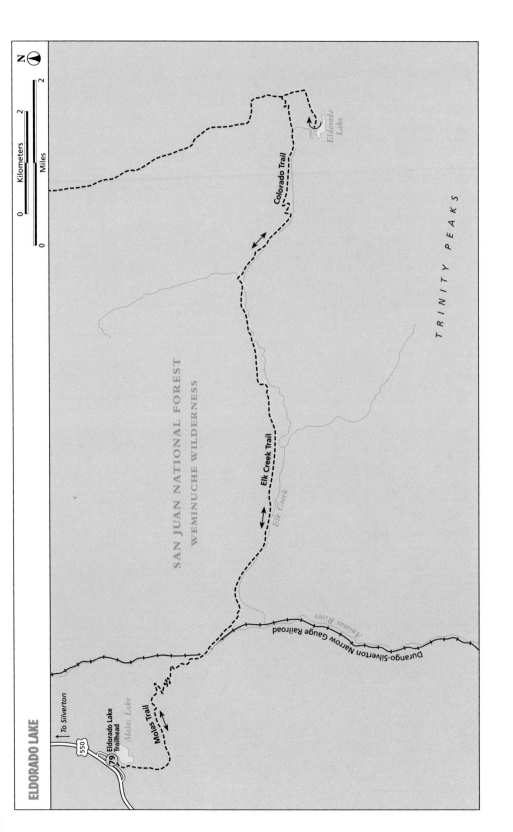

ELDORADO LAKE

To Silverton

550

Eldorado Lake
Trailhead

Molas Lake

Molas Trail

Durango-Silverton Narrow Gauge Railroad

Animas River

SAN JUAN NATIONAL FOREST
WEMINUCHE WILDERNESS

Elk Creek Trail

Elk Creek

Colorado Trail

Eldorado
Lake

T R I N I T Y   P E A K S

N

Kilometers
0   2

Miles
0   2

MILES AND DIRECTIONS

0.0 Start on the Molas Trail and follow it south along the west side of Molas Lake.

3.8 Cross the Animas River on a footbridge—the trail becomes the Elk Creek Trail.

4.0 Cross the Durango and Silverton Railroad tracks and the wilderness boundary.

5.1 The Elk Creek Trail descends to Elk Creek.

7.2 Bench and small, unnamed lake.

12.3 Ridge at the head of Elk Creek; turn right (south) on an informal trail.

12.6 Turn right on another informal trail, and hike west down the slope toward Eldorado Lake.

13.1 Eldorado Lake; return the way you came.

26.2 Trailhead.

80 HIGHLAND MARY LAKES

The day hike or multiday backpack trip takes you into an area of high alpine lakes in the San Juan Mountains with many possibilities for extended exploration.

Start: 9.1 miles east of Silverton
Distance: 4.8-mile out-and-back
Hiking time: About 3 hours
Difficulty: Moderate
Trail surface: Dirt and rocks
Best seasons: Summer through fall
Water: Highland Mary Creek and lakes
Other trail users: Horses
Canine compatibility: Leashed dogs permitted

Fees and permits: None
Schedule: The access road is closed in winter.
Maps: CalTopo.com MapBuilder Topo layer; Gaia GPS Trails Illustrated layer
Trail contacts: San Juan National Forest, 15 Burnett Ct., Durango, CO 81301; (970) 247-4874; https://www.fs.usda.gov/sanjuan

FINDING THE TRAILHEAD

From Silverton, drive about 1 mile east on CR 20, then turn left on CR 2. Drive 3.5 miles, then turn right on CR 4. Drive 4.6 miles to the end of the road and the Highland Mary Lakes Trailhead. GPS: N37 46.962' / W107 34.838'

THE HIKE

Although the approach to the trailhead involves a long gravel road, it's worth it as this hike starts from a high trailhead and takes you to a beautiful complex of alpine lakes set in a 12,000-foot glacial basin. There are many possibilities for extended exploration and multiday backpack trips in this area.

Hike south on the Highland Mary Lakes Trail, which climbs up the headwaters of Cunningham Creek through patches of alpine forest. As it reaches timberline, the trail swings southwest for a bit, then turns southeast and reaches the first of the Highland Mary Lakes. It then passes along the east side of a larger lake, and then climbs slightly onto the low ridge west of the largest of the lakes. This is the destination for our day hike, but you can continue and connect to other trails in the area, including the Continental Divide Trail. Cross-country exploration is also easy, but make sure you bring a topographic map, compass, and GPS unit.

For backpackers, water and gorgeous campsites are plentiful.

MILES AND DIRECTIONS

0.0   From the trailhead, hike south on the Highland Mary Lakes Trail.

0.9   Wilderness boundary.

1.9   First of the Highland Mary Lakes.

2.1   Second lake.

2.4   Third lake; return the way you came.

4.8   Trailhead.

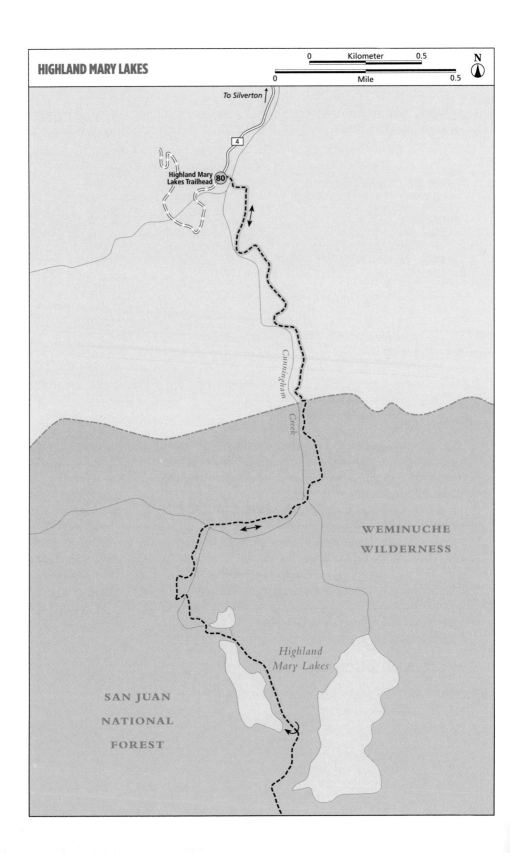

0   Kilometer   0.5

0   Mile   0.5

N

To Silverton

4

Highland Mary
Lakes Trailhead   80

Cunningham Creek

WEMINUCHE
WILDERNESS

Highland
Mary Lakes

SAN JUAN

NATIONAL

FOREST

81 ENDLICH MESA

This backpack trip starts from an 11,000-foot trailhead, and is at or above timberline for much of the way. It avoids the long hike through dense forest of other approaches to the high peaks of the San Juan Mountains.

Start: 30.9 miles northeast of Durango
Distance: 24.4-mile out-and-back
Hiking time: About 3 days
Difficulty: Strenuous
Trail surface: Dirt and rocks
Best seasons: Summer through fall
Water: City Reservoir, Columbine Lake
Other trail users: Horses
Canine compatibility: Leashed dogs permitted

Fees and permits: None
Schedule: Access road closed in winter
Maps: CalTopo.com MapBuilder Topo layer; Gaia GPS Trails Illustrated layer
Trail contacts: San Juan National Forest, 15 Burnett Ct., Durango, CO 81301; (970) 247-4874; https://www.fs.usda.gov/sanjuan

FINDING THE TRAILHEAD

From Durango, drive 14 miles north on Florida Road (CR 240) to the junction with CR 243, then turn left. Follow CR 243 for 6.6 miles, then turn right on FR 597, a gravel road. Drive 10.3 miles to the end of the road at the trailhead. A high-clearance vehicle is recommended. The road is closed in winter. GPS: N27 28.624' / W107 37.890'

THE HIKE

The trail heads east and soon reaches a junction. The trail on the right is the southern extension of the Endlich Mesa Trail and eventually goes to Vallecito Reservoir, but it hasn't been maintained since the Missionary Ridge fire in 2002 and may be impassable. Luckily the fire didn't affect the northern portion of the trail, which lies at or above timberline.

After the junction, the trail turns north and follows the broad ridge. Views are outstanding in all directions. The trail descends to the Florida River and City Reservoir, then climbs west onto another broad mesa and heads north. At Trimble Pass, the trail descends into the headwaters of Johnson Creek, then climbs slightly to Columbine Pass. Turn right on the Johnson Creek Trail and descend to Columbine Lake, the end of the hike.

Columbine Lake is a popular base camp for climbers attempting the surrounding high peaks and can be very busy. You might want to consider camping away from the lake, or possibly at Lille Lake just below Trimble Pass.

There are many opportunities for longer backpack trips from the end of this hike. Many involve informal trails and cross-country hiking across mountain passes, so you should be experienced and carry a topo map, compass, and GPS unit.

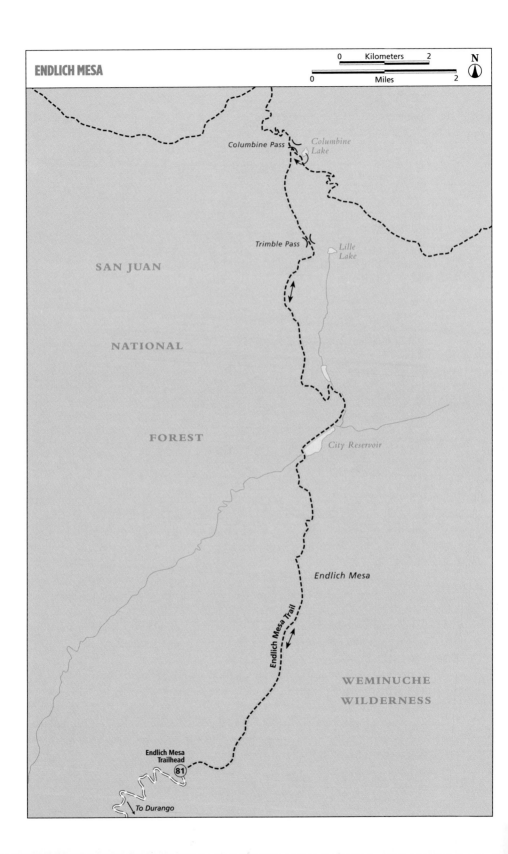

ENDLICH MESA

0 Kilometers 2
0 Miles 2

N

Columbine Pass
Columbine
Lake

Trimble Pass
Lille
Lake

SAN JUAN

NATIONAL

FOREST

City Reservoir

Endlich Mesa

Endlich Mesa Trail

WEMINUCHE

WILDERNESS

Endlich Mesa
Trailhead
81

To Durango

MILES AND DIRECTIONS

0.0   Hike east on the Endlich Mesa Trail.

0.6   Junction; the right fork goes to Vallecito Reservoir; turn left and hike north on the Endlich Mesa Trail.

6.0   City Reservoir.

10.4 Trimble Pass and side trail to Lille Lake.

11.9 Columbine Pass.

12.2 Columbine Lake; return the way you came.

24.4 Trailhead.

82 VALLECITO CREEK

This backpack trip takes you up a long, beautiful canyon into the heart of the San Juan Mountains. It's crowned by a loop over the Continental Divide past several alpine lakes.

Start: 29.4 miles northeast of Durango
Distance: 46.7-mile out-and-back with a 17-mile loop section
Hiking time: 5–8 days
Difficulty: Strenuous
Trail surface: Dirt and rocks
Best seasons: Summer through fall
Water: Vallecito Creek and numerous side creeks
Other trail users: Horses

Canine compatibility: Leashed dogs permitted
Fees and permits: None
Schedule: Open all year
Maps: CalTopo.com MapBuilder Topo layer; Gaia GPS Trails Illustrated layer
Trail contacts: San Juan National Forest, 15 Burnett Ct., Durango, CO 81301; (970) 247-4874; https://www.fs.usda.gov/sanjuan

FINDING THE TRAILHEAD

From Durango, drive 17 miles north on Florida Road, CR 240. Turn left on CR 501 and continue 9.7 miles through the community of Vallecito. Turn left onto CR 500 and drive 2.7 miles to the Vallecito campground entrance. The trailhead is on your left. GPS: N37 28.496' / W107 32.887'

THE HIKE

The well-used and popular trail skirts the campground on the west, then climbs west above the creek for a short distance. After it returns to creekside, the trail is never far from the creek as it passes through dense spruce, fir, and aspen forest. Camping is limited until you are about 7 miles up Vallecito Creek, then the canyon floor opens up and the trail passes through numerous meadows. At 9.2 miles, the Needle Creek Trail forks left; stay right on the Vallecito Trail. More meadows offer some scenic campsites and a break from the forest. At 12.6 miles, the trail climbs away from Vallecito Creek on the east, and not long after, you come to the junction with the Rock Creek Trail, where the loop portion of the hike begins.

Turn right on the Rock Creek Trail and follow it as it climbs generally southeast up Rock Creek. At 18.8 miles, the trail reaches timberline and levels out a bit just below Rock Lake, which is out of sight just to the south of the main trail. A short informal trail leads to the aptly named lake. It's a scenic spot but the rocky shore of the lake offers very poor campsites. Much better campsites lie ahead.

After the lake, the trail turns more to the north and climbs to a broad saddle and the junction with the Flint Lakes Trail. Stay left, on the Rock Creek Trail. A steeper climb leads to an unnamed pass on the Continental Divide, and then a short descent to Twin Lakes, where there are some good campsites. Just after passing the second Twin Lake, the trail meets the Continental Divide Trail; turn left.

The trail descends to cross Middle Ute Creek, then climbs to a pass. It is a short descent to West Ute Lake, where there are good campsites. Next, the trail turns northwest and

Balsam Lake, San Juan Mountains

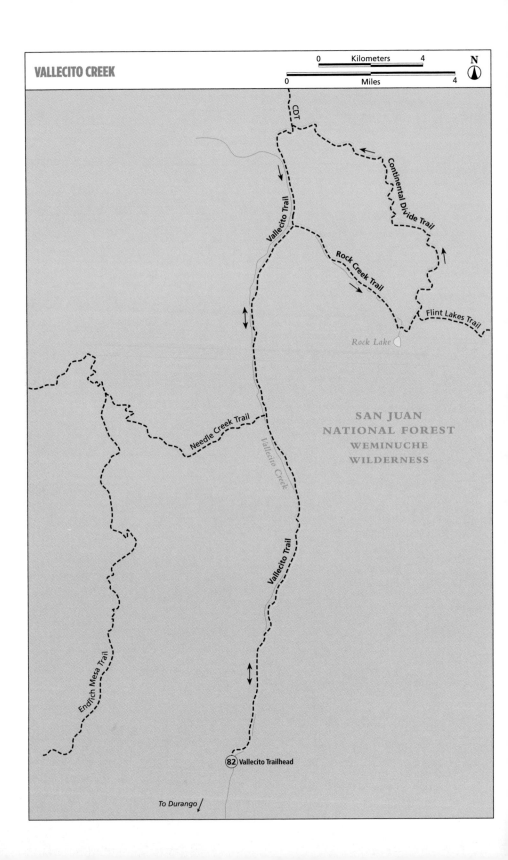

0   Kilometers   4

0   Miles   4

N

CDT

Continental Divide Trail

Vallecito Trail

Rock Creek Trail

Flint Lakes Trail

Rock Lake

SAN JUAN
NATIONAL FOREST
WEMINUCHE
WILDERNESS

Needle Creek Trail

Vallecito Creek

Vallecito Trail

Endlich Mesa Trail

82 Vallecito Trailhead

To Durango

climbs steadily back to the Continental Divide. It descends past a small unnamed lake then continues down Nebo Creek to meet the Vallecito Trail. Turn left and follow the Vallecito Trail south down Vallecito Creek.

At 31.9 miles, the Rock Creek Trail comes on the left, completing the loop. Hike south on the Vallecito Trail to return to the trailhead.

There are many opportunities for side hikes and exploration off the main hike. A number of informal trails lead to high cirques that climbers use to access the summits of the Needle Mountains and Grenadier Ranges. These peaks offer some of the most challenging summits in Colorado. And for non-climbers, other informal trails lead to alpine lakes set in glacial cirques.

MILES AND DIRECTIONS

0.0 Follow the Vallecito Trail around the campground, then north along Vallecito Creek.

0.6 Just north of the campground, the trail climbs away from the creek on the west.

1.8 The trail returns to creekside.

9.2 Needle Creek Trail forks left; stay right on the Vallecito Trail.

12.6 The trail climbs away from Vallecito Creek on the east.

14.8 Junction; the Vallecito Trail continues straight ahead, which will be our return from the loop portion of the hike. Turn right on the Rock Creek Trail.

18.8 An informal trail goes right a short distance to Rock Lake.

19.5 Pass. Flint Lakes Trail goes right; stay left on Rock Creek Trail.

20.3 Pass and the Continental Divide.

21.4 Twin Lakes.

21.6 Junction; turn left on the Continental Divide and the Continental Divide Trail.

24.2 Pass.

25.2 West Ute Lake.

27.3 Pass and the Continental Divide.

28.8 Junction; turn left on the Vallecito Trail.

31.9 Rock Creek Trail joins from the left, closing the loop. Stay right on the Vallecito Trail.

46.7 Trailhead.

83 LAKE EILEEN TRAIL

This short day hike takes you to a small lake overlooking Vallecito Canyon and the miles-long expanse of Vallecito Reservoir.

Start: 26.5 miles northeast of Durango
Distance: 2.6-mile out-and-back
Hiking time: About 2 hours
Difficulty: Easy
Trail surface: Dirt and rocks
Best seasons: Summer through fall
Water: Lake Eileen
Other trail users: Horses
Canine compatibility: Leashed dogs permitted

Fees and permits: None
Schedule: Open all year
Maps: CalTopo.com Forest Service 2016 (green) layer; Gaia GPS Trails Illustrated layer
Trail contacts: San Juan National Forest, 15 Burnett Ct., Durango, CO 81301; (970) 247-4874; https://www.fs.usda.gov/sanjuan

FINDING THE TRAILHEAD

From Durango, drive 17 miles on Florida Road, CR 240. Turn left onto CR 501, then drive 9.5 miles north of the Vallecito Reservoir, through the community of Vallecito. Look for the Forest Service Work Center; a trailhead sign is visible from the road. Park on the east side of the road; the trailhead is on the west (opposite) side. GPS: N37 26.584' / W107 33.502'

THE HIKE

The trail starts on the west side of the road and climbs north through aspen groves to the small, shallow lake, which is perched on a bench. The lake is set in a small meadow surrounded by aspens, and it's a short walk east to the edge of the bench, where there are great views of Vallecito Canyon and Vallecito Reservoir.

Vallecito Reservoir was constructed by the Bureau of Reclamation in 1940 to provide water for irrigation. There are numerous Forest Service campgrounds along its eastern shore, and it is also popular with boaters and anglers.

MILES AND DIRECTIONS

0.0 Trailhead.

1.3 Lake Eileen; return the way you came.

2.6 Trailhead.

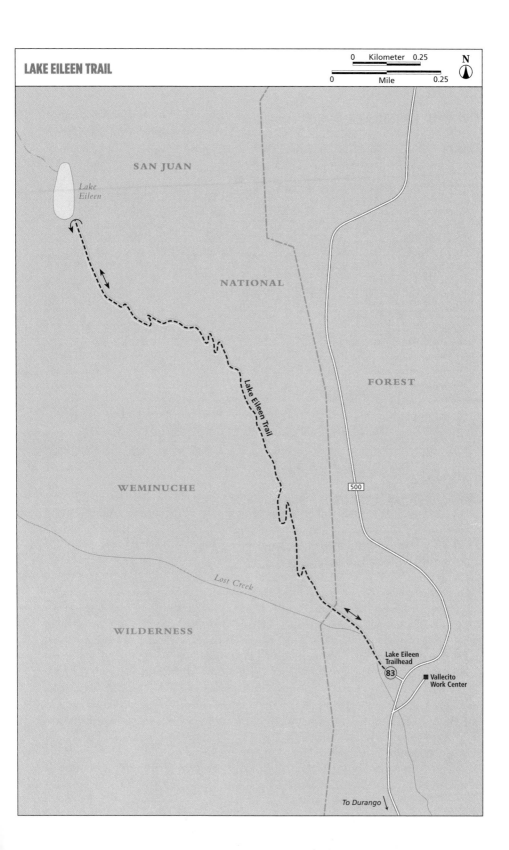

LAKE EILEEN TRAIL

0   Kilometer   0.25

0   Mile   0.25

N

SAN JUAN

Lake
Eileen

NATIONAL

FOREST

Lake Eileen Trail

WEMINUCHE

500

Lost Creek

WILDERNESS

Lake Eileen
Trailhead

83

Vallecito
Work Center

To Durango

84 CONTINENTAL DIVIDE

This loop backpack trip in the eastern Weminuche Wilderness takes you through scenic glacial canyons and along a section of the Continental Divide National Scenic Trail in the San Juan Mountains of southwestern Colorado.

Start: 56 miles west of South Fork
Distance: 28.7-mile loop
Hiking time: About 5 days
Difficulty: Strenuous
Trail surface: Dirt and rocks
Best seasons: Summer and fall
Water: Numerous sources, including Squaw Creek, small lakes and creeks along the Continental Divide Trail, and Weminuche Creek
Other trail users: Horses
Canine compatibility: Leashed dogs permitted

Fees and permits: None
Schedule: Open all year
Maps: CalTopo.com MapBuilder Topo layer; Gaia GPS Trails Illustrated layer
Trail contacts: Rio Grande National Forest, 1803 W. Hwy. 160, Monte Vista, CO 81144; (719) 657-3321; https://www.fs.usda.gov/riogrande. San Juan National Forest, 15 Burnett Ct., Durango, CO 81301; (970) 247-4874; https://www.fs.usda.gov/sanjuan

FINDING THE TRAILHEAD

 From South Fork, drive 56 miles west on CO 156, then turn left into Thirtymile Campground. Park at the Squaw Creek Trailhead, on the right. GPS: N37 43.397' / W107 15.535'

THE HIKE

Walk south along the west side of the campground to a trail junction where the Weminuche Trail goes right—this will be our return from the loop. Turn left and follow the Squaw Creek Trail south into the mouth of Squaw Creek Canyon. About 2 miles up the creek, the dense forest opens up a bit and there are meadows along the creek. At 6.4 miles, the Squaw Lake Trail forks right; stay left on the Squaw Creek Trail and continue south up Squaw Creek.

Finally, the trail starts climbing up the headwaters of Squaw Creek toward Squaw Pass, and meets the Continental Divide Trail (CDT) just before the pass. Turn right on the CDT and follow it to the broad pass, then up a slope to the west that leads onto a high bench at timberline. Now the CDT turns northwest and works its way through several glacial cirques containing small lakes. The CDT finally climbs onto the crest (the actual Continental Divide). Squaw Lake will be visible below to the northeast, and then the Squaw Lake Trail joins from the right; go left to remain on the CDT. After working its way farther along the broad crest of the Divide, the Snowslide Trail joins from the left; stay right and follow the CDT as leaves the crest, turns west, and drops into the North Fork of Los Pinos River.

When the trail emerges into the broad meadow at Weminuche Pass, turn right on the Weminuche Trail, leaving the CDT. Follow the Weminuche Trail north down Weminuche Creek.

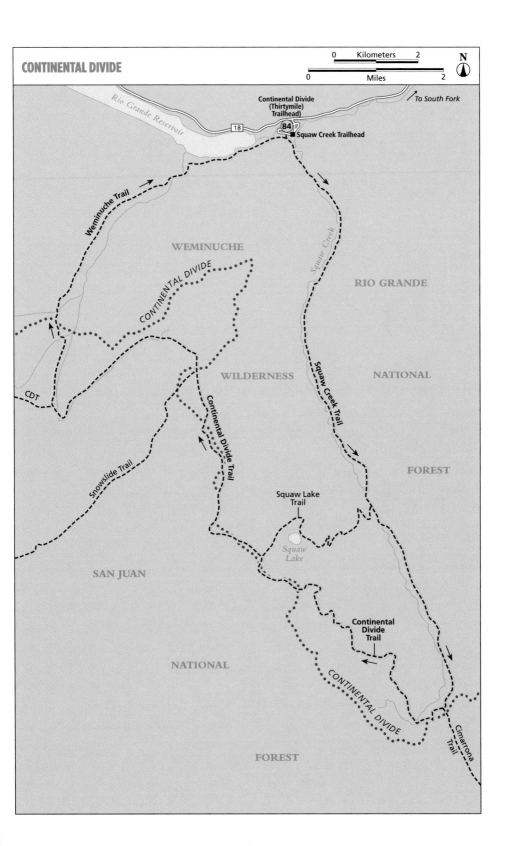

CONTINENTAL DIVIDE

0 Kilometers 2
0 Miles 2

N

Rio Grande Reservoir

Continental Divide (Thirtymile) Trailhead

To South Fork

18

84

Squaw Creek Trailhead

Weminuche Trail

WEMINUCHE

CONTINENTAL DIVIDE

Squaw Creek

RIO GRANDE

CDT

WILDERNESS

NATIONAL

Continental Divide Trail

Snowslide Trail

Squaw Creek Trail

FOREST

Squaw Lake Trail

Squaw Lake

SAN JUAN

Continental Divide Trail

NATIONAL

CONTINENTAL DIVIDE

Cimarrona Trail

FOREST

MILES AND DIRECTIONS

0.0 Walk south along the west side of the campground.

0.1 Junction; Weminuche Trail, on the right, will be your return from the loop. Turn left and follow the Squaw Creek Trail.

0.4 Wilderness boundary.

6.4 Squaw Lake Trail forks right; stay left on the Squaw Creek Trail.

9.6 The Continental Divide Trail (CDT) joins from the left; hike south on the CDT.

10.0 Cimarrona Trail goes left; stay right on the CDT.

15.4 Squaw Lake Trail joins from the right; stay left on the CDT.

19.0 Snowslide Trail joins from the left; stay right on the CDT.

22.2 Junction; leave the CDT and turn right on the Weminuche Trail.

27.0 The trail leaves Weminuche Creek and turns east above Rio Grande Reservoir.

28.0 Wilderness boundary.

28.6 Junction with the Squaw Creek Trail; turn left to return to the trailhead.

28.7 Trailhead.

85 PETROGLYPH POINT TRAIL

This loop day hike takes you through the rugged terrain of Mesa Verde National Park to a petroglyph panel. Interpretive signs explain features and artifacts along the trail.

Start: 31 miles southeast of Cortez
Distance: 2.7-mile loop
Hiking time: About 2 hours
Difficulty: Moderate
Trail surface: Paved and dirt trail, rocky, some scrambling
Best seasons: Spring through fall
Water: None
Other trail users: None
Canine compatibility: Dogs not permitted

Fees and permits: Entrance fee
Schedule: All year except for New Year's Day, Thanksgiving Day, and Christmas
Maps: CalTopo.com MapBuilder Topo layer; Gaia GPS Trails Illustrated layer
Trail contacts: Mesa Verde National Park, PO Box 8, Mesa Verde National Park, CO 81330; (970) 529-4465; https://www.nps.gov/meve

FINDING THE TRAILHEAD

From Cortez, drive 10.5 miles east on US 160, then turn right on Mesa Verde National Park road. Stop at the visitor center here to pay the park entrance fee. Then drive 20.5 miles on the park road to the parking lot for Spruce Tree House and Chapin Mesa Museum. GPS: N37 11.050' / W108 29.344'

THE HIKE

Start on the paved trail to Spruce Tree House, then turn right onto the Petroglyph Point Trail, which heads south and climbs along Spruce Tree Canyon. The trail works its way along ledges through the piñon-juniper woodland, finally reaching Petroglyph Point.

The trail climbs a short rock face with good handholds, and then reaches the rim of the canyon, which it follows to the north. Several open areas of slickrock give good views. The trail descends west of the canyon rim, then meets the paved Spruce Tree House Trail. Turn left to return to the trailhead.

Mesa Verde was home to a thriving population of the Ancestral Puebloan people, who lived in the area from about 600 to 1300 AD. Because they had no written language, traditions and knowledge were passed down orally to new generations. Artists did carve and paint images on rock faces, such as the panel along this hike.

MILES AND DIRECTIONS

0.0 Start on the paved trail from the Spruce Tree House Trailhead.

0.1 Junction; turn right onto the Petroglyph Point Trail.

0.3 Spruce Canyon Trail on right; stay left on Petroglyph Point Trail.

1.4 Petroglyph Point.

1.5 Mesa rim.

2.6 Spruce Tree House Trail; turn left to return to the trailhead.

2.7 Trailhead.

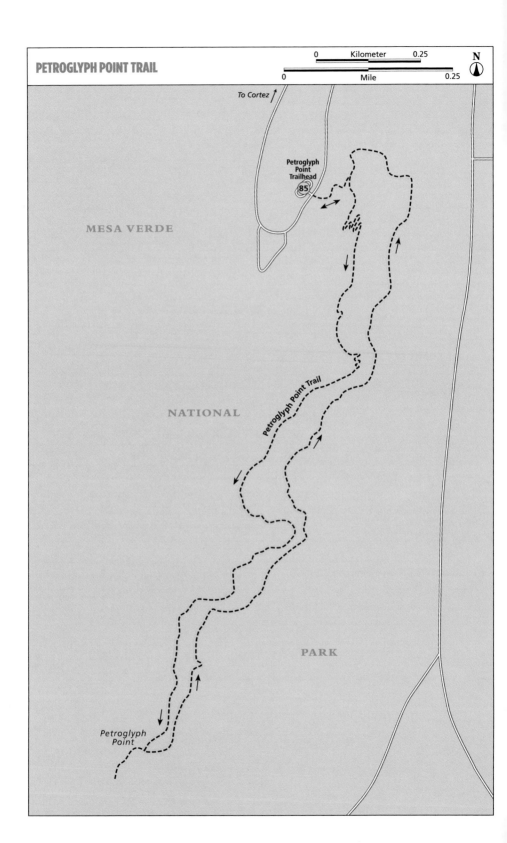

PETROGLYPH POINT TRAIL

0   Kilometer   0.25

0   Mile   0.25

N

To Cortez

MESA VERDE

Petroglyph
Point
Trailhead
85

NATIONAL

Petroglyph Point Trail

PARK

Petroglyph
Point

SOUTHERN UTAH

86 PINE VALLEY MOUNTAINS

This loop takes you along the crest of the Pine Valley Mountains, which reach over 10,000 feet and tower above the surrounding Colorado Plateau and Great Basin Desert.

Start: 65.5 miles southwest of Cedar City
Distance: 17.1-mile loop
Hiking time: About 2 days
Difficulty: Strenuous
Trail surface: Dirt and rocks
Best seasons: Summer through fall
Water: Seasonal in Hop Canyon on both the Whipple and Summit Trails, Whipple Valley, and Nay Canyon
Other trail users: Horses

Canine compatibility: Leashed dogs permitted
Fees and permits: Parking fee
Schedule: Open all year
Maps: CalTopo.com MapBuilder Topo layer; Gaia GPS Trails Illustrated layer
Trail contacts: Dixie National Forest Information, 345 E. Riverside Dr., St. George, UT 84790; (435) 688-3246; https://www.fs.usda.gov/dixie

FINDING THE TRAILHEAD

From I-15 in Cedar City, drive 30 miles west on UT 56. At Newcastle, turn left and drive 9 miles southwest. Turn left on UT 18 and drive 15 miles south to Central. Turn on FR 35 and drive 8 miles to Pine Valley Church. Turn left and drive 3.5 miles to the Pine Valley Campground and Recreation Area and the Whipple Trailhead. GPS: N37 22.240' / W113 27.305'

THE HIKE

Start out by heading east on the Whipple Trail. A section of gradual climbing along the Middle Fork of the Santa Clara River ends all too soon and the trail starts a steady climb up a series of switchbacks, finally reaching an unnamed 8,400-foot saddle. The relief from the relentless ascent is short-lived, because as soon as the trail crosses Hop Valley it starts climbing again, finally crossing a 9,300-foot saddle. A short descent leads down to the South Valley, and the Left Fork Santa Clara River, where you'll turn right on Summit Trail.

Head southwest on the Summit Trail as it climbs gradually and enters Whipple Valley. During the spring and early summer, the entire grassland can effectively be a marsh, with a lot of standing water surrounding the main stream channel. At the junction with the Wet Sandy Trail, stay right on the Summit Trail and continue southwest. A short climb leads to a 9,200-foot pass, and the trail descends into a tributary of Hop Canyon. After following the drainage west for a short distance, the trail contours southwest then climbs south up another tributary of Hop Canyon. Crossing a 9,300-foot saddle, the trail descends briefly to the southwest then crosses the Middle Fork Santa Clara River very near its headwaters.

Now the Summit Trail climbs steadily west along the broad crest of the Pine Valley Mountains, working its way through a beautiful forest of mixed quaking aspen, Engelmann spruce, and Douglas fir, and climbing over two ridges. The second of these is the

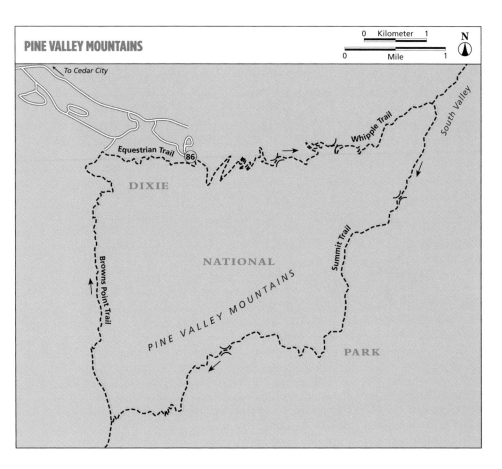

high point of the loop hike at 10,000 feet. Follow the Summit Trail west as it descends to meet the Browns Point Trail in Nay Canyon.

Turn right on the Browns Point Trail, which descends north along the bottom of the canyon for only a short distance before climbing up the eastern slope. The trail soon tops out on a ridge, which it descends to the north. After the trail drops off the ridge onto the gentle slope above Pine Valley, it meets the Equestrian Trail just before the Browns Point Trailhead. Turn right and follow the Equestrian Trail as it gently contours along the slope to reach Whipple Trailhead and the end of the loop hike.

MILES AND DIRECTIONS

0.0 Whipple Trailhead—head east on the Whipple Trail.

5.6 Turn right (south) onto the Summit Trail.

6.3 Wet Sandy Trail; stay right on the Summit Trail.

12.3 Turn right (north) onto the Browns Point Trail.

16.0 Turn right (east) onto the Equestrian Trail.

17.1 Arrive back at the trailhead.

87 EAST RIM TRAIL

This classic Zion trail climbs out of Zion Canyon to the east, connecting with several other trails, and ends at Observation Point, which has a stunning view of Zion Canyon. Several sections of the trail are cut into steep cliffs with serious dropoffs—this trail is not for those bothered by heights.

Start: 6 miles north of Zion Visitor Center
Distance: 6.8-mile out-and-back
Hiking time: About 6 hours
Difficulty: Strenuous
Trail surface: Dirt and rocks
Best seasons: Spring and fall
Water: None
Other trail users: None
Canine compatibility: Dogs not permitted
Fees and permits: None for day hikes
Schedule: Open all year
Maps: CalTopo.com MapBuilder Topo layer; Gaia GPS Trails Illustrated layer
Trail contacts: Zion National Park, 1 Zion Park Blvd., Springdale, UT 84767; (435) 772-3256; https://www.nps.gov/zion/

FINDING THE TRAILHEAD

Park in one of the paid parking lots in Springdale, just outside the park. Then ride the Springdale shuttle to the Zion Canyon Village stop, then walk across the pedestrian bridge to the visitor center. From the park visitor center, take the free shuttle up Zion Canyon to stop 7, Weeping Rock. Personal vehicles may only be driven in Zion Canyon when the shuttle is not operating. GPS: N37 16.257' / W112 56.306'

THE HIKE

After passing the Weeping Rock Trail right after leaving the trailhead, follow the East Rim Trail as it switchbacks up the piñon-juniper covered slope to the southeast. At the end of a switchback, the Hidden Canyon Trail goes right; stay left and follow the East Canyon Trail up a couple more switchbacks and then down into the drainage of Echo Canyon. After about a third of a mile, the trail climbs onto the bench north of Echo Canyon and climbs gradually to the east, where it meets the Hayduke Trail.

Turn left to remain on the East Rim Trail, which climbs northwest up a series of short switchbacks. Some parts of the trail have been cut out of the steeply sloping slickrock and would not be enjoyable to anyone afraid of heights. The trail finally ascends onto the east rim where it meets the East Mesa Trail.

Stay right on the East Rim Trail and follow it west and then south to trail's end at Observation Point. After soaking in the expansive view of Zion Canyon, return the way you came.

Zion Canyon

GEOLOGY

As you ride the free shuttle up Zion Canyon, take advantage of the time spent not driving to really look at the canyon. All of the rocks that make up the spectacular cliffs and buttes of Zion Canyon are sedimentary and were deposited underwater or as great sand dunes about 110 to 270 million years ago. But only in the last few million years has uplift of the Colorado Plateau and erosion exposed these rock layers to view. As you enter the park and proceed up Zion Canyon, you'll get a great view of the rock layers from lowest and oldest to highest and youngest.

The Kaibab Limestone is the oldest layer of rock exposed in the park, but is found in the Kolob section, not Zion Canyon. It is a hard, resistant rock that often forms white cliffs. The Kaibab Limestone forms the rims of the Grand Canyon, where it is one of the youngest rocks found in that park.

The Moenkopi Formation is composed of layers of reddish-brown siltstone, mudstone, and sandstone that were deposited on tidal flats. These soft rocks form slopes, which are visible on the drive along UT 9 from Hurricane to Springdale. Ripple marks and the tracks of ancient reptiles and amphibians are preserved in the layers.

The upper portion of the Chinle Formation is visible near the park entrance. These soft purple, gray, blue, and yellow mudstones erode into badlands, steep slopes, and hills often bare of plant life. The Chinle is best known in Petrified Forest National Park, where it contains the world's greatest concentration of petrified wood.

Forming the higher slopes in lower Zion Canyon, the Moenave Formation consists of thin layers of reddish siltstone, sandstone, and mudstone that were deposited in ancient lakes, streams, and rivers. Dinosaur footprints are common in the Moenave.

Above the Moenave, the Kayenta Formation consists of similar rock layers, but tends to have a few more resistant cliff-forming units. It forms the slopes just below the towering cliffs in Zion Canyon.

The Navajo Sandstone forms the dramatic White Cliffs of Zion Canyon, and marks an abrupt change in the ancient environment. Tidal flats and shallow seas gave way to a vast Sahara-like desert of windblown sand dunes. When the dunes were later buried under younger sediments, the sand was compressed into a buff-colored massive sandstone that still preserves the slopes of the ancient dunes as cross-bedding, sloping layers that reveal the direction of the ancient winds.

The Temple Cap Formation marks the transition back to a wet environment, and contains tidal flat mudstones, sandstones deposited as coast dunes, and even limestone formed in deeper water. It forms the tops of many of the temples in Zion Canyon, notably East Temple and West Temple.

EAST RIM TRAIL

Observation
Point

ZION

NATIONAL

PARK

East Rim Trail

Weeping Rock Trail

Weeping Rock
Shuttle Stop

87 East Rim
Trailhead

To Springdale

MILES AND DIRECTIONS

0.0 From the trailhead, stay right on the East Rim Trail.

0.5 Meet the Hidden Canyon Trail at a switchback; stay left on the East Rim Trail.

1.7 Meet the Hayduke Trail; turn left to remain on the East Rim Trail.

3.4 Observation Point; return the way you came.

6.8 Arrive back at Weeping Rock Trailhead.

88 RIVERWALK

This is an easy walk along the Virgin River in Zion Canyon. The first half of the trail is accessible, though sand may cover the paved trail in places after rainstorms.

Start: 8.5 miles north of Springdale
Distance: 1.8-mile out-and-back
Hiking time: About 2 hours
Difficulty: Easy
Trail surface: Paved
Best seasons: All year
Water: At trailhead
Other trail users: None
Canine compatibility: Dogs not permitted on trails in the park

Fees and permits: None
Schedule: Open all year
Maps: CalTopo.com MapBuilder Topo layer; Gaia GPS Trails Illustrated layer
Trail contacts: Zion National Park, 1 Zion Park Blvd., Springdale, UT 84767; (435) 772-3256; https://www.nps.gov/zion

FINDING THE TRAILHEAD

Park in one of the paid parking lots in Springdale, just outside the park. Then ride the Springdale shuttle to the Zion Canyon Village stop, then walk across the pedestrian bridge to the visitor center. Now, board the Zion Canyon shuttle and take it to the last stop, the Temple of Sinawava. GPS: N37 17.110' / W112 56.861'

THE HIKE

This very easy hike nevertheless takes you away from the crowds at the shuttle stops in Zion Canyon, and gives you a taste of the Zion Narrows and the park backcountry. From the trailhead, walk north on the paved trail. As you continue, Zion Canyon gradually becomes narrower, but so subtly that you may not notice until you are very near the end of the trail. The end of the trail is the starting point for the Zion Narrows hike, a multiday backpack trip that involves wading the Virgin River and the North Fork Virgin River for many miles.

MILES AND DIRECTIONS

0.0   Hike north on the Riverwalk Trail.

0.9   End of trail—return the way you came.

1.8   Arrive back at the trailhead.

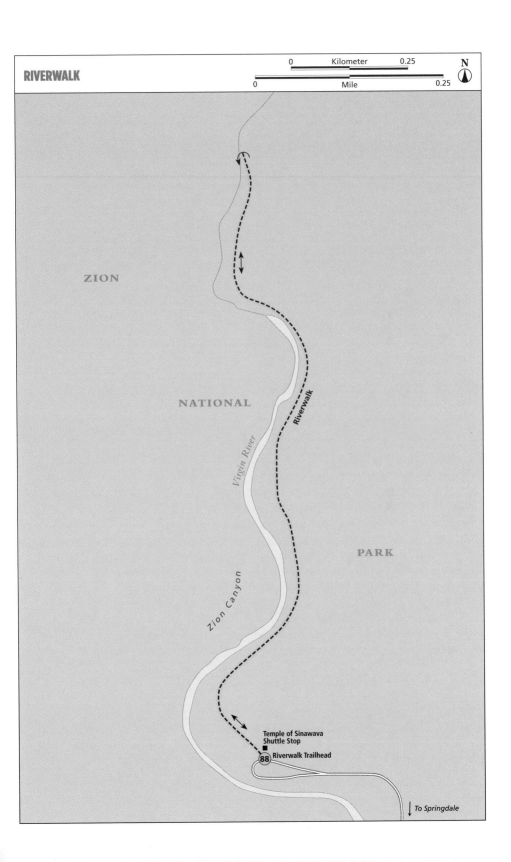

ZION

NATIONAL

PARK

Virgin River

Riverwalk

Zion Canyon

Temple of Sinawava
Shuttle Stop
88 Riverwalk Trailhead

To Springdale

0   Kilometer   0.25
0   Mile   0.25

N

89 RAMPARTS OVERLOOK, CEDAR BREAKS

This day hike takes you along the south rim of Cedar Breaks to one of the best viewpoints in the national monument.

Start: 21.4 miles east of Cedar City
Distance: 4.8-mile out-and-back
Hiking time: 2–3 hours
Difficulty: Moderate
Trail surface: Dirt and rocks
Best seasons: Summer and fall
Water: None
Other trail users: None
Canine compatibility: Dogs not permitted

Fees and permits: None
Schedule: Open June through Oct, depending on snowfall
Maps: CalTopo.com MapBuilder Topo layer; Gaia GPS Trails Illustrated layer
Trail contacts: Cedar Breaks National Monument, 2390 W. Hwy. 56 Suite #11, Cedar City, UT 84720; (435) 986-7120; https://www.nps.gov/cebr

FINDING THE TRAILHEAD

From Cedar City, drive 17.9 miles east on UT 14, then turn left on UT 148 (UT 148 is closed in winter). Drive 3.5 miles north and park at the Ramparts Trailhead, on the left. GPS: N37 36.740' / W112 50.276'

THE HIKE

The trail closely follows the south rim of Cedar Breaks, also known as the Wasatch Rampart. The trail climbs to the 10,400-foot high point of the hike, then descends to Spectra Point. Follow the trail west along the rim as it gradually descends to a saddle, then climbs slightly to The Bartizan and the end of the trail. Return the way you came.

Because the trail follows a ridge to the west, you'll get great views of Cedar Breaks stretching away to the north. The sedimentary rock layers here are the culmination of the "Grand Staircase," a series of south-facing cliffs that start at the bottom of the Grand Canyon, far to the south in Arizona, and expose ever-younger rock layers in northward progression. The rocks of the Grand Staircase represent more than half of the Earth's 4.6-billion-year history.

The cliffs, hoodoos, and steep slopes of Cedar Breaks drop away more than 5,000 feet to the valley floor near Cedar City. This west-facing escarpment causes winter storms to drop an immense amount of snow on Cedar Breaks, up to 245 inches per year.

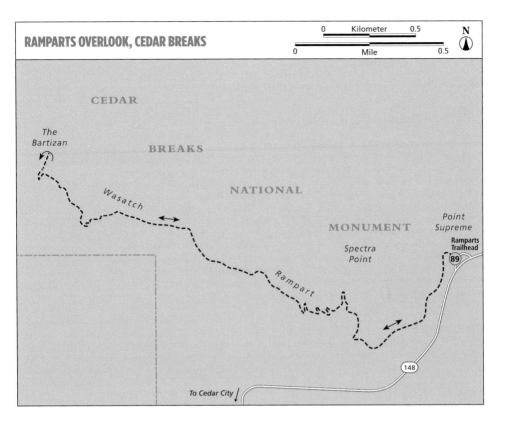

MILES AND DIRECTIONS

0.0 Start by hiking southwest on the Ramparts Trail.

0.7 Spectra Point.

2.4 The Bartizan; return the way you came.

4.8 Trailhead.

90 BRYCE RIM LOOP

This delightful day hike starts and ends with easy walking along the Rim Trail, and loops below the rim past colorful hoodoos and weirdly eroded formations and canyons.

Start: 26.3 miles southeast of Panguitch
Distance: 7.5-mile loop
Hiking time: About 5 hours
Difficulty: Moderate
Trail surface: Dirt, rocks, pavement
Best seasons: Summer through fall
Water: Sunset Point
Other trail users: Horses on the Peek-A-Boo Loop Trail

Canine compatibility: Leashed dogs permitted
Fees and permits: Entrance fee
Schedule: Open all year; trails are snow-covered during the winter
Maps: CalTopo.com MapBuilder Topo layer; Gaia GPS Trails Illustrated layer
Trail contacts: Bryce Canyon National Park, PO Box 640201, Bryce, UT 84764; (435) 834-5322; https://www.nps.gov/brca

FINDING THE TRAILHEAD

From Panguitch, drive 6.9 miles south on US 89, then turn left on UT 12. Continue 13.6 miles, then turn right on UT 63. Drive 5.4 miles, then turn left on Bryce Point Road. After 0.1 mile, turn left on Inspiration Point Road and drive 0.3 mile to the end of the road at Inspiration Point. GPS: N37 36.905' / W112 10.242'

THE HIKE

From the parking lot, walk out to the rim and turn right on the Rim Trail. The trail skirts the very edge of the rim and gives you ever-changing views of the famous and colorful erosional forms of the park. Although the main viewpoints can be very crowded, far fewer people venture very far from the parking lots.

So that you don't miss any of the named formations along the hike, bring the park brochure and map along on your hike (you can get a copy at the entrance station), or print the portion of the Gaia GPS Trails Illustrated layer that covers the hike.

The Rim Trail reaches Bryce Point, the southernmost viewpoint overlooking Bryce Amphitheater, skirts the parking lot, and then reaches a junction. The Under-the-Rim Trail goes right; turn left and descend east and then northwest below the rim. Below Bryce Point, you'll meet the Peek-A-Boo Loop Trail, which is a one-way, clockwise loop. Turn left to hike the western side of the loop.

The eastern portion of the Peek-A-Boo Trail comes in from the right just as you reach the floor of Bryce Canyon. Turn left, and then left again, on the Bryce Canyon Trail. Hike less than a mile west up the canyon, where you'll meet the Navajo Loop Trail at a four-way junction. Take the rightmost trail, the Queens Garden Trail. This trail ascends to the north, working its way up to a ridge where a horse trail joins from the right. Stay left, and follow the trail to the rim at Sunrise Point. This point is the northernmost viewpoint overlooking Bryce Amphitheater.

Bryce Canyon in winter

Bryce Canyon

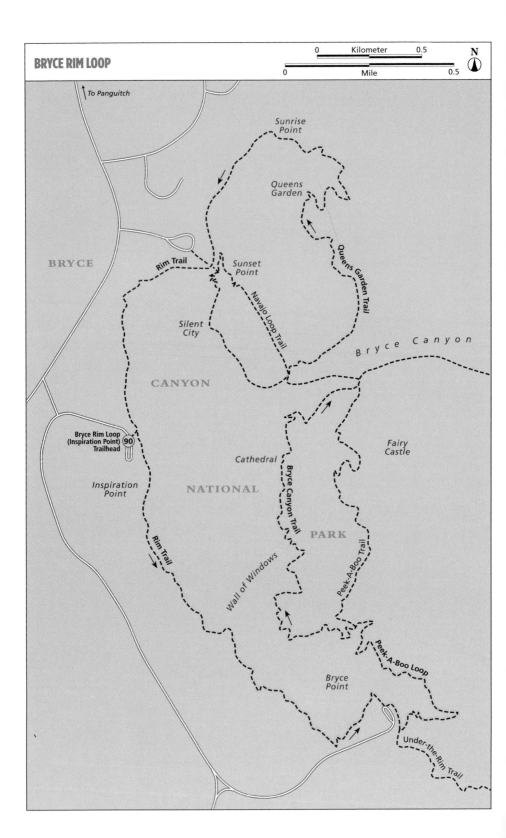

Turn left on the Rim Trail and follow it south to Sunset Point. If you need water, it is available at the parking lot for this viewpoint. Otherwise, continue south and west on the Rim Trail to Inspiration Point and your vehicle.

MILES AND DIRECTIONS

0.0 From the parking lot, walk the short spur trail to the rim, then turn right (south) on the Rim Trail.

1.6 Bryce Point.

1.7 Junction; turn left.

2.7 Peek-A-Boo Loop Trail; turn left and descend below the rim.

4.4 Peek-A-Boo loop continues right; turn left, and then left again on the Bryce Canyon Trail.

4.6 Navajo Loop Trail (four-way junction); stay right on the Queens Garden Trail.

5.7 A horse trail joins from the right; stay left on the Queens Garden Trail.

6.2 Sunrise Point; turn left on the Rim Trail.

6.7 Sunset Point.

7.5 Inspiration Point and Trailhead.

91 **PARIA CANYON**

This 4- or 5-day backpack trip takes you down the longest slot canyon in the world, through the Paria Canyon–Vermilion Cliffs Wilderness. Although spectacular, the hiking is easy along the sandy riverbed. Hiking must be done north to south, and requires a car shuttle. Commercial shuttle services are available in Page, Arizona, and Kanab, Utah.

Start: 42.8 miles west of Page
Distance: 36.2-mile one way with a shuttle
Hiking time: About 4 days
Difficulty: Moderate
Trail surface: Sandy trails, sand and cobble riverbed
Best seasons: Late spring and early fall
Water: Paria River, several springs
Other trail users: None
Canine compatibility: Leashed dogs permitted, must be on permit
Fees and permits: Fee and permit required for overnight hikes—must be reserved in advance. Day hikes require a permit that can be obtained at either trailhead by scanning a QR code on your phone.
Schedule: Open all year
Maps: CalTopo.com MapBuilder Topo layer; Gaia GPS Trails Illustrated layer
Trail contacts: Bureau of Land Management, 345 E. Riverside Dr., St. George, UT 84790-6714; (435) 688-3200; https://www.blm.gov/visit/paria-canyon-vermilion-cliffs-wilderness-area

FINDING THE TRAILHEAD

To reach the Lees Ferry (south) Trailhead from Page, drive 23 miles south on US 89, then turn right on US 89A. Continue 14.3 miles, then turn right on Lees Ferry Road. Continue 5.5 miles to the trailhead and boat ramp parking lot on the right. GPS: N36 51.950' / W111 35.522'

To reach the White House (north) Trailhead from Page, drive 29 miles west on US 89, then turn left onto dirt White House Road. Continue 2 miles to White House Trailhead and Campground at the end of the road. You must pick up your reserved permit at the BLM ranger station located at the turnoff. GPS: N37 4.786' / W111 53.434'

THE HIKE

You must have a solid forecast of good weather for at least the first 2 days of the hike, so that you can get through the narrows without risk of a flash flood. The headwaters of the Paria River lie far to the north at Bryce Canyon, and rain in the watershed can cause violent floods in Paria Canyon. Even when you are safely downstream of the narrows, floods can trap you at your campsite for several days.

Although walking is easy along the shallow Paria River, you'll cross it many times on this hike. Do not wear leather hiking boots—they will be destroyed. Good water shoes are the best footwear, but not river sandals—your feet will be abraded by the sand getting between your soles and the foot bed.

Bring a topo map to track your progress, but don't bother with a GPS unit. It won't work in the narrow canyon.

Narrows, Paria Canyon

The Paria River can be drunk but it is not very palatable due to silt and alkaline minerals. Fortunately, there are springs just about a day's hike apart. Plan on carrying water for a full day at at time.

From the White House Trailhead, walk down to the broad Paria River and follow it downstream. About 2 miles downstream, the broad wash enters Paria Canyon, and the walls start to close in. After another couple of miles, the canyon walls are so steep and close that there is no way to climb out of the canyon bottom without technical climbing gear. You'll reach the narrowest part of the canyon, where the walls are less than 20 feet apart and more than 500 feet high, just before Buckskin Gulch, a major side canyon, comes in from the right. This also marks the spot where you cross the state line into Arizona, a fact that seems totally irrelevant at this point. There is a campsite on a bench about 0.2 mile up Buckskin Gulch, but it is reserved for those holding a Buckskin Gulch permit and is off limits to Paria Canyon permit holders.

As you continue down Paria Canyon, the walls widen gradually. Soon you'll come to the first alluvial bench, marked by green cottonwood trees, which marks the end of the narrows and the first place to camp safely above any floodwaters. Often the first few benches and campsites are taken, but there are plenty more downstream, and also a spring on the right canyon wall.

This section is arguably the most spectacular, as the walls tower more than 800 feet above you but are still so close together as to reveal only a narrow strip of sky. As the canyon bends right and left, the undercut cliffs on the outside of the bends tower over the river in huge scalloped overhangs. There are plentiful campsites along the rest of the hike. A good strategy is to hike until you find one of the springs, fill up your bottles, then hike until the next good campsite.

Judd Hollow, on the left, is marked by an old car engine and pipes where ranchers once attempted to pump water from the river up to the east rim to provide water for their cattle on the dry Paria Plateau. In a little more than a mile, you'll come to The Hole, a narrow slot canyon on the right that usually has spring water.

After this, watch for a large side canyon opening out on the right—this is Wrather Arch Canyon. You can do an easy side hike on a use trail to within sight of the arch, which resembles a giant jug handle.

Continue down Paria Canyon, which continues to gradually widen. Fill your water bottles at any spring you encounter, as there are no springs in the lower canyon.

Finally, at about mile 27.2, the canyon walls recede and the river flows through shale hills. Watch for the start of a foot trail here, which stays on the alluvial benches and avoids the slower going along the riverbed. You'll come around a final right bend and get your first distant views of the hike. The red peaks in the distance are the Echo Peaks, which lie just across the Colorado River from Lees Ferry, your destination.

As you near Lees Ferry, you'll pass the remains of Lonely Dell, the ranch established by John D. Lee in 1870 at the mouth of the Paria River. Lee established the first permanent ferry across the Colorado River at this site, which served until replaced by Navajo Bridge in 1929.

The trail ends at Lees Ferry Road. Turn left and walk to the Lees Ferry Trailhead.

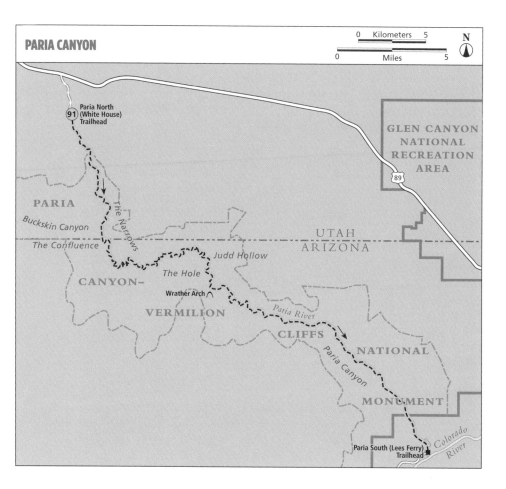

PARIA CANYON

GLEN CANYON
NATIONAL
RECREATION
AREA

89

Paria North
(White House)
Trailhead
91

PARIA

Buckskin Canyon

The Confluence

The Narrows

CANYON-

VERMILION

Judd Hollow

The Hole

Wrather Arch

CLIFFS

Paria River

UTAH
ARIZONA

NATIONAL

Paria Canyon

MONUMENT

Paria South (Lees Ferry)
Trailhead

Colorado
River

MILES AND DIRECTIONS

0.0 From the trailhead, drop into the broad bed of the Paria River and follow it south, downstream.

2.0 Approximate start of Paria Canyon.

4.1 Approximate start of the narrows.

7.1 Buckskin Canyon enters from the right; stay left and continue down Paria Canyon.

8.2 Approximate end of the narrows.

17.4 Judd Hollow, on the left.

18.8 The Hole, a slot canyon on the right, usually has water.

20.0 Wrather Arch Canyon, on the right.

27.2 Canyon walls recede; follow the foot trail along the river benches.

35.8 Lees Ferry Road; turn left on the road.

36.2 Lees Ferry Trailhead.

92 **CASSIDY ARCH**

This day hike takes you through a spectacular, narrow canyon that cuts through the Waterpocket Fold, and then to a natural arch named for a famous outlaw and train robber.

Start: 15.2 miles east of Torrey
Distance: 7.0-mile out-and-back
Hiking time: About 4 hours
Difficulty: Moderate
Trail surface: Sand, cobbles, and slickrock
Best seasons: Spring through fall
Water: None
Other trail users: None

Canine compatibility: Dogs not permitted
Fees and permits: Entrance fee
Schedule: Open all year
Maps: CalTopo.com MapBuilder Topo layer; Gaia GPS Trails Illustrated layer
Trail contacts: Capitol Reef National Park, HC 70, Box 15, Torrey, UT 84775; (435) 425-3791; https://www.nps.gov /care

FINDING THE TRAILHEAD

From Torrey, drive 15.2 miles east on UT 24 and park at the small trailhead on the right. GPS: N38 16.694' / W111 11.562'

THE HIKE

Start by hiking west from the trailhead, following the bed of Grand Wash. About a mile up the canyon, you'll reach a section called "The Narrows," where the canyon walls close in. As you continue, the canyon floor opens up. Just over 2 miles up the canyon, turn right on the Cassidy Arch Trail, which climbs out of the canyon on the right. The trail works its way along a bend on the north side of Grand Wash, then meets the Frying Pan Trail; stay left here and follow the Cassidy Arch Trail to its end at the arch. Return the way you came.

Butch Cassidy (Robert Parker) was made famous by the 1969 movie *Butch Cassidy and the Sundance Kid*, starring Paul Newman and Robert Redford.

MILES AND DIRECTIONS

- **0.0** Hike west up the bed of Grand Wash.
- **1.0** The Narrows.
- **2.2** Turn right on Cassidy Arch Trail.
- **3.2** Junction with the Frying Pan Trail; stay left on the Cassidy Arch Trail.
- **3.5** Cassidy Arch; return the way you came.
- **7.0** Arrive back at the trailhead.

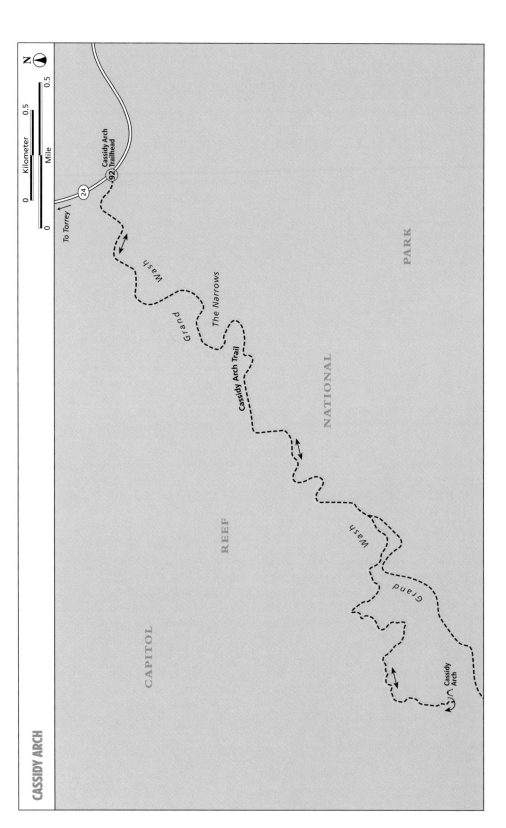

CASSIDY ARCH

N

Kilometer
0   0.5

Mile
0   0.5

To Torrey

24

92 Cassidy Arch Trailhead

CAPITOL

REEF

NATIONAL

PARK

Grand Wash

The Narrows

Cassidy Arch Trail

Grand Wash

Cassidy Arch

93 HOLE IN THE ROCK

This short but spectacular day hike takes you down an unlikely pioneer wagon route to the shores of Lake Powell. The Hole-in-the-Rock Road also provides access to Escalante Canyon and several of its side canyons.

Start: 61.3 miles southeast of Escalante
Distance: 0.8-mile out-and-back
Hiking time: About 2 hours
Difficulty: Moderate
Trail surface: Sand and slickrock
Best seasons: Spring and fall
Water: Lake Powell
Other trail users: None
Canine compatibility: Dogs permitted, must be on a leash 6 feet or less

Fees and permits: None
Schedule: Open all year
Maps: CalTopo.com MapBuilder Topo layer; Gaia GPS Trails Illustrated layer
Trail contacts: Glen Canyon National Recreation Area, PO Box 1507, Page, AZ 86040; (928) 608-6200; https://www.nps.gov/glca

FINDING THE TRAILHEAD

From Escalante, drive 5.5 miles east on UT 12, then turn right onto Hole-in-the-Rock Road. Drive 55.8 miles to the end of the road at the rim of Glen Canyon above Lake Powell. Sections of the road are impassible when wet, and the last 5 miles require a high-clearance vehicle. GPS: N37 15.404' / W110 54.082'

THE HIKE

Although this is a long drive with a short hike at the end, the whole adventure is spectacular. Hole-in-the-Rock Road follows the route of the 1879 San Juan Expedition, which was sent from Salt Lake City to found a settlement on the banks of the San Juan River in southeast Utah. The descendants of those pioneers still live in the small town of Bluff, on the north bank of the San Juan River. Much of the route was straightforward for the wagons and livestock, but the cliffs of Glen Canyon (now partially filled by Lake Powell) presented a 1,200-foot obstacle to crossing the Colorado River. While the main group camped at Dance Hall Rock (on the left 36.8 miles south of UT 12), the trailblazers worked for months to blast open the notch and prepare a route down the sloping sandstone below. A ledge was cut into the rock for the uphill wheels of the wagons, and the lower wheels were supported on logs lashed to steel bars driven into the rock. After the dangerous crossing of the Colorado River, the expedition ascended Wilson Canyon through terrain that was nearly as difficult, before reaching easy going on top of Wilson Mesa. The route was so difficult that it was abandoned by 1901 in favor of an easier route upstream at Hall's Crossing.

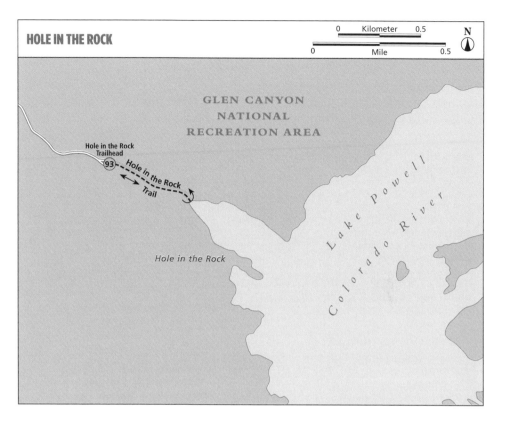

As you descend the notch, you'll have to squeeze between boulders that have fallen since the trail was abandoned. Even so, it's difficult to imagine getting loaded wagons down here. Below the notch, follow the ledges cut out of the sloping sandstone. Although the slope isn't too steep to hike, it would have been very dangerous for the wagons and livestock. The route finally emerges on talus slopes, and it's an easy walk to the edge of the lake. Return the way you came.

MILES AND DIRECTIONS

0.0 Hike down the notch in the rim toward the lake.

0.4 Lake Powell; return the way you came.

0.8 Arrive back at the trailhead.

94 UPHEAVAL DOME

This loop with an out-and-back section has it all—spectacular geology and beautiful slickrock scenery, starting from the rim of Island in the Sky and including an optional walk to the Green River.

Start: 55.3 miles west of Moab
Distance: 11.3 miles; 8.7-mile loop with 2.6-mile out-and back section
Hiking time: About 8 hours or 2–3 days
Difficulty: Strenuous
Trail surface: Dirt and rocks
Best seasons: Spring and fall
Water: Green River
Other trail users: None
Canine compatibility: Dogs not permitted

Fees and permits: Entry fee; permit required for overnight or longer hikes. Reservations for permits at recreation.gov.
Schedule: Open all year
Maps: CalTopo.com MapBuilder Topo layer; Gaia GPS Trails Illustrated layer
Trail contacts: Canyonlands National Park, 2282 Resource Rd., Moab, UT 84532; (435) 719-2313; https://www .nps.gov/cany

FINDING THE TRAILHEAD

From Moab, drive north on US 191 about 9 miles, then turn left on UT 313. Continue 14 miles. At this junction, UT 313 goes left to Deadhorse Point State Park; continue straight ahead 21 miles on Island in the Sky Road (CR 143) to the park entrance station. Continue 6.5 miles, then turn right on Upheaval Dome Road, and continue 4.8 miles to the Upheaval Dome Trailhead. GPS: N35 25.581' / W109 55.528'

THE HIKE

The trail heads northwest then north, descending gradually along the dry wash of Syncline Valley. The east rim of Upheaval Dome forms the skyline to the west. After the trail swings to the northwest, the descent steepens as the trail drops into the canyon formed in the lower Syncline Valley. The trail continues around Upheaval Dome, turning to the southwest, and then meets the Upheaval Dome Trail. This is the designated campsite area for those who are backpacking.

Turn left at this junction and follow the Upheaval Dome Trail east into the heart of the dome. You are 1,300 feet below the overlook near the trailhead. Retrace your steps to the Syncline Loop Trail. Hike 0.3 miles south to the junction with the Upheaval Canyon Trail.

At this point you can optionally do the 7.6-mile side hike down Upheaval Canyon to the Green River—see below.

To continue on the main hike, walk south on the Syncline Loop Trail, which climbs gradually up the bed of a broad canyon. After the trail turns to the southeast, it climbs steeply out of the lower canyon, then ascends along a a ridge. Switchbacks lead to the plateau south of Upheaval Dome, where the ascent moderates. Finally, you'll arrive back at the Upheaval Dome Trailhead.

UPHEAVAL DOME

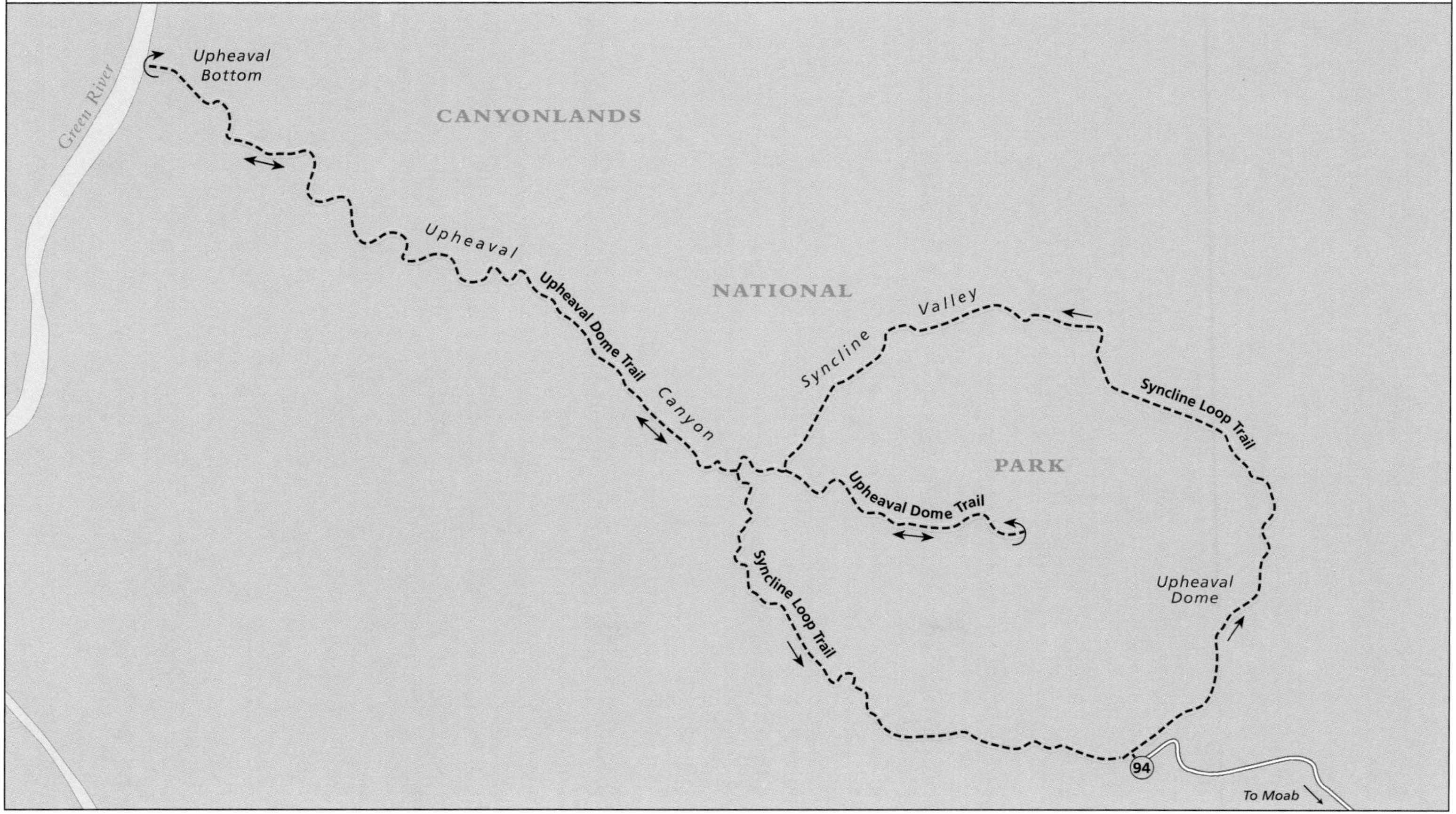

N

CANYONLANDS

NATIONAL

PARK

Green River

Upheaval Bottom

Upheaval

Upheaval Dome Trail

Canyon

Syncline

Valley

Syncline Loop Trail

Syncline Loop Trail

Upheaval Dome Trail

Upheaval Dome

94

To Moab

DOMES

At Upheaval Dome, the normally horizontal layers of sedimentary rock have been uplifted into a blister-like dome. There are several theories on the formation of the dome—the most likely is that it is a salt dome, where a plug of salt pushed up from below, bending the sedimentary layers into a dome shape while all the rocks were still deeply buried under younger rocks. Then, erosion exposed the ring of upturned rock layers. There are many salt-related formations in the Canyonlands country, including the sunken graben valleys of the Needles District of the park. A graben is a valley formed when layers of salt buried in the rock strata beneath the valley are dissolved and carried away by groundwater, causing the valley floor to sink. The orientation of the valley may have no relationship to the surface drainage patterns and erosion features.

Another theory is that the dome is the eroded remnants of a meteorite impact crater. One study found shocked quartz, a mineral only found at impact sites.

MILES AND DIRECTIONS

0.0 From the Upheaval Dome Trailhead, hike northeast on the Syncline Loop Trail.

4.5 Turn left on the Upheaval Dome Trail.

5.8 End of trail at base of Upheaval Dome—return the way you came.

7.1 Reach Syncline Loop Trail; turn left to continue the loop portion. This is the designated campsite for those who are backpacking.

7.4 Junction with optional Upheaval Canyon Trail; stay left on Syncline Loop Trail.

11.3 Arrive back at the Upheaval Dome Trailhead.

OPTIONAL HIKE TO GREEN RIVER

This out-and-back side hike adds 7.6 miles to the hike and would be a great option to make the hike into a 3-day backpack trip. Camp at the designated site at the junction of the Syncline Loop Trail and the Upheaval Dome Trail—mile 4.5. From this campsite, continue 0.3 mile, then turn right and follow the trail downstream along Upheaval Canyon to the White Rim Trail. Here, cross the trail (a jeep road) and walk 0.3 mile to the Green River.

0.0 Junction of Syncline Loop Trail and Upheaval Canyon Trail; head northwest and follow the Upheaval Canyon Trail down Upheaval Canyon.

3.5 Cross the White Rim Trail and continue down Upheaval Canyon, a broad dry wash.

3.8 Green River; return the way you came.

7.6 Rejoin the Syncline Loop Trail and turn right to continue the main hike.

95 **CONFLUENCE OVERLOOK**

This day hike takes you through the weird graben valleys and slick-rock of the Needles section of Canyonlands National Park to a point overlooking the confluence of the Green and Colorado Rivers.

Start: 80.6 miles southwest of Moab
Distance: 9.8-mile out-and-back
Hiking time: About 7 hours
Difficulty: Strenuous
Trail surface: Sand and rocks
Best seasons: Spring and fall
Water: None
Other trail users: None
Canine compatibility: Dogs not permitted

Fees and permits: Entrance fee
Schedule: Open all year
Maps: CalTopo.com MapBuilder Topo layer; Gaia GPS Trails Illustrated layer
Trail contacts: Canyonlands National Park, 2282 Resource Blvd., Moab, UT 84532; (435) 719-2313; https://www .nps.gov/cany

FINDING THE TRAILHEAD

From Moab, drive 39.8 miles south on US 191, then turn right on UT 211 and drive 34.4 miles to the park entrance. Continue on the main park road 6.4 miles to the Confluence Trailhead at the end of the road. GPS: N38 10.690' / W109 49.019'

THE HIKE

Hike west on the Confluence Overlook Trail. The trail is clear where it crosses sandy flats, but is marked by rock cairns where it crosses areas of bare slickrock. Pay close attention to the cairns and always have the next cairn in sight before leaving the last one. A map, compass, and GPS unit are a good idea.

At 3.1 miles, you'll emerge into a broad valley and cross a two-track road. Continue west and northwest on the footpath. At 3.8 miles a footpath merges from the left and, almost immediately, the footpath ends at a two-track road. Turn left on the two-track. When the two-track ends, continue northwest and then southwest to the Confluence Overlook.

Here in the wild heart of Canyonlands National Park, two of the Southwest's major rivers meet, the Green and the Colorado. The Colorado River starts in Rocky Mountain National Park, and the Green River has its beginnings in the Wind River Range in Wyoming. Originally, the Colorado River was called the Grand River above the confluence, but in 1921 Congress responded to pressure from the Colorado congressional delegation and changed the name of the Grand River to the Colorado. But despite that, the Green is actually the longer river above the confluence, and really the main river.

The weird landscape of the Needles District of Canyonlands National Park is a result of erosion, primarily by water, that attacks weaknesses, or joints, in the sedimentary rock as the rock layers are exposed on the surface. Erosion along these parallel joints creates tall fins and pinnacles. At the same time, layers of salt deep below the surface have been gradually removed by the action of groundwater, causing some areas to sink

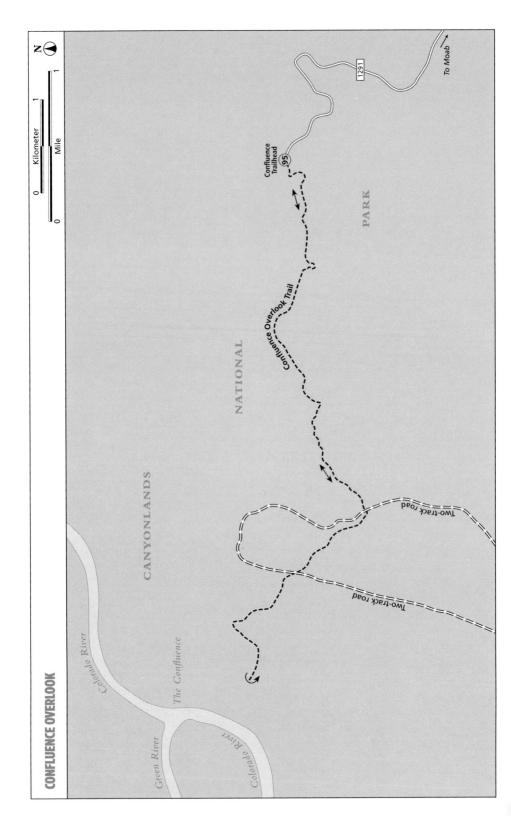

CONFLUENCE OVERLOOK

N

0   Kilometer   1

0   Mile   1

Colorado River

Green River

The Confluence

Colorado River

CANYONLANDS

NATIONAL

PARK

Confluence Overlook Trail

Confluence Trailhead

95

1291

To Moab

Two-track road

Two-track road

and form valleys that seemingly don't have any connection to surface drainage. The resulting landscape may seem completely chaotic, but there is order here, created by running water from the occasional flash flood. Every drainage, no matter how small, leads downstream into a larger drainage, and in turn into a still larger drainage, and then into the Colorado or Green River.

MILES AND DIRECTIONS

0.0   Hike west on the Confluence Overlook Trail.

3.1   Cross a two-track road and continue west, then northwest on the Confluence Overlook Trail.

3.8   A trail merges from the left, then you'll meet a two-track road. Turn left (west) on the two-track.

4.1   The two-track ends; continue on the footpath.

4.9   Confluence Overlook; return the way you came.

9.8   Trailhead.

96 DEVILS GARDEN

This day hike takes you through a fine selection of Arches National Park's famous natural arches and features excellent views.

Start: 23 miles north of Moab
Distance: 6.8-mile out-and-back with a loop portion and several spur trails to the arches
Hiking time: About 4 hours
Difficulty: Moderate
Trail surface: Sand and slickrock
Best seasons: Spring and fall
Water: Trailhead only
Other trail users: None

Canine compatibility: Dogs not permitted
Fees and permits: Entrance fee
Schedule: Open all year
Maps: CalTopo.com MapBuilder Topo layer; Gaia GPS Trails Illustrated layer
Trail contacts: Arches National Park, PO Box 907, Moab, UT 84532; (435) 719-2299; https://www.nps.gov/arch

FINDING THE TRAILHEAD

From Moab, drive 4.6 miles north on US 191, then turn right on Arches National Park Road. Continue 18.4 miles to the end of the road at the Devils Garden Trailhead. GPS: N38 46.955' / W109 35.705'

THE HIKE

This hike has several side trails to the arches, and every single one is worth the time and effort, as no two of the hundreds of arches in the park are the same. This hike is the longest trail in the park and takes you to some of the best arches.

Just after you pass Tunnel Arch, take the spur trail on the right to beautiful Pine Tree Arch, named for the piñon pine growing in the opening. The arch frames a sweeping view of the canyon country to the northeast.

Back on the main trail, continue to a junction, where a primitive trail forks right. This will be the return from the loop portion of the hike. For now, stay left and continue a short distance to Landscape Arch, which is above the trail to the left. This thin ribbon of sandstone impossibly spans more than 300 feet.

Beyond this point, the trail traverses areas of bare sandstone (known as slickrock) and is marked by rock cairns. Hikers wishing an easy hike should turn around here.

Next, you'll come to a spur trail on the left, which leads to Navajo and Partition Arches. Turn left, then right at the next fork to reach Navajo Arch. Retrace your steps, then turn right on the spur trail to Partition Arch. Now, retrace your steps to the Navajo Arch Trail, turn right, and then left on the main trail.

Finally, you'll reach a junction where the main trail goes left and the primitive loop trail goes right. Stay left here and hike a short distance to Double O Arch. Then retrace your steps to the main trail, and turn left on the primitive trail (from this point, you can optionally retrace your steps on the main trail to return to the trailhead).

The next junction is a spur trail to Private Arch; turn left here. From the arch, retrace your steps to the junction and turn left on the primitive trail. The trail wanders through the sandstone fins east of the main trail, then rejoins it just southeast of Landscape Arch. Turn left on the main trail to return to the trailhead.

Pine Tree Arch, Devils Garden

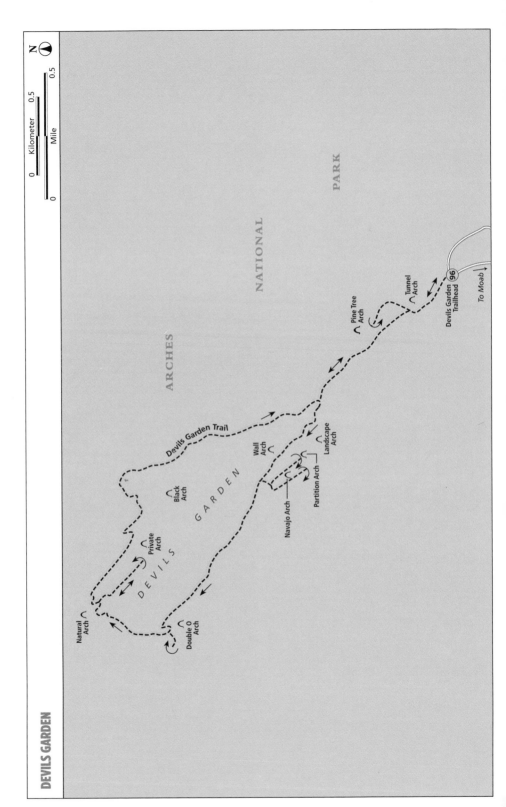

DEVILS GARDEN

N

| 0 | Kilometer | 0.5 |
| 0 | Mile | 0.5 |

ARCHES

NATIONAL

PARK

Devils Garden Trail

DEVILS GARDEN

Natural Arch

Private Arch

Black Arch

Double O Arch

Wall Arch

Navajo Arch

Partition Arch

Landscape Arch

Pine Tree Arch

Tunnel Arch

Devils Garden Trailhead

96

To Moab

MILES AND DIRECTIONS

0.0   Hike northwest on the Devils Garden Trail.

0.2   Tunnel Arch on the right.

0.3   Take the spur trail to Pine Tree Arch, on the right.

0.4   Pine Tree Arch; retrace your steps to the main trail.

0.5   Turn right on the main trail.

1.2   Junction with a primitive trail on the right—this will be the return from the loop portion of the hike. For now, stay left on the main trail.

1.3   Landscape Arch on the left.

1.6   Turn left on the spur trail to Navajo and Partition Arches on the left.

1.7   Stay right on the trail to Navajo Arch.

1.9   Navajo Arch; return the way you came.

2.1   Turn right on the trail to Partition Arch.

2.2   Partition Arch; retrace your steps.

2.3   Turn right to return to the main trail.

2.4   Reach the main trail and turn left.

3.3   Turn left on the spur trail to Double O Arch.

3.4   Double O Arch; retrace your steps.

3.5   Main trail; turn left to start the primitive loop portion of the trail.

3.8   Turn right on the spur trail to Private Arch.

4.1   Private Arch; retrace your steps.

4.4   Turn right on the main trail.

6.0   End of the loop portion; turn left to return to the trailhead.

6.8   Trailhead.

97 MORNING GLORY NATURAL ARCH

This beautiful and easily accessed hike follows Grandstaff Canyon to the sixth largest natural arch in the country.

Start: 5.1 miles northeast of Moab
Distance: 4.2-mile out-and-back
Hiking time: About 2 hours
Difficulty: Easy
Trail surface: Dirt and rocks
Best seasons: Spring and fall
Water: Grandstaff Canyon
Other trail users: None
Canine compatibility: Leashed dogs permitted

Fees and permits: None
Schedule: Open all year
Maps: CalTopo.com MapBuilder Topo layer; Gaia GPS Trails Illustrated layer
Trail contacts: Bureau of Land Management, 82 E. Dogwood, Moab, UT 84532; (435) 259-2100; https://www.blm.gov/office/moab-field-office

FINDING THE TRAILHEAD

 From Moab, drive to the north end of town on US 191, then, just before crossing the bridge over the Colorado River, turn right on UT 128. Drive 5.1 miles to the Morning Glory Natural Arch Trailhead, on the right. GPS: N38 36.586' / W109 32.018'

THE HIKE

This is an easy hike suitable for families and children that meanders up the floor of a beautiful sandstone canyon. Bring footwear that can get wet as you'll be crossing the creek several times. Just over a mile into the gradual climb, the main canyon swings sharply left where a side canyon enters from the right. Be sure to stay left on the main trail. After another half-mile, the trail turns right, leaving the main canyon, and climbs a short distance to the natural arch.

NATURAL ARCHES VS. BRIDGES

People are often confused by the difference between natural arches and bridges. Both tend to form in sandstone where fins of rock become separated from the main cliffs, and then erosion works its way through the thin fin from below, creating an opening. Bridges are formed when a stream erodes away at the sides of a meander, eventually cutting through and diverting the stream. Thus, bridges always span a watercourse. Arches are formed where rock fins become separated from cliffs by erosion along joints (cracks) in the rock, and don't span a watercourse.

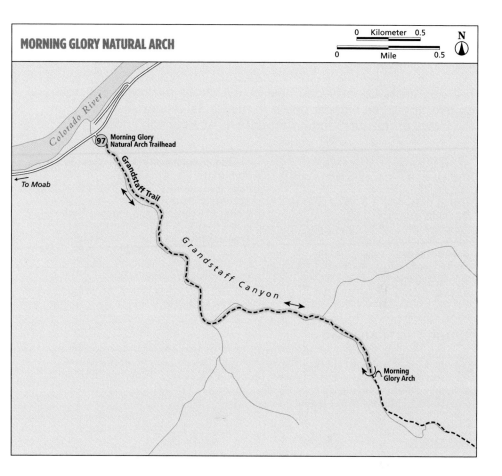

MILES AND DIRECTIONS

0.0 Follow the trail southeast up Grandstaff Canyon.

1.2 A major side canyon enters from the right; stay left and follow the trail up the main canyon.

1.7 Turn right, leaving the main canyon, and follow the trail up a side canyon.

2.1 Morning Glory Natural Arch; return the way you came.

4.2 Trailhead.

98 MOUNT PEALE

This long cross-country day hike or overnight backpack trip takes you over the three highest peaks in the La Sal Mountains, with stunning views of the surrounding mountains and canyonlands.

Start: 27.9 miles east of Moab
Distance: 10.3-mile loop with side hikes to the summits
Hiking time: About 8 hours or 2 days
Difficulty: Strenuous
Trail surface: Cross-country, old roads, maintained road
Best seasons: Summer and fall
Water: Gold Basin and Horse Creek
Other trail users: Vehicles on the road portion of the hike

Canine compatibility: Leashed dogs permitted
Fees and permits: None
Schedule: Open all year
Maps: CalTopo.com MapBuilder Topo layer; Gaia GPS Trails Illustrated layer
Trail contacts: Manti-La Sal National Forest, 599 W. Price River Dr., Price, UT 84501; (435) 636-3500; https://www.fs.usda.gov/mantilasal

FINDING THE TRAILHEAD

From Moab, drive 8 miles south on US 191, then turn left on Old Airport Road (CR 127). Continue 5.7 miles, then turn left on Geyser Pass Road (CR 127). At the forest boundary, this road becomes FR 46. Drive 6.3 miles, then turn right to remain on Geyser Pass Road (now FR 71). Continue 7.9 miles to Geyser Pass, and park. GPS: N38 29.114' / W109 13.964'

THE HIKE

This hike involves cross-country hiking through forest and along rocky ridges. Only experienced hikers who are carrying a topo map, compass, and GPS unit should attempt this loop. Much of the hike is above timberline—hikers should be prepared for sudden changes in the weather, including thunderstorms, lightning, and snow, and be prepared to retreat or at least to drop below timberline.

From Geyser Pass, hike south through the forest toward Mount Mellenthin, clearly visible above the trees. Climb the north slopes of the mountain to reach the summit. Then head south along the ridge toward Mount Peale. The walking along the high ridges is easy for the most part, and the views of the nearby La Sal Mountains and the surrounding red deserts of the canyonlands are incredible—well worth the 2,000-foot climb from Geyser Pass.

Continue up to Peak 12145, northwest of Mount Peale. Then turn southeast and climb Mount Peale, the highest point in the La Sal Mountains at 12,721 feet. Now, retrace your steps to Peak 12145.

Head west down the ridge toward Mount Tukuhnikivatz. At the saddle (where you'll return to resume the loop), continue west to Mount Tukuhnikivatz. Then retrace your steps east to the saddle. Descend the ravine north toward a small lake at timberline. This high basin right on the edge of the forest makes a good campsite for those doing this as an overnight.

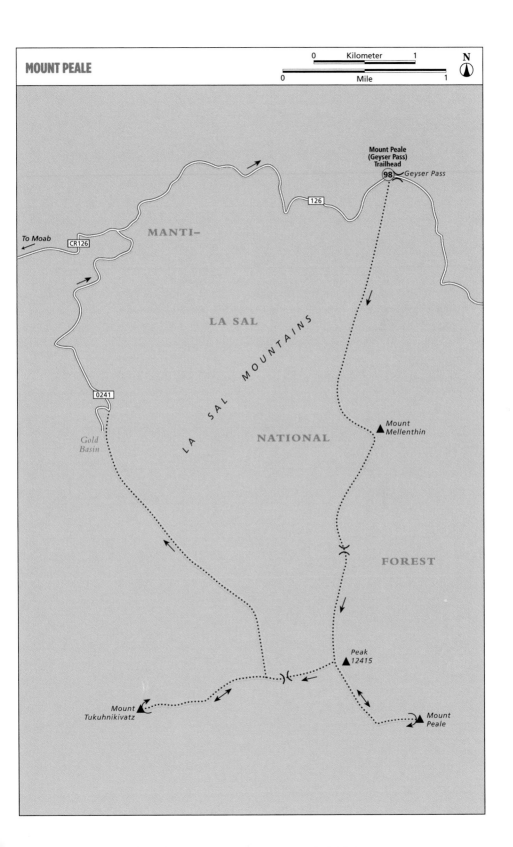

MOUNT PEALE

To Moab

MANTI–

CR126

0241

Gold
Basin

LA SAL

LA SAL MOUNTAINS

NATIONAL

FOREST

126

Mount Peale
(Geyser Pass)
Trailhead

98 Geyser Pass

Mount
Mellenthin

Peak
12415

Mount
Tukuhnikivatz

Mount
Peale

0   Kilometer   1

0   Mile   1

N

Hike northwest along the stream to Gold Basin and the end of FR 0241. Follow the road north to the Geyser Pass Road, where you'll turn right to return to Geyser Pass and your vehicle.

MILES AND DIRECTIONS

0.0　From the pass, hike cross-country south through the forest and up the north ridge of Mount Mellenthin.

0.9　Timberline.

1.7　Mount Mellenthin; descend south along the main ridge toward Mount Peale.

3.1　Peak 12145; turn left and follow the northwest ridge of Mount Peale toward the summit.

3.8　Mount Peale; retrace your steps to Peak 12145.

4.6　Peak 12145; turn west along the ridge toward Mount Tukuhnikivatz.

5.0　Saddle between Mount Peale and Mount Tukuhnikivatz; continue west up the ridge.

5.8　Mount Tukuhnikivatz; retrace your steps east to the saddle.

6.6　Saddle; descend north down the ravine.

7.1　Reach timberline at a small lake; descend northwest along the stream toward Gold Basin.

8.6　Gold basin and the south end of FR 0241; hike north on FR 0241. GPS: N38 27.913' / W109 15.839'

10.3　Geyser Pass Road; turn right.

99 DARK CANYON

This is a fine multiday loop backpack trip through a remote canyon complex that is part of Bears Ears National Monument. There is a short shuttle between the two trailheads, so a second vehicle is useful.

Start: 43.4 miles west of Blanding
Distance: 40.3-mile loop (37.9 miles with a shuttle vehicle)
Hiking time: 5–7 days
Difficulty: Strenuous
Trail surface: Sand, dirt trails, dirt roads, and slickrock
Best seasons: Late spring, and fall
Water: Seasonal along the canyon bottoms and at springs. Be prepared to carry at least a full day's supply of water.
Other trail users: None
Canine compatibility: Leashed dogs permitted

Fees and permits: None
Schedule: Open all year
Maps: CalTopo.com MapBuilder Topo layer; Gaia GPS Trails Illustrated layer
Trail contacts: Bureau of Land Management, 365 N. Main St., Monticello, UT 84535; (435) 587-1500; https://www.blm.gov/visit /bears-ears-national-monument. Manti-La Sal National Forest, 397 N. Main St., Monticello, UT 84535; (435) 587-2637, https://www.fs.usda.gov /visit/bears-ears-national-monument

FINDING THE TRAILHEAD

From Blanding, drive about 3 miles south on US 191, then turn right on UT 95. Continue 6.3 miles, then turn right on CR 228, a maintained dirt road. Drive 23.8 miles, then turn left on CR 256. Drive 7.9 miles to the Peavine Trailhead. This is the end of the hike—if you have a shuttle vehicle, leave it here. GPS: N37 39.619' / W109 52.985'

To reach the starting point, continue on CR 256 for 1.7 miles, then turn right on the Woodenshoe Road 0.7 mile to its end at the Woodenshoe Trailhead. GPS: N37 40.132' / W109 55.095'

If you don't have a second vehicle, it's only a 2.4-mile road walk from the Peavine Trailhead to the Woodenshoe Trailhead.

THE HIKE

Follow the trail, marked with rock cairns, northwest into Woodenshoe Canyon. At 4.7 miles, Cheery Canyon enters from the right. There is seasonal water up Cherry Canyon and good camping at the confluence.

At 12.3 miles, you'll reach Wates Pond, which also has good camping. About 0.5 mile farther downstream, a seep spring on the east wall is known as "Hanging Garden." Soon after, you'll reach Dark Canyon. Turn right and hike northeast up Dark Canyon. About a mile past the point where Warren and Trail Canyons come in, there is good camping. Prehistoric artifacts show that this campsite has been used for thousands of years.

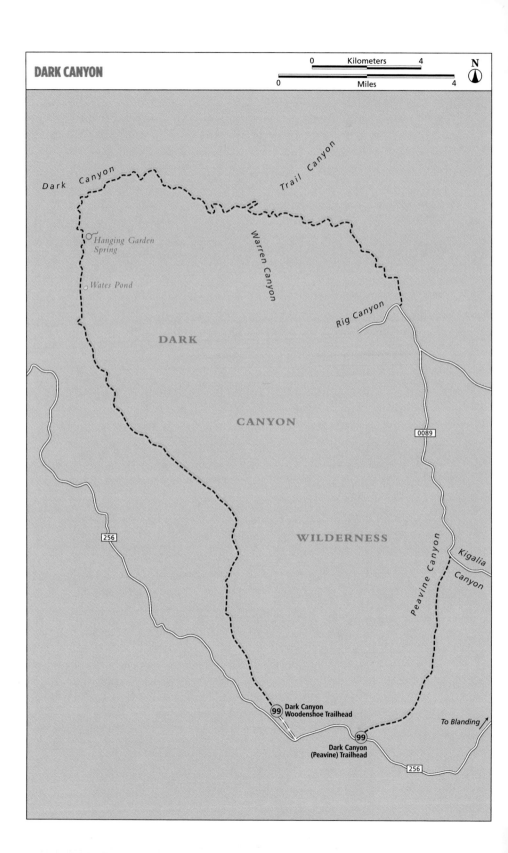

DARK CANYON

0 Kilometers 4
0 Miles 4

N

Dark   Canyon

Trail   Canyon

Warren Canyon

Hanging Garden
Spring

Wates Pond

Rig Canyon

DARK

0089

CANYON

256

WILDERNESS

Peavine Canyon

Kigalia
Canyon

Dark Canyon
99 Woodenshoe Trailhead

To Blanding

99
Dark Canyon
(Peavine) Trailhead

256

Continue up Dark Canyon past where Rig Canyon enters from the right to Peavine Canyon. Here, turn right on FR 0089, and follow it south up Peavine Canyon. After about 5 miles FR 0089 goes left into Kigalia Canyon. Turn right and follow the Peavine Trail south up Peavine Canyon to Peavine Trailhead and your shuttle vehicle. If you didn't leave a vehicle, hike 2.4 miles west on the road to Woodenshoe Trailhead.

MILES AND DIRECTIONS

0.0 From the Woodenshoe Trailhead, follow the trail northwest down into Woodenshoe Canyon.

4.7 Cherry Canyon enters from the right; continue northwest down Woodenshoe Canyon.

12.3 Wates Pond.

12.8 Hanging Garden Spring.

14.0 Dark Canyon; turn right and hike northeast up the canyon.

20.9 Warren Canyon enters from the right and then Trail Canyon from the left.

26.3 Rig Canyon enters from the right.

27.4 Turn right on FR 0089 and follow it south up Peavine Canyon (Dark Canyon goes left).

33.0 Kigalia Canyon; turn right on the Peavine Trail and follow it south up Peavine Canyon.

37.9 Peavine Trailhead and your shuttle vehicle.

100 NATURAL BRIDGES LOOP

This is an easy loop day hike past three large natural bridges, also featuring beautiful canyons and pre-Columbian ruins.

Start: 41.2 miles west of Blanding
Distance: 8.2-mile loop
Hiking time: About 5 hours
Difficulty: Moderate
Trail surface: Sand, dirt, and rocks
Best seasons: Spring through fall
Water: None
Other trail users: None
Canine compatibility: Dogs not permitted

Fees and permits: Entrance fee
Schedule: Open all year
Maps: CalTopo.com MapBuilder Topo layer; Gaia GPS Trails Illustrated layer
Trail contacts: Natural Bridges National Monument, HC-60 Box 1, Lake Powell, UT 84533-0001; (435) 692-1234 x616; https://www.nps.gov /nabr

FINDING THE TRAILHEAD

From Blanding, drive 4.0 miles south on US 191, then turn right on UT 95. Continue 30.2 miles, then turn right on UT 275. Drive 3.8 miles to the park boundary, then continue 1.2 miles, passing the visitor center, to Bridge View Drive. Turn right on this one-way road and drive 2.0 miles to the Sipapu Bridge Trailhead, on the right. GPS: N37 36.791' / W110 0.568'

THE HIKE

Descend the Sipapu Trail into the canyon. A staircase and several wooden ladders aid in the descent, which is the steepest section of the hike. Sipapu Natural Bridge is the second largest in the world, surpassed only by Rainbow Bridge. After enjoying the view, turn left and hike down White Canyon. Just after you pass Deer Canyon, Horse Collar Ruin is visible on the right wall.

You'll reach Kachina Bridge just before the junction with the Kachina Trail and Armstrong Canyon. Kachina is a young bridge, judging by the relatively small size of its opening.

Continue south and southeast up Armstrong Canyon. Just before Tuwa Canyon joins from the left, you'll reach Owachomo Bridge. Turn left (north) and follow the Owachomo Trail out of the canyon to the Owachomo Trailhead.

Cross Bridge View Drive and follow the Loop Trail north through pleasant piñon-juniper woodland, crossing the road two more times, before returning to the Sipapu Trailhead and your vehicle.

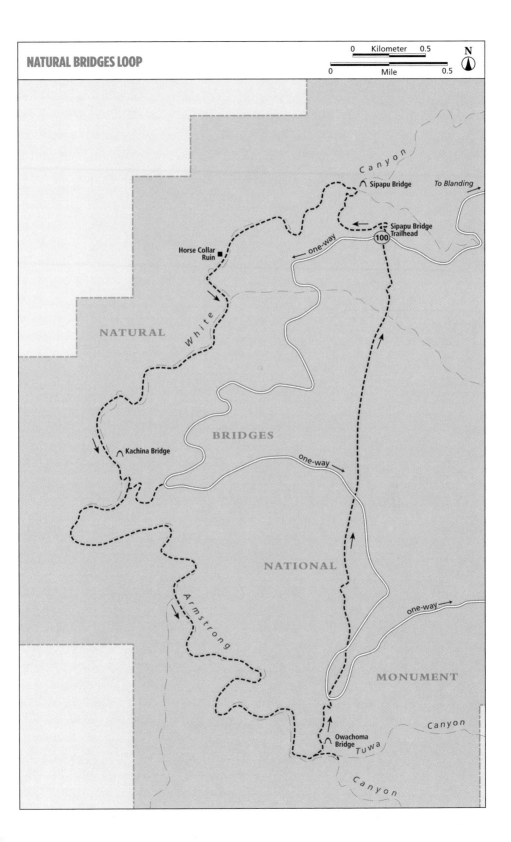

NATURAL BRIDGES LOOP

0   Kilometer   0.5
0   Mile   0.5

N

Canyon

Sipapu Bridge

To Blanding

Sipapu Bridge
Trailhead

100

one-way

Horse Collar
Ruin

NATURAL

White

BRIDGES

Kachina Bridge

one-way

NATIONAL

Armstrong

one-way

MONUMENT

Canyon

Owachoma
Bridge

Tuwa

Canyon

MILES AND DIRECTIONS

0.0   Hike north on the Sipapu Trail.

0.5   Sipapu Bridge; turn left, downstream, and walk down the wash.

1.3   Horse Collar Ruin, on the right.

2.6   Kachina Bridge.

2.9   Kachina Trail forks left; stay right and walk south up Armstrong Canyon.

5.8   Owachomo Bridge; follow the Owachomo Trail north out of the canyon.

6.1   Owachomo Trailhead; cross the road and continue north on the Loop Trail.

6.3   Cross Bridge View Drive.

7.0   Cross Bridge View Drive again.

8.2   Sipapu Trailhead.

101 **TODIE CANYON**

This day hike takes you down a side canyon into Grand Gulch and one of the best cliff dwellings in the Grand Gulch area. The entire area has many cliff dwellings and rock art panels.

Start: 27.4 miles north of Mexican Hat
Distance: 7.6-mile out-and-back
Hiking time: About 5 hours
Difficulty: Moderate
Trail surface: Sand and slickrock
Best seasons: Spring and fall
Water: Season in canyon bottoms
Other trail users: None
Canine compatibility: Dogs not permitted

Fees and permits: Self-serve permit and fee at trailhead
Schedule: Open all year
Maps: CalTopo.com MapBuilder Topo layer; Gaia GPS Trails Illustrated layer
Trail contacts: Bureau of Land Management, Monticello Field Office, 365 N. Main, Monticello, UT 84535; (435) 587-1500; https://www.blm .gov/visit/grand-gulch

FINDING THE TRAILHEAD

From Mexican Hat, drive north on US 163 for 3.8 miles. Turn left onto UT 261 and continue 22.4 miles north to CR 2361, marked with a sign for Todie Canyon Trailhead. Turn left (west) and drive 1.2 miles to the Todie Canyon trailhead.
GPS: N37 28.911' / W109 55.718'

THE HIKE

Grand Gulch and its many tributaries are home to hundreds of Ancient Puebloan cliff dwellings and rock art. Although Split Level Ruin is one of the finest in the canyons, keep a sharp eye out as you hike and you'll find many more, as well as petroglyphs and pictographs. Ruins are no longer shown on the USGS topo maps in an effort to keep pot hunters from illegally destroying them. Please respect these remnants of ancient cultures and be very careful not to damage them. Rock art in particular can be damaged by your skin oil. All artifacts are protected by the American Antiquities Act.

The initial descent into Todie Canyon follows rock cairns and some rock scrambling is required. Once in the canyon bottom, follow the wash downstream. Walking is easy but can be slow in soft sand.

Eventually, you'll reach Grand Gulch, where you'll turn left and hike downstream. At about 3.8 miles you reach Split Level Ruin. Return the way you came.

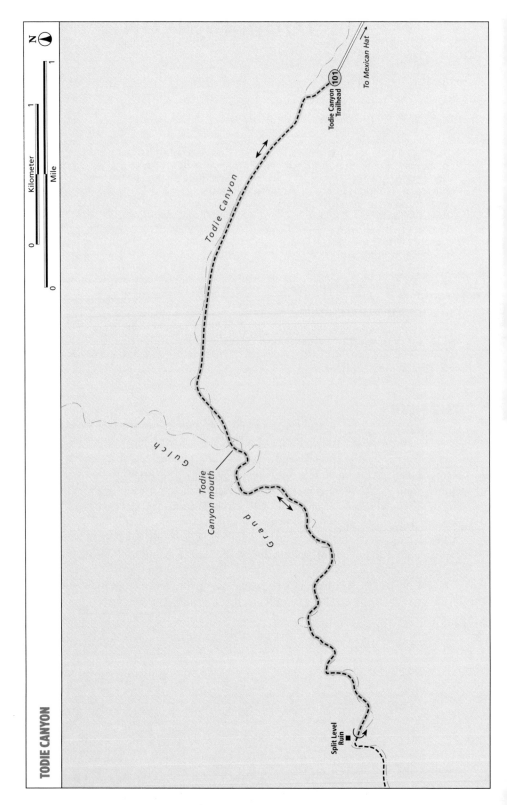

TODIE CANYON

Todie Canyon

Todie Canyon mouth

Gulch

Grand

Split Level Ruin

Todie Canyon Trailhead

101

To Mexican Hat

N

Kilometer

Mile

0   1

0   1

Ruins in Grand Gulch

MILES AND DIRECTIONS

0.0 Head northwest down Todie Canyon.

1.9 Grand Gulch enters from the right (GPS: N37 29.314' / W109 57.505'); stay left and hike down Grand Gulch.

3.8 Split Level Ruin (GPS: N37 29.314' / W109 57.505'); return the way you came.

7.6 Todie Canyon Trailhead.

Ruins in Grand Gulch

THE ART OF HIKING

When standing nose to nose with a mountain lion, you're probably not too concerned with the issue of ethical behavior in the wild. No doubt you're just terrified. But let's be honest. How often are you nose to nose with a mountain lion? For most of us, a hike into the "wild" means loading up the SUV with expensive gear and driving to a toileted trailhead. Sure, you can mourn how civilized we've become—how GPS units have replaced natural instinct and Gore-Tex stands in for true-grit—but the silly gadgets of civilization aside, we have plenty of reason to take pride in how we've matured. With survival now on the back burner, we've begun to understand that we have a responsibility to protect, no longer just conquer, our wild places: that they, not we, are at risk. So please, do what you can. The following section will help you understand better what it means to "do what you can" while still making the most of your hiking experience. Anyone can take a hike, but hiking safely and well is an art requiring preparation and proper equipment.

TRAIL ETIQUETTE

LEAVE NO TRACE
Always leave an area just like you found it—if not better than you found it. Avoid camping in fragile, alpine meadows and along the banks of streams and lakes. Use a camp stove versus building a wood fire. (All of the areas in this book prohibit backcountry campfires.) Pack up all of your trash and extra food. Bury human waste at least 100 feet from open water and dry desert washes under 6 to 8 inches of topsoil. Don't bathe with soap in a lake or stream—use prepackaged moistened towels to wipe off sweat and dirt, or bathe in the water without soap.

STAY ON THE TRAIL
It's true, a path anywhere leads nowhere new, but purists will just have to get over it. Paths serve an important purpose; they limit impact on natural areas. Straying from a designated trail may seem innocent but it can cause damage to sensitive areas—damage that may take years to recover, if it can recover at all. Even simple shortcuts can be destructive. So, please, stay on the trail, whether officially constructed or made by hikers.

LEAVE NO WEEDS
Noxious weeds tend to overtake other plants, which in turn affects animals and birds that depend on them for food. To minimize the spread of noxious weeds, hikers should regularly clean their boots, tents, packs, and hiking poles of mud and seeds. Also brush your dog to remove any weed seeds before heading off into a new area.

KEEP YOUR DOG UNDER CONTROL

You can buy a flexi-lead that allows your dog to go exploring along the trail, while allowing you the ability to reel him in should another hiker approach or should he decide to chase a rabbit. (But remember that some areas limit leashes to 6 feet.) Always obey leash laws and be sure to bury your dog's waste or pack it in resealable plastic bags.

RESPECT OTHER TRAIL USERS

Often you're not the only one on the trail. With the rise in popularity of multiuse trails, you'll have to learn a new kind of respect, beyond the nod and "hello" approach you may be used to. First investigate whether you're on a multiuse trail, and assume the appropriate precautions. When you encounter motorized vehicles (ATVs, motorcycles, and 4WDs), be alert. Though they should always yield to the hiker, often they're going too fast or are too lost in the buzz of their engine to react to your presence. If you hear activity ahead, step off the trail just to be safe. Note that you're not likely to hear a mountain biker coming, so be prepared and know ahead of time whether you share the trail with them. Cyclists should always yield to hikers, but that's little comfort to the hiker. Be aware. When you approach horses or pack animals on the trail, always step quietly off the trail, preferably on the downhill side, and let them pass. If you're wearing a large backpack, it's often a good idea to sit down. To some animals, a hiker wearing a large backpack might appear threatening. Many national forests allow domesticated grazing, usually for sheep and cattle. Make sure your dog doesn't harass these animals, and respect ranchers' rights while you're enjoying yours.

GETTING INTO SHAPE

Unless you want to be sore—and possibly have to shorten your trip or vacation—be sure to get in shape before a big hike. If you're terribly out of shape, start a walking program early, preferably 8 weeks in advance. Start with a 15-minute walk during your lunch hour or after work and gradually increase your walking time to an hour. You should also increase your elevation gain. Walking briskly up hills really strengthens your leg muscles and gets your heart rate up. If you work in a storied office building, take the stairs instead of the elevator. If you prefer going to a gym, walk the treadmill or use a stair machine. You can further increase your strength and endurance by walking with a loaded backpack. Stationary exercises you might consider are squats, leg lifts, sit-ups, and push-ups. Other good ways to get in shape include biking, running, aerobics, and, of course, short hikes. Stretching before and after a hike keeps muscles flexible and helps avoid injuries.

PREPAREDNESS

It's been said that failing to plan means planning to fail. So do take the necessary time to plan your trip. Whether going on a short day hike or an extended backpack trip, always prepare for the worst. Simply remembering to pack a copy of the US Army Survival Manual is not preparedness. Although it's not a bad idea if you plan on entering truly wild places, it's merely the tourniquet answer to a problem. You need to do your best to prevent the problem from arising in the first place. In order to survive—and to stay reasonably comfortable—you need to concern yourself with the basics: water, food, and shelter. Don't go on a hike without having these bases covered. And don't go on a hike expecting to find these items in the woods.

WATER

Even in frigid conditions, you need at least 2 quarts of water a day to function efficiently. Add heat and taxing terrain and you can bump that figure up to 2 gallons. That's simply a base to work from—your metabolism and your level of conditioning can raise or lower that amount. Unless you know your level, assume that you need 1 gallon of water a day. Now, where do you plan on getting the water?

PREFERABLY NOT FROM NATURAL WATER SOURCES

These sources can be loaded with intestinal disturbers, such as bacteria, viruses, and fertilizers. *Giardia lamblia*, the most common of these disturbers, is a protozoan parasite that lives part of its life cycle as a cyst in water sources. The parasite spreads when mammals defecate in water sources. Once ingested, *Giardia* can induce cramping, diarrhea, vomiting, and fatigue within 2 days to 2 weeks after ingestion. Giardiasis is treatable with prescription drugs. If you believe you've contracted giardiasis, see a doctor immediately.

TREATING WATER

The best and easiest solution to avoid polluted water is to carry your water with you. Yet, depending on the nature of your hike and the duration, this may not be an option—1 gallon of water weighs 8½ pounds. In that case, you'll need to look into treating water. Regardless of which method you choose, you should always carry some water with you in case of an emergency. Save this reserve until you absolutely need it.

There are three methods of treating water: boiling, chemical treatment, and filtering. If you boil water, current studies show that bringing water to a boil—at any altitude—is sufficient to kill all disease organisms. After boiling, remove the flat taste by pouring the water back and forth between two containers several times. You can opt for chlorine dioxide tablets or iodine chemical treatment, which will kill all dangerous organisms but will not take care of chemical pollutants. Another drawback to chemical treatments is the unpleasant taste of the water after it's treated. You can remedy this by adding powdered drink mix to the water. Filters do not remove viruses such as hepatitis unless they are labeled as water purifiers, but they do remove *Giardia* and organic and inorganic contaminants, and they don't leave an aftertaste. Water filters are far from perfect as they can easily become clogged or leak if a gasket wears out. It's always a good idea to carry a backup supply of chemical treatment tablets in case your filter decides to quit on you.

FOOD

If we're talking about survival, you can go days without food, as long as you have water. But we're also talking about comfort. Try to avoid foods that are high in sugar and fat like candy bars and potato chips. These food types are harder to digest and are low in nutritional value. Instead, bring along foods that are easy to pack, nutritious, and high in energy (e.g., bagels, nutrition bars, dehydrated fruit, gorp, and jerky). If you are on an overnight trip, easy-to-fix dinners include mixes with dehydrated rice, potatoes, corn, pasta with cheese sauce, and soup mixes. For a tasty breakfast, you can fix hot oatmeal with brown sugar and reconstituted milk powder topped off with banana chips. If you like a hot drink in the morning, bring along herbal tea bags or hot chocolate. If you are a coffee junkie, you can purchase coffee that is packaged like tea bags. You can prepackage all of your meals in heavy-duty resealable plastic bags to keep food from spilling in your pack. These bags can be reused to pack out trash.

SHELTER

The type of shelter you choose depends less on the conditions than on your tolerance for discomfort. Shelter comes in many forms—tent, tarp, lean-to, bivy sack, cabin, cave, etc. If you're camping in the desert, a bivy sack may suffice, but if you're above the treeline and a storm is approaching, a better choice is a three- or four-season tent. Tents are the logical and most popular choice for most backpackers as they're lightweight and packable—and you can rest assured that you always have shelter from the elements. Before you leave on your trip, anticipate what the weather and terrain will be like and plan for the type of shelter that will work best for your comfort level (see Equipment later in this section).

FINDING A CAMPSITE

If there are established campsites, stick to those. If not, start looking for a campsite early— around 3:30 or 4:00 p.m. Stop at the first decent site you see. Depending on the area, it could be a long time before you find another suitable location. Pitch your camp in an area that's level. Make sure the area is at least 200 feet from fragile areas like lakeshores, meadows, and streambanks. And try to avoid areas thick in underbrush, as they can harbor insects and provide cover for approaching animals.

If you are camping in stormy, rainy weather, look for a rock outcrop or a shelter in the trees to keep the wind from blowing your tent all night. Be sure that you don't camp under trees with dead limbs that might break off on top of you. Also, try to find an area that has an absorbent surface, such as sandy soil or forest duff. This, in addition to camping on a surface with a slight angle, will provide better drainage. By all means, don't dig trenches to provide drainage around your tent—remember you're practicing zero-impact camping.

If you're in bear country, steer clear of creekbeds or animal paths. If you see any signs of a bear's presence (i.e., scat, footprints), relocate. You'll need to find a campsite near a tall tree where you can hang your food and other items that may attract bears such as deodorant, toothpaste, or soap. Carry a lightweight nylon rope with which to hang your food. As a rule, you should hang your food at least 20 feet from the ground and 5 feet away from the tree trunk. You can put food and other items in a waterproof stuff sack and tie one end of the rope to the stuff sack. To get the other end of the rope over the tree branch, tie a good size rock to it, and gently toss the rock over the tree branch. Pull the stuff sack up until it reaches the top of the branch and tie it off securely. Don't hang your food near your tent! If possible, hang your food at least 100 feet away from your campsite. Alternatives to hanging your food are bear-proof plastic tubes and metal bear boxes.

Lastly, think of comfort. Lie down on the ground where you intend to sleep and see if it's a good fit. For morning warmth (and a nice view to wake up to), have your tent face east.

FIRST AID

I know you're tough, but get 10 miles into the woods and develop a blister and you'll wish you had carried that first-aid kit. Face it, it's just plain good sense. Many companies produce lightweight, compact first-aid kits. Just make sure yours contains at least the following:

- adhesive bandages
- moleskin or duct tape
- various sterile gauze and dressings
- white surgical tape
- an Ace bandage
- an antihistamine
- aspirin
- Betadine solution
- a first-aid book
- antacid tablets
- tweezers
- scissors
- antibacterial wipes
- triple-antibiotic ointment
- plastic gloves
- sterile cotton tip applicators
- syrup of ipecac (to induce vomiting)
- thermometer
- wire splint

Here are a few tips for dealing with and hopefully preventing certain ailments.

Sunburn

Take along sunscreen or sun block, protective clothing, and a wide-brimmed hat. If you do get a sunburn, treat the area with aloe vera gel, and protect the area from further sun exposure. At higher elevations, the sun's radiation can be particularly damaging to skin. Remember that your eyes are vulnerable to this radiation as well. Sunglasses can be a good way to prevent headaches and permanent eye damage from the sun, especially in places where light-colored rock or patches of snow reflect light up in your face. They should be considered essential in the Southwest during the spring and summer.

Blisters

Be prepared to take care of these hike-spoilers by carrying moleskin (a lightly padded adhesive), gauze and tape, or adhesive bandages. An effective way to apply moleskin is to cut out a circle of moleskin and remove the center—like a doughnut—and place it over the blistered area. Cutting the center out will reduce the pressure applied to the sensitive skin. Other products can help you combat blisters. Some are applied to suspicious hot spots before a blister forms to help decrease friction to that area, while others are applied to the blister after it has popped to help prevent further irritation.

Insect bites and stings

You can treat most insect bites and stings by applying hydrocortisone 1 percent cream topically and taking a pain medication such as ibuprofen or acetaminophen to reduce swelling. If you forgot to pack these items, a cold compress or a paste of mud and ashes can sometimes assuage the itching and discomfort. Remove any stingers by using tweezers or scraping the area with your fingernail or a knife blade. Don't pinch the area as you'll only spread the venom.

Some hikers are highly sensitive to bites and stings and may have a serious allergic reaction that can be life threatening. Symptoms of a serious allergic reaction can include wheezing, an asthmatic attack, and shock. The treatment for this severe type of reaction is epinephrine. If you know that you are sensitive to bites and stings, carry a pre-packaged kit of epinephrine, which can be obtained only by prescription from your doctor.

Ticks

Ticks can carry diseases such as Rocky Mountain spotted fever and Lyme disease. The best defense is, of course, prevention. If you know you're going to be hiking through an area littered with ticks, wear long pants and a long sleeved shirt. You can apply a permethrin repellent to your clothing and a Deet repellent to exposed skin. At the end of your hike, do a spot check for ticks (and insects in general). If you do find a tick, grab the head of the tick firmly—with a pair of tweezers if you have them—and gently pull it away from the skin with a twisting motion. Sometimes the mouth parts linger, embedded in your skin. If this happens, try to remove them with a disinfected needle. Clean the affected area with an antibacterial cleanser and then apply triple antibiotic ointment. Monitor the area for a few days. If irritation persists or a white spot develops, see a doctor for possible infection.

Poison ivy, oak, and sumac

These skin irritants can be found most anywhere in North America and come in the form of a bush or a vine, having leaflets in groups of three, five, seven, or nine. Learn how to spot the plants. The oil they secrete can cause an allergic reaction in the form of blisters, usually about 12 hours after exposure. The itchy rash can last from 10 days to several weeks. The best defense against these irritants is to wear clothing that covers the arms, legs, and torso. For summer, zip-off cargo pants come in handy. There are also nonprescription lotions you can apply to exposed skin that guard against the effects of poison ivy/oak/sumac and can be washed off with soap and water. If you think you were in contact with the plants, after hiking (or even on the trail during longer hikes) wash with soap and water. Taking a hot shower with soap after you return home from your hike will also help to remove any lingering oil from your skin. Should you contract a rash from any of these plants, use an antihistamine to reduce the itching. If the rash is localized, create a light bleach/water wash to dry up the area. If the rash has spread, either tough it out or see your doctor about getting a dose of cortisone (available both orally and by injection).

Snakebites

Snakebites are rare in North America. Unless startled or provoked, the majority of snakes will not bite. If you are wise to their habitats and keep a careful eye on the trail, you should be just fine. When stepping over logs, first step on the log, making sure you can see what's on the other side before stepping down. Though your chances of being struck are slim, it's wise to know what to do in the event you are.

If a nonvenomous snake bites you, allow the wound to bleed a small amount and then cleanse the wounded area with a Betadine solution (10 percent povidone iodine). Rinse the wound with clean water (preferably) or fresh urine (it might sound ugly, but it's sterile). Once the area is clean, cover it with triple antibiotic ointment and a clean bandage. Remember, most residual damage from snakebites, venomous or otherwise, comes from infection, not the snake's venom. Keep the area as clean as possible and get medical attention immediately.

If somebody in your party is bitten by a venomous snake, follow these steps:

1. Calm the patient.

2. Remove jewelry, watches, and restrictive clothing, and immobilize the affected limb. Do not elevate the injury. Medical opinions vary on whether the area should be lower or level with the heart, but the consensus is that it should not be above it.

3. Make a note of the circumference of the limb at the bite site and at various points above the site as well. This will help you monitor swelling.

4. Evacuate your victim. Ideally they should be carried out to minimize movement. If the victim appears to be doing okay, they can walk. Stop and rest frequently, and if the swelling appears to be spreading or the patient's symptoms increase, change your plan and find a way to get your patient transported.

5. If you are waiting for rescue, make sure to keep your patient comfortable and hydrated (unless the person begins vomiting).

Snakebite treatment is rife with old-fashioned remedies: You used to be told to cut and suck the venom out of the bite site or to use a suction cup extractor for the same purpose; applying an electric shock to the area was even in vogue for a while. Do not do any of these things. Do not apply ice, do not give your patient painkillers, and do not apply a tourniquet. All you really want to do is keep your patient calm and get help. If you're alone and have to hike out, don't run—you'll only increase the flow of blood throughout your system. Instead, walk calmly. Rattlesnake bites are very rarely fatal.

Dehydration

Have you ever hiked in hot weather and had a roaring headache and felt fatigued after only a few miles? More than likely you were dehydrated. Symptoms of dehydration include fatigue, headache, and decreased coordination and judgment. When you are hiking, your body's rate of fluid loss depends on the outside temperature, humidity, altitude, and your activity level. On average, a hiker walking in warm weather will lose 4 liters of fluid a day. That fluid loss is easily replaced by normal consumption of liquids and food. However, if a hiker is walking briskly in hot, dry weather in the desert, they can lose 1 to 3 liters of water an hour. It's important to always carry plenty of water and to stop often and drink fluids regularly, even if you aren't thirsty.

Heat exhaustion is the result of a loss of large amounts of electrolytes and often occurs if a hiker is dehydrated and has been under heavy exertion. Common symptoms of heat exhaustion include cramping, exhaustion, fatigue, lightheadedness, and nausea. You can treat heat exhaustion by getting out of the sun and drinking an electrolyte solution made up of 1 teaspoon of salt and 1 tablespoon of sugar dissolved in a liter of water. Drink this solution slowly over a period of 1 hour. Drinking plenty of fluids (preferably an electrolyte solution/sports drink) can prevent heat exhaustion. Avoid hiking during the hottest parts of the day, and wear breathable clothing, a wide-brimmed hat, and sunglasses.

Hypothermia

Cold is one of the biggest dangers in the backcountry, especially for day hikers in the summertime. That may sound strange, but imagine starting out on a hike in midsummer when it's sunny and 80 degrees out. You're clad in nylon shorts and a cotton T-shirt. About halfway through your hike, the sky begins to cloud up, and in the next hour a light drizzle begins to fall and the wind starts to pick up. Before you know it, you are soaking wet and shivering—the perfect recipe for hypothermia. More advanced signs include decreased coordination, slurred speech, and blurred vision. When a victim's temperature falls below 92 degrees, the blood pressure and pulse plummet, possibly leading to coma and death.

To avoid hypothermia, always bring a windproof/rainproof shell, a fleece jacket, long underwear made of a breathable, synthetic fiber, gloves, and hat when you are hiking in the mountains. Learn to adjust your clothing layers based on the temperature. If you are climbing uphill at a moderate pace you will stay warm, but when you stop for a break you'll become cold quickly, unless you add more layers of clothing.

If a hiker is showing advanced signs of hypothermia, dress them in dry clothes and make sure they are wearing a hat and gloves. Place the person in a sleeping bag in a tent or shelter that will protect them from the wind and other elements. Give the person warm fluids to drink and keep them awake.

Frostbite

When the mercury dips below 32 degrees, your extremities begin to chill. If a persistent chill attacks a localized area, say, your hands or your toes, the circulatory system reacts by cutting off blood flow to the affected area—the idea being to protect and preserve the body's overall temperature. And so it's death by attrition for the affected area. Ice crystals start to form from the water in the cells of the neglected tissue. Deprived of heat, nourishment, and now water, the tissue literally starves. This is frostbite.

Prevention is your best defense against this situation. Most prone to frostbite are your face, hands, and feet, so protect these areas well. Wool is the traditional material of choice because it provides ample air space for insulation and draws moisture away from the skin. Synthetic fabrics, however, have made great strides in the cold weather clothing market. Do your research. A pair of light silk liners under your regular gloves is a good trick for keeping warm. They afford some additional warmth, but more important they'll allow you to remove your mitts for detail work without exposing the skin.

If your feet or hands start to feel cold or numb due to the elements, warm them as quickly as possible. Place cold hands under your armpits or bury them in your crotch. If your feet are cold, change your socks. If there's plenty of room in your boots, add another pair of socks. Do remember, though, that constricting your feet in tight boots can restrict blood flow and actually make your feet colder more quickly. Your socks need to have breathing room if they're going to be effective. Dead air provides insulation. If your face is cold, place your warm hands over your face, or simply wear a head stocking.

Should your skin go numb and start to appear white and waxy, chances are you've got or are developing frostbite. Don't try to thaw the area unless you can maintain the warmth. In other words, don't stop to warm up your frostbitten feet only to head back on the trail. You'll do more damage than good. Tests have shown that hikers who walked on thawed feet did more harm, and endured more pain, than hikers who left the affected areas alone. Do your best to get out of the cold entirely and seek medical attention—which usually consists of performing a rapid rewarming in water for 20 to 30 minutes.

The overall objective in preventing both hypothermia and frostbite is to keep the body's core warm. Protect key areas where heat escapes, like the top of the head, and maintain the proper nutrition level. Foods that are high in calories aid the body in producing heat. Never smoke or drink when you're in situations where the cold is threatening. By affecting blood flow, these activities ultimately cool the body's core temperature.

Altitude sickness (AMS)

High lofty peaks, clear alpine lakes, and vast mountain views beckon hikers to the high country. But those who like to venture high may become victims of altitude sickness (also known as Acute Mountain Sickness—AMS). Altitude sickness is your body's reaction to insufficient oxygen in the blood due to decreased barometric pressure. While some hikers may feel lightheaded, nauseous, and experience shortness of breath at 7,000 feet, others may not experience these symptoms until they reach 10,000 feet or higher.

Slowing your ascent to high places and giving your body a chance to acclimatize to the higher elevations can prevent altitude sickness. For example, if you live at sea level and are planning a weeklong backpacking trip to elevations between 7,000 and 12,000 feet, start by staying below 7,000 feet for one night, then move to between 7,000 and 10,000 feet for another night or two. Avoid strenuous exertion and alcohol to give your body a chance to adjust to the new altitude. It's also important to eat light food and drink plenty of nonalcoholic fluids, preferably water. Loss of appetite at altitude is common, but you must eat!

Most hikers who experience mild to moderate AMS develop a headache and/or nausea, grow lethargic, and have problems sleeping. The treatment for AMS is simple: stop heading uphill. Keep eating and drinking water and take meds for the headache. You actually need to take more breaths at altitude than at sea level, so breathe a little faster without hyperventilating. If symptoms don't improve over 24 to 48 hours, descend. Once a victim descends about 2,000 to 3,000 feet, the signs will usually begin to diminish.

Severe AMS comes in two forms: High Altitude Pulmonary Edema (HAPE) and High Altitude Cerebral Edema (HACE). HAPE, an accumulation of fluid in the lungs, can occur above 8,000 feet. Symptoms include rapid heart rate, shortness of breath at rest, AMS symptoms, dry cough developing into a wet cough, gurgling sounds, flu-like or bronchitis symptoms, and lack of muscle coordination. HAPE is life threatening so descend immediately, at least 2,000 to 4,000 feet. HACE usually occurs above 12,000 feet but sometimes occurs above 10,000 feet. Symptoms are similar to HAPE but also include seizures, hallucinations, paralysis, and vision disturbances. Descend immediately—HACE is also life threatening.

Hantavirus Pulmonary Syndrome (HPS)

Deer mice spread the virus that causes HPS, and humans contract it from breathing it in, usually when they've disturbed an area with dust and mice feces from nests or surfaces with mice droppings or urine. Exposure to large numbers of rodents and their feces or urine presents the greatest risk. As hikers, we sometimes enter old buildings, and often deer mice live in these places. We may not be around long enough to be exposed, but do be aware of this disease. About half the people who develop HPS die. Symptoms are flu-like and appear about two to three weeks after exposure. After initial symptoms, a dry cough and shortness of breath follow. Breathing is difficult. If you even think you might have HPS, see a doctor immediately!

NATURAL HAZARDS

Besides tripping over a rock or tree root on the trail, there are some real hazards to be aware of while hiking. Even if where you're hiking doesn't have the plethora of venomous snakes and plants, insects, and grizzly bears found in other parts of the United States, there are a few weather conditions and predators you may need to take into account.

Lightning

Thunderstorms build over the mountains almost every day during the summer. Lightning is generated by thunderheads and can strike without warning, even several miles away from the nearest overhead cloud. The best rule of thumb is to start leaving exposed peaks, ridges, and canyon rims by about noon. This time can vary a little depending on storm buildup. Keep an eye on cloud formation and don't underestimate how fast a storm can build. The bigger they get, the more likely a thunderstorm will happen. Lightning takes the path of least resistance, so if you're the high point, it might choose you. Ducking under a rock overhang is dangerous as you form the shortest path between the rock and ground. If you dash below treeline, avoid standing under the only or the tallest tree. If you are caught above treeline, stay away from anything metal you might be carrying, Move down off the ridge slightly to a low, treeless point and squat until the storm passes. If you have an insulating pad, squat on it. Avoid having both your hands and feet touching the ground at once and never lay flat. If you hear a buzzing sound or feel your hair standing on end, move quickly as an electrical charge is building up.

Flash floods

On July 31, 1976, a torrential downpour unleashed by a thunderstorm dumped tons of water into the Big Thompson watershed near Estes Park. Within hours, a wall of water moved down the narrow canyon killing 139 people and causing more than $30 million in property damage. The spooky thing about flash floods, especially in western canyons, is that they can appear out of nowhere from a storm many miles away. While hiking or driving in canyons, keep an eye on the weather. Always climb to safety if danger threatens. Flash floods usually subside quickly, so be patient and don't cross a swollen stream.

Bears

Most of the United States (outside of the Pacific Northwest and parts of the Northern Rockies) does not have a grizzly bear population, although some rumors exist about sightings where there should be none. Black bears are plentiful, however. Here are some tips in case you and a bear scare each other. Most of all, avoid surprising a bear. Talk or sing where visibility or hearing is limited, such as along a rushing creek or in thick brush. In grizzly country especially, carry bear spray in a holster on your pack belt where you can quickly grab it. While hiking, watch for bear tracks (five toes), droppings (sizable with leaves, partly digested berries, seeds, and/or animal fur), or rocks and roots along the trail that show signs of being dug up (this could be a bear looking for bugs to eat). Keep a clean camp, hang food or use bearproof storage containers, and don't sleep in the clothes you wore while cooking. Be especially careful to avoid getting between a mother and her cubs. In late summer and fall bears are busy eating to fatten up for winter, so be extra careful around berry bushes and oakbrush. If you do encounter a bear, move away slowly while facing the bear, talk softly, and avoid direct eye contact. Give the bear room to escape. Since bears are very curious, it might stand upright to get a better whiff of you, and it may even charge you to try to intimidate you. Try to stay calm. If a black bear attacks you, fight back with anything you have handy. If a grizzly bear attacks you, your best option is to "play dead" by lying face down on the ground and covering the back of your neck and head with your hands. Unleashed dogs have been known to come running back to their owners with a bear close behind. Keep your dog on a leash or leave it at home.

Mountain lions

These large cats appear to be getting more comfortable around humans as long as deer (their favorite prey) are in an area with adequate cover. Usually elusive and quiet, lions rarely attack people. If you meet a lion, give it a chance to escape. Stay calm and talk firmly to it. Back away slowly while facing the lion. If you run, you'll only encourage the cat to chase you. Make yourself look large by opening a jacket, if you have one, or waving your hiking poles. If the lion behaves aggressively throw stones, sticks, or whatever you can while remaining tall. If a lion does attack, fight for your life with anything you can grab.

Africanized bees

This variant of the common honeybee has spread into the desert Southwest. Although their sting is no worse than that of a European honeybee, Africanized bees are much more aggressive. When hiking, avoid all bees and especially any that are swarming. Avoid anything that is scented, including scented soap, shampoo, hair spray, perfumes and colognes, and chewing gum. If you're hiking with a dog, keep it on a leash and do not let it roam through brush. Dogs have triggered a number of attacks.

If attacked, seek the shelter of a vehicle or building if available. In the backcountry, run and keep running. Africanized bees commonly pursue for a quarter- to a half-mile. Don't fight or flail at the bees—the scent of crushed bees further incites their attack. Africanized bees go for your head and face, so cover your head with loose clothing and protect your face. Run through brush or dense foliage if it is handy—dense vegetation confuses bees.

Hunting

This is a popular sport in the United States, especially during rifle season in October and November. Hiking is still enjoyable in those months in many areas, so just take a few precautions. First, learn when the different hunting seasons start and end in the area in which you'll be hiking. During this time frame, be sure to wear at least a blaze orange hat, and possibly put an orange vest over your pack. Don't be surprised to see hunters in camo outfits carrying bows or rifles around during their season. If you would feel more comfortable without hunters around, hike in national parks and monuments or state and local parks where hunting is not allowed.

NAVIGATION

Whether you are going on a short hike in a familiar area or planning a week-long backpack trip, you should always be equipped with the proper navigational equipment—at the very least a detailed map and a sturdy compass.

Maps

Computer-based, digital maps have significant advantages over traditional maps. Services such as GaiaGPS.com and CalTopo.com are web-based and also available on phone apps. Basic mapping is free and advanced features are available with a paid subscription. You can view and overlay many different map layers, including USGS 7.5-minute topo maps, US Forest Service topo maps, Trails Illustrated recreational maps, satellite and aerial images, wildfire history, and many more. Mapping tools allow you to plan your hike, noting distances and elevation changes. And you can print a copy of your custom map for your hike—always a good idea in case your electronic maps fail.

The art of map reading is a skill that you can develop by first practicing in an area you are familiar with. To begin, orient the map so the map is lined up in the correct direction (i.e., north on the map is lined up with true north). Next, familiarize yourself with the map symbols and try to match them up with terrain features around you such as a high ridge, mountain peak, river, or lake. If you are practicing with a topographic map, notice the contour lines. On gentler terrain these contour lines are spaced farther apart, and on steeper terrain they are closer together. Pick a short loop trail, and stop frequently to check your position on the map. As you practice map reading, you'll learn how to anticipate a steep section on the trail or a good place to take a rest break, and so on.

Compasses

First off, the sun is not a substitute for a compass. So, what kind of compass should you have? Here are some characteristics you should look for: an orienteering-type compass, which has a rectangular base with detailed scales, a liquid-filled housing, protective housing, a sighting line on the mirror, luminous alignment and back-bearing arrows, a luminous north-seeking arrow, and a well-defined bezel ring.

You can learn compass basics by reading the detailed instructions included with your compass. If you want to fine-tune your compass skills, sign up for an orienteering class or purchase a book on compass reading. Once you've learned the basic skills of using a compass, remember to practice these skills before you head into the backcountry.

Global Positioning System (GPS)

Once you have learned basic compass skills, you may be interested in checking out the technical wizardry of GPS. The GPS was developed by the US Department of Defense and works off twenty-four NAVSTAR satellites orbiting 12,000 miles above the Earth. A trail GPS receiver is a handheld unit that continuously calculates your precise location, within 30 feet or less—which is more accurate than the best topographic maps.

There are many different types of GPS units available and they range in price from $100 to $600. In general, all GPS units have a display screen and keypad where you input information. All units allow you to plot your route, easily retrace your path, track your traveling speed, find the mileage between waypoints, and calculate the total mileage of your route. Better units have built-in or downloadable topographic maps showing roads and trails. They also receive the Russian GLONASS and European Galileo satellites, further increasing accuracy and the likelihood of maintaining a position fix where the view of the sky is limited.

Keep in mind that GPS isn't perfect and doesn't always work. GPS receivers have difficulty picking up signals indoors, in heavily wooded areas, or in narrow canyons. Also, batteries can die or the unit can be dropped and broken. A GPS unit should be always used in conjunction with a map and compass, not in place of those items.

All cell phones have built-in GPS, and there are many backcountry navigation apps that use phone GPS. Dedicated trail GPS units still have several advantages—the GPS electronics and antenna are generally military grade and are much better at working when the sky is partially obscured, battery life is much longer and batteries can be changed in the field, and the unit is generally water-resistant and dustproof. And the unit isn't dependent on cell service to display maps.

Pedometers

A pedometer is a small, clip-on unit with a digital display that calculates your hiking distance in miles or kilometers based on your walking stride. Some units also calculate the calories you burn and your total hiking time. Pedometers are available at most large outdoor stores and range in price from $20 to $40. There are also pedometer apps for phones, as well as fitness watches that track not only distance and time but also heart rate and other parameters.

TRIP PLANNING

Planning your hiking adventure begins with letting a friend or relative know your trip itinerary so they can call for help if you don't return at your scheduled time. Your next task is to make sure you are outfitted to experience the risks and rewards of the trail. This section highlights gear and clothing you may want to take with you to get the most out of your hike.

Day Hikes

- camera
- printed map
- compass
- GPS unit
- pedometer
- daypack
- first-aid kit
- food
- guidebook
- LED headlamp/flashlight with extra batteries and bulbs
- hat
- insect repellent
- knife/multipurpose tool
- map
- matches in waterproof container and fire starter
- fleece jacket
- rain gear
- space blanket
- sunglasses
- sunscreen
- swimsuit and/or fishing gear (if hiking to a lake or swimming hole)
- watch
- water
- water bottles/water hydration system

Overnight Trip

- backpack and waterproof rain cover
- backpacker's trowel
- bandanna
- biodegradable soap
- pot scrubber
- multiple collapsible water containers (1 or 2 quarts each)
- clothing—extra wool socks, shirt, and shorts
- cook set/utensils
- ditty bags to store gear
- extra plastic resealable bags
- gaiters
- garbage bag
- ground cloth
- journal/pen
- nylon rope to hang food
- long underwear
- permit (if required)
- rain jacket and pants
- sandals to wear around camp and to ford streams

- sleeping bag
- waterproof stuff sack
- sleeping pad
- small bath towel
- stove and fuel

- tent
- toiletry items
- water filter
- whistle

EQUIPMENT

With the outdoor market currently flooded with products, many of which are pure gimmickry, it seems impossible to both differentiate and choose. Do I really need a tropical-fish-lined collapsible shower? (No, you don't.) The only defense against the maddening quantity of items thrust in your face is to think practically—and to do so before you go shopping. The worst buys are impulsive buys. Since most name brands will differ only slightly in quality, it's best to know what you're looking for in terms of function. Buy only what you need. You will, don't forget, be carrying what you've bought on your back. One hundred pounds of ultralight hiking gear is still 100 pounds! Here are some things to keep in mind before you go shopping.

Clothes

Clothing is your armor against Mother Nature's little surprises. Hikers should be prepared for any possibility, especially when hiking in mountainous areas. Adequate rain protection and extra layers of clothing are a good idea. In summer, a wide-brimmed hat is essential in the desert. In the winter months the first layer you'll want to wear is a "wicking" layer of long underwear that keeps perspiration away from your skin. Wear long underwear made from synthetic fibers that wick moisture away from the skin and draw it toward the next layer of clothing, where it then evaporates. Avoid wearing long underwear made of cotton as it is slow to dry and keeps moisture next to your skin.

The second layer you'll wear is the "insulating" layer. Aside from keeping you warm, this layer needs to "breathe" so you stay dry while hiking. A fabric that provides insulation and dries quickly is fleece. It's interesting to note that this one-of-a-kind fabric is made out of recycled plastic. Purchasing a zip-up jacket made of this material is highly recommended.

The last line of layering defense is the "shell" layer. You'll need some type of waterproof, windproof, breathable jacket that will fit over all of your other layers. It should have a large hood that fits over a hat. You'll also need a good pair of rain pants made from a similar waterproof, breathable fabric, such as Gore-Tex or one of the alternatives.

Now that you've learned the basics of layering, you can't forget to protect your hands and face. In cold, windy, or rainy weather you'll need a hat made of wool or fleece and insulated, waterproof gloves that will keep your hands warm and toasty. As mentioned earlier, buying an additional pair of light silk liners to wear under your regular gloves is a good idea.

Footwear

If you have any extra money to spend on your trip, put that money into boots or trail shoes. Poor shoes will bring a hike to a halt faster than anything else. To avoid this annoyance, buy shoes that provide support and are lightweight and flexible. A lightweight hiking boot is better than a heavy, leather mountaineering boot for most day hikes and backpacking. Trail running shoes provide a little extra cushion and are made in a high-top style that many people wear for hiking. These running shoes are lighter, more flexible, and more breathable than hiking boots. If you know you'll be hiking in wet weather often, purchase boots or shoes with a Gore-Tex or equivalent waterproof and breathable liner, which will help keep your feet dry.

When buying your hiking shoes, be sure to wear the same type of socks you'll be wearing on the trail. If the boots you're buying are for cold weather hiking, try the boots on while wearing two pairs of socks. Speaking of socks, a good cold weather sock combination is to wear a thinner sock made of wool or polypropylene covered by a heavier outer sock made of wool or a synthetic/wool mix. The inner sock protects the foot from the rubbing effects of the outer sock and prevents blisters. Many outdoor stores have some type of ramp to simulate hiking uphill and downhill. Be sure to take advantage of this test, as toe-jamming boot fronts can be very painful and debilitating on the downhill trek.

Once you've purchased your footwear, be sure to break the footwear in before you hit the trail. New footwear is often stiff and needs to be stretched and molded to your foot.

Hiking poles

Hiking poles help with balance and, more importantly, take pressure off your knees. The ones with shock absorbers are easier on your elbows and knees. Some poles even come with a camera attachment to be used as a monopod. And heaven forbid you meet a mountain lion, bear, or unfriendly dog, the poles can make you look a lot bigger. Some people prefer a single walking stick, because it's easier to free up your hands for activities such as rock scrambling and photography. A walking stick or trekking poles can also be used as a tarp support in the treeless desert, saving the weight of poles. In either case, make sure your stick or poles has rubber, not metal tips. In the rocky desert, rubber grips much better than metal and is far quieter.

Backpacks

No matter what type of hiking you do, you'll need a pack of some sort to carry the basic trail essentials. There are a variety of backpacks on the market, but let's first discuss what you intend to use it for. Day hikes or overnight trips?

If you plan on doing a day hike, a daypack should have some of the following characteristics: a padded hip belt that's at least 2 inches in diameter (avoid packs with only a small nylon piece of webbing for a hip belt); a chest strap (the chest strap helps stabilize the pack against your body); external pockets to carry items that you want easy access to; an internal pocket to hold keys, a knife, a wallet, and other miscellaneous items; an external lashing system to hold a jacket; and, if you so desire, a hydration pocket for carrying a hydration system (which consists of a water bladder with an attachable drinking hose). In the desert, don't put water bottles in outside pockets—the sun will quickly heat the water. Instead, put your bottles inside your pack under a jacket or other insulation.

For short hikes, some hikers like to use a fanny pack to store just a camera, food, a compass, a map, and other trail essentials. Most fanny packs have pockets for two water bottles and a padded hip belt. But fanny packs can't carry the gear needed to safely do longer or more remote hikes.

If you intend to do an extended, overnight trip, there are multiple considerations. First off, you need to decide what kind of framed pack you want. There are two backpack types for backpacking: the internal frame and the external frame. An internal frame pack rests closer to your body, making it more stable and easier to balance when hiking over rough terrain, a consideration if you like to hike remote, rough trails or cross-country. An external frame pack is just that, an aluminum frame attached to the exterior of the pack. Some hikers consider an external frame pack to be better for long backpack trips because it distributes the pack weight better and allows you to carry heavier loads. It's often easier to pack, and your gear is more accessible. It also offers better back ventilation in the desert.

The most critical measurement for fitting a pack is torso length. The pack needs to rest evenly on your hips without sagging. A good pack will come in two or three sizes and have straps and hip belts that are adjustable according to your body size and characteristics.

When you purchase a backpack, go to an outdoor store with salespeople who are knowledgeable in how to properly fit a pack. Once the pack is fitted for you, load the pack with the amount of weight you plan on taking on the trail (extra water bottles can substitute for heavy items such as food). The weight of the pack should be distributed evenly and you should be able to swing your arms and walk briskly without feeling out of balance. Another good technique for evaluating a pack is to walk up and down stairs and make quick turns to the right and to the left to be sure the pack doesn't feel out of balance. Other features that are nice to have on a backpack include a removable day pack or fanny pack, external pockets for items that need to be handy, and extra lash points to attach a jacket or other items. However, avoid getting a pack that is too small. You'll end up lashing gear to the outside, where it puts you off balance and catches on brush and tree limbs.

Sleeping bags and pads

Sleeping bags are more or less rated by temperature. You can purchase a bag made with synthetic insulation, or you can buy a goose down bag. Goose down bags are more expensive, but they have a higher insulating capacity by weight and will keep their loft longer. You'll want to purchase a bag with a temperature rating that fits the time of year and conditions you are most likely to camp in. One caveat: The techno-standard for temperature ratings is far from perfect. Ratings vary from manufacturer to manufacturer, so to protect yourself you should purchase a bag rated 10 to 15 degrees below the temperature you expect to be camping in. Synthetic bags are more resistant to water than down bags, but most down bags are now made from down that is treated to make it highly water repellent. Down bags are also more compressible than synthetic bags and take up less room in your pack, which is an important consideration if you are planning a multiday backpack trip. Features to look for in a sleeping bag include a mummy-style bag, a hood you can cinch down around your head in cold weather, and draft tubes along the zippers that help keep heat in and drafts out.

You'll also want a sleeping pad to provide insulation and padding from the cold ground. There are different types of sleeping pads available, from the more expensive self-inflating air mattresses to the less expensive closed-cell foam pads. Self-inflating air mattresses are usually heavier than closed-cell foam mattresses and are prone to punctures, especially in cactus country.

Tents

The tent is your home away from home while on the trail. It provides protection from wind, rain, snow, and insects. A three-season tent with a separate waterproof fly is a good choice for backpacking and can range in price from $100 to $500. A tent with net panels in the canopy provides more ventilation and is more comfortable in the desert. These lightweight and versatile tents provide protection in all types of weather, except heavy snowstorms or high winds, and range in weight from 4 to 8 pounds. Look for a tent that's easy to set up and will easily fit two people with gear. Dome-type tents usually offer more headroom and places to store gear. Other handy tent features include a vestibule where you can store wet boots and backpacks. Some nice-to-have items in a tent include interior pockets to store small items and lashing points to hang a clothesline. Even if your tent is completely self-supporting, always stake it securely so that it doesn't blow away in the wind while you're outside enjoying the sunset. Before you purchase a tent, set it up and take it down a few times to be sure it is easy to handle. Also, sit inside the tent and make sure it has enough room for you and your gear.

Cell phones

Many hikers are carrying their cell phones into the backcountry these days in case of emergency. That's fine and good, but please know that cell phone coverage is often poor to nonexistent in valleys, canyons, and thick forest. The companies providing cell phone coverage build towers where the customers are—cities and major highways. Coverage in wilderness areas is incidental to their business model. More importantly, people have started to call for help because they're just tired and don't feel like hiking out. Let's go back to being prepared. You are responsible for yourself in the backcountry—which is one of the major attractions of being a hiker! Use your brain to avoid problems, and if you do encounter one, first use your brain to try to correct the situation. Only use your cell phone, if it works, in true emergencies. If it doesn't work down low in a valley, try hiking to a high point where you might get reception.

HIKING WITH CHILDREN

Hiking with children isn't a matter of how many miles you can cover or how much elevation gain you make in a day; it's about seeing and experiencing nature through their eyes.

Kids like to explore and have fun

They like to stop and point out bugs and plants, look under rocks, jump in puddles, and throw sticks. If you're taking a toddler or young child on a hike, start with a trail that you're familiar with. Trails that have interesting things for kids, like piles of leaves to play in or a small stream to wade through during the summer, will make the hike much more enjoyable for them and will keep them from getting bored.

You can keep your child's attention if you have a strategy before starting on the trail. Using games is not only an effective way to keep a child's attention, it's also a great way to teach your child about nature. Quiz children on the names of plants and animals. Pick up a family-friendly outdoor hobby like geocaching (www.geocaching.com) or letter-boxing (www.atlasquest.com), both of which combine the outdoors, clue-solving, and treasure hunting. If your children are old enough, let them carry their own daypack filled with snacks and water. So that you are sure to go at their pace and not yours, let them lead the way. Playing follow the leader works particularly well when you have a group of children. Have each child take a turn at being the leader.

With children, a lot of clothing is key. The only thing predictable about weather is that it will change. Especially in mountainous areas, weather can change dramatically in a very short time. Always bring extra clothing for children, regardless of the season. In the winter, have your children wear wool socks and warm layers such as long underwear, a fleece jacket and hat, wool mittens, and good rain gear. It's not a bad idea to have these along in late fall and early spring as well. Good footwear is also important. A sturdy pair of high- top tennis shoes or lightweight hiking boots are the best bet for little ones. If you're hiking in the summer near a lake or stream, bring along a pair of old sneakers that children can put on when they want to go exploring in the water. Remember when you're near any type of water, always watch your child at all times. Also, keep a close eye on teething toddlers who may decide a rock or leaf of poison oak is an interesting item to put in their mouth.

From spring through fall, you'll want your kids to wear a wide-brimmed hat to keep their face, head, and ears protected from the hot sun. Also, make sure your children wear sunscreen at all times. Choose a brand without Paba—children have sensitive skin and may have an allergic reaction to sunscreen that contains Paba. If you are hiking with a child younger than six months, don't use sunscreen or insect repellent. Instead, be sure that their head, face, neck, and ears are protected from the sun with a wide-brimmed hat, and that all other skin exposed to the sun is protected with the appropriate clothing.

Remember that food is fun. Kids like snacks, so it's important to bring a lot of munchies for the trail. Stopping often for snack breaks is a fun way to keep the trail interesting. Raisins, apples, granola bars, crackers and cheese, cereal, and trail mix all make great snacks. Also, a few of their favorite candy treats can go a long way toward heading off a fit of fussing. If children are old enough to carry their own backpack, let them fill it with some lightweight "comfort" items such as a doll, a small stuffed animal, or a little toy (you'll have to draw the line at bringing the 10-pound Tonka truck). If your kids don't like drinking water, you can bring some powdered drink mix or a juice box.

Avoid poorly designed child-carrying packs—you don't want to break your back carrying your child. Most child-carrying backpacks designed to hold a 40-pound child will contain a large carrying pocket to hold diapers and other items. Some have an optional rain/sun hood.

HIKING WITH YOUR DOG

Bringing your furry friend with you is always more fun than leaving him behind. Our canine pals make great trail buddies because they never complain and always make good company. Hiking with your dog can be a rewarding experience, especially if you plan ahead.

Getting your dog in shape

Before you plan outdoor adventures with your dog, make sure he's in shape for the trail. Getting your dog into shape takes the same discipline as getting yourself into shape, but, luckily, your dog can get in shape with you. Take your dog with you on your daily runs or walks. If there is a park near your house, hit a tennis ball or play Frisbee with your dog.

Swimming is also an excellent way to get your dog into shape. If there is a lake or river near where you live and your dog likes the water, have him retrieve a tennis ball or stick. Gradually build your dog's stamina up over a 2- to 3-month period. A good rule of thumb is to assume that your dog will travel twice as far as you will on the trail. If you plan on doing a 5-mile hike, be sure your dog is in shape for a 10-mile hike.

Training your dog for the trail

Before you go on your first hiking adventure with your dog, be sure he has a firm grasp on the basics of canine etiquette and behavior. Make sure he can sit, lie down, stay, and come. One of the most important commands you can teach your canine pal is to "come" under any situation. It's easy for your friend's nose to lead him astray or possibly get lost. Another helpful command is the "get behind" command. When you're on a hiking trail that's narrow, you can have your dog follow behind you when other trail users approach. Nothing is more bothersome than an enthusiastic dog that runs back and forth on the trail and disrupts the peace of the trail for others—or, worse, jumps up on other hikers and gets them muddy. Remember that some people have had bad experiences with dogs and are frightened when a dog approaches or jumps up on them. When you see other trail users approaching you on the trail, give them the right of way by quietly stepping off the trail and making your dog lie down and stay until they pass.

Equipment for your dog

The most critical pieces of equipment you can invest in for your dog are proper identification and a sturdy leash. Flexi-leads work well for hiking because they give your dog more freedom to explore but still leave you in control. (Some areas restrict the length of leashes.) Make sure your dog has identification that includes your name and address and a number for your veterinarian. Other forms of identification for your dog include a tattoo or a microchip. You should consult your veterinarian for more information on these last two options.

The next piece of equipment you'll want to consider is a pack for your dog. By no means should you hold all of your dog's essentials in your pack—let him carry his own gear! Dogs that are in good shape can carry 30 to 40 percent of their own weight.

Most packs are fitted by a dog's weight and girth measurement. Companies that make dog packs generally include guidelines to help you pick out the size that's right for your dog. Some characteristics to look for when purchasing a pack for your dog include a harness that contains two padded girth straps, a padded chest strap, leash attachments, removable saddle bags, internal water bladders, and external gear cords.

You can introduce your dog to the pack by first placing the empty pack on his back and letting him wear it around the yard. Keep an eye on him during this first introduction. He may decide to chew through the straps if you aren't watching him closely. Once he learns to treat the pack as an object of fun and not a foreign enemy, fill the pack evenly on both sides with a few ounces of dog food in resealable plastic bags. Have your dog wear his pack on your daily walks for a period of 2 to 3 weeks. Each week add a little more weight to the pack until your dog will accept carrying the maximum amount of weight he can carry.

You can also purchase collapsible water and dog food bowls for your dog. These bowls are lightweight and can easily be stashed into your pack or your dog's. If you are hiking on rocky terrain or in the snow, you can purchase footwear for your dog that will protect his feet from cuts and bruises.

Always carry plastic bags to remove feces from the trail. It is a courtesy to other trail users and helps protect local wildlife.

The following is a list of items to bring when you take your dog hiking: collapsible water bowls, a comb, a collar and a leash, dog food, plastic bags for feces, a dog pack, flea/tick powder, paw protection, water, and a first-aid kit that contains eye ointment, tweezers, scissors, stretchy foot wrap, gauze, antibacterial wash, sterile cotton tip applicators, antibiotic ointment, and cotton wrap.

First aid for your dog
Your dog is just as prone—if not more prone—to getting in trouble on the trail as you are, so be prepared. Here's a rundown of the more likely misfortunes that might befall your little friend.

Bees and wasps
If a bee or wasp stings your dog, remove the stinger with a pair of tweezers and place a mudpack or a cloth dipped in cold water over the affected area. If you spot bees, especially a swarm, keep your dog on a leash and close to you because of the danger from Africanized bees. Dogs are commonly killed when they disturb Africanized bees, and the bees may attack you too.

Porcupines
One good reason to keep your dog on a leash is to prevent it from getting a nose full of porcupine quills. You may be able to remove the quills with pliers, but a veterinarian is the best person to do this nasty job because most dogs need to be sedated.

Heat stroke
Avoid hiking with your dog in really hot weather. Dogs with heat stroke will pant excessively, lie down and refuse to get up, and become lethargic and disoriented. If your dog shows any of these signs on the trail, have him lie down in the shade. If you are near a stream, pour cool water over your dog's entire body to help bring his body temperature back to normal.

Heartworm
Dogs get heartworms from mosquitoes, which carry the disease in the prime mosquito months of July and August. Giving your dog a monthly pill prescribed by your veterinarian easily prevents this condition.

Plant pitfalls
One of the biggest plant hazards for dogs on the trail are foxtails. Foxtails are pointed grass seed heads that bury themselves in your friend's fur, between his toes, and even get in his ear canal. If left unattended, these nasty seeds can work their way under the skin and cause abscesses and other problems. If you have a long-haired dog, consider trimming the hair between his toes and giving him a summer haircut to help prevent foxtails from attaching to his fur. After every hike, always look over your dog for these seeds—especially between his toes and his ears.

Other plant hazards include burrs, thorns, thistles, and poison oak. If you find any burrs or thistles on your dog, remove them as soon as possible before they become an unmanageable mat. Thorns can pierce a dog's foot and cause a great deal of pain. If you see that your dog is lame, stop and check his feet for thorns. Dogs are immune to poison oak but they can pick up the sticky, oily substance from the plant and transfer it to you.

Protect those paws

Be sure to keep your dog's nails trimmed so he avoids getting soft tissue or joint injuries. If your dog slows and refuses to go on, check to see that his paws aren't torn or worn. You can protect your dog's paws from trail hazards such as sharp gravel, foxtails, lava scree, and thorns by purchasing dog boots.

Sunburn

If your dog has light skin, he is an easy target for sunburn on his nose and other exposed skin areas. You can apply a nontoxic sunscreen to exposed skin areas that will help protect him from overexposure to the sun.

Ticks and fleas

Ticks can easily give your dog Lyme disease, as well as other diseases. Before you hit the trail, treat your dog with a flea and tick spray or powder. You can also ask your veterinarian about a once-a-month pour-on treatment that repels fleas and ticks.

Mosquitoes and deer flies

These little flying machines can do a job on your dog's snout and ears. Best bet is to spray your dog with fly repellent for horses to discourage both pests.

Giardia

Dogs can get giardiasis, which results in diarrhea. It is usually not debilitating, but it's definitely messy. A vaccine against giardiasis is available.

Mushrooms

Make sure your dog doesn't sample mushrooms along the trail. They could be poisonous to him, but he doesn't know that.

When you are finally ready to hit the trail with your dog, keep in mind that national parks and many wilderness areas do not allow dogs on trails. Your best bet is to hike in national forests, BLM lands, and state parks. Always call ahead to see what the restrictions are.

HIKE INDEX

ABOUT THE AUTHOR

Bruce Grubbs is an avid hiker, mountain biker, paddler, and cross-country skier who has been exploring the American West for decades. He has used high-technology gear in the backcountry in his work as a professional pilot, an amateur radio operator, and a mountain rescue team member. Bruce holds Airline Transport Pilot and Instrument Flight Instructor certificates, and is the chief pilot for an air charter company. He lives in Flagstaff, Arizona, and is the author of more than thirty-five books.